Spring Boot 2.0 Cookbook
Second Edition

Configure, test, extend, deploy, and monitor your Spring Boot
application both outside and inside the cloud

Alex Antonov

BIRMINGHAM - MUMBAI

Spring Boot 2.0 Cookbook
Second Edition

Commissioning Editor: Aaron Lazar
Acquisition Editor: Chaitanya Nair
Content Development Editor: Zeeyan Pinheiro
Technical Editor: Vibhuti Gawde
Copy Editor: Safis Editing
Project Coordinator: Vaidehi Sawant
Proofreader: Safis Editing
Indexer: Tejal Daruwale Soni
Graphics: Jason Monteiro
Production Coordinator: Shraddha Falebhai

First published: September 2015
Second edition: February 2018

Production reference: 1230218

Published by Packt Publishing Ltd.
Livery Place
35 Livery Street
Birmingham
B3 2PB, UK.

ISBN 978-1-78712-982-5

www.packtpub.com

This book is dedicated to my son, Evan!

I hope it inspires you to learn, create, reach your goals, conquer challenges, dream big, and to reach for the skies!

– Your loving dad!

`mapt.io`

Mapt is an online digital library that gives you full access to over 5,000 books and videos, as well as industry leading tools to help you plan your personal development and advance your career. For more information, please visit our website.

Why subscribe?

- Spend less time learning and more time coding with practical eBooks and Videos from over 4,000 industry professionals

- Improve your learning with Skill Plans built especially for you

- Get a free eBook or video every month

- Mapt is fully searchable

- Copy and paste, print, and bookmark content

PacktPub.com

Did you know that Packt offers eBook versions of every book published, with PDF and ePub files available? You can upgrade to the eBook version at `www.PacktPub.com` and as a print book customer, you are entitled to a discount on the eBook copy. Get in touch with us at `service@packtpub.com` for more details.

At `www.PacktPub.com`, you can also read a collection of free technical articles, sign up for a range of free newsletters, and receive exclusive discounts and offers on Packt books and eBooks.

Contributors

About the author

Alex Antonov is a very passionate technologist with a hunger to learn new tools, languages, techniques, and concepts behind enterprise application design. His specialty lies in designing highly scalable distributed large-scale enterprise systems. He is also a frequent presenter on the topics of architecture and design at conferences such as UberConference, JavaOne, and SpringOne 2GX.

Alex joined Orbitz Worldwide in 2004 and in his current role of senior principal engineer, he is responsible for providing technical leadership and guidance in the development of foundational technologies, core libraries, and APIs for enterprise-wide use, as well as being responsible for web application frameworks and developing common practices.

Alex has been a long-time Spring user, starting with Spring 2.0.8 all the way to the latest and greatest—Spring Boot. Besides Java, he is also proficient in Ruby/Rails, PHP, and Groovy, and is currently learning Erlang and Go.

I would like to thank all the people who have inspired, supported, and encouraged me through the book writing process. For me, this book represents the ability to take my passion for building software, my appreciation of the Spring family of frameworks, and the amazing work that was done by their creators, combine it with my many years of first-hand experience building complex applications, and share all the thoughts and best practices that I've developed over time and always wanted to share, with the community to help them build better, more elegant, robust, and performant applications.

I want to specially thank my wife, Alla, for constantly being there for me, for supporting me in writing this book, for being understanding when I spent countless evenings and weekends working on the chapters, for giving me an extra push to the finish line when I was close to being done, and for just being there for me! Honey, I love you very much!!!

A special thank you goes to my parents for giving me the opportunity to pursue my career dreams, for my education, and for raising me to become the person I am. All your hard work is now paying off and I would not be able to achieve what I have, or written this book, if it weren't for you. I love you guys a lot, and while you are around, I can still be a child.

About the reviewers

Ricky Yim is a passionate software engineer who has over 17 years of industry experience. Ricky is a firm believer in building quality software and using agile practices to solve problems. He takes a flexible approach to software delivery and applies innovative solutions. He is currently the head of technology and delivery at DiUS Computing.

Tejaswini Mandar Jog is a passionate and enthusiastic Java trainer. She has more than 9 years of experience in the IT training field, specializing in Java, J2EE, Spring, and relevant technologies. She has worked with many renowned corporate companies on training and skill enhancement programs. She is also involved in the development of projects using Java, Spring, and Hibernate. She has written two books. In her first book, *Learning Modular Java Programming*, the reader explores the power of modular programming to build applications with Java and Spring. Her second book, *Learning Spring 5.0*, explores building an application using the Spring 5.0 framework with the latest modules, such as WebFlux for dealing with reactive programming. Her recent book, Reactive Programming with Java 9, explains how to build robust, asynchronous, and event-driven applications with ease.

Packt is searching for authors like you

If you're interested in becoming an author for Packt, please visit `authors.packtpub.com` and apply today. We have worked with thousands of developers and tech professionals, just like you, to help them share their insight with the global tech community. You can make a general application, apply for a specific hot topic that we are recruiting an author for, or submit your own idea.

Table of Contents

Preface 1

Chapter 1: Getting Started with Spring Boot 7
  Introduction 7
  Using a Spring Boot template and starter 8
    How to do it... 8
    How it works... 8
  Creating a simple application 10
    How to do it... 11
    How it works... 11
  Launching an application using Gradle 15
    How to do it... 15
    How it works... 16
  Using the command-line runners 17
    How to do it... 17
    How it works... 18
  Setting up a database connection 18
    Getting ready 19
    How to do it... 20
    How it works... 20
  Setting up a data repository service 22
    How to do it... 22
    How it works... 25
  Scheduling executors 26
    Getting ready 26
    How to do it... 26
    How it works... 27

Chapter 2: Configuring Web Applications 29
  Creating a basic RESTful application 29
    How to do it... 30
    How it works... 31

Creating Spring Data REST service   32
  How to do it...   32
  How it works...   34
Configuring custom servlet filters   34
  How to do it...   35
  How it works...   35
Configuring custom interceptors   36
  How to do it...   37
  How it works...   38
Configuring custom HttpMessageConverters   38
  How to do it...   39
  How it works...   40
Configuring custom PropertyEditors   41
  How to do it...   41
  How it works...   45
Configuring custom type formatters   45
  How to do it...   45
  How it works...   48
Chapter 3: Web Framework Behavior Tuning   49
Introduction   49
Configuring route matching patterns   50
  How to do it...   50
  How it works...   52
Configuring custom static path mappings   52
  How to do it...   53
  How it works...   53
Tuning Tomcat via ServletWebServerFactory   54
  How to do it...   55
  How it works...   56
Choosing embedded servlet containers   56
  How to do it...   56
  How it works...   57
Adding custom connectors   58
  Getting ready   58
  How to do it...   59

How it works... 61

Chapter 4: Writing Custom Spring Boot Starters 63
Introduction 63
Understanding Spring Boot autoconfiguration 64
How to do it... 64
How it works... 65
Creating a custom Spring Boot autoconfiguration starter 66
How to do it... 67
How it works... 69
Configuring custom conditional bean instantiations 71
How to do it... 72
How it works... 73
Using custom @Enable annotations to toggle configuration 74
How to do it... 74
How it works... 76

Chapter 5: Application Testing 79
Introduction 79
Creating tests for MVC controllers 80
How to do it... 80
How it works... 84
Configuring a database schema and populating it 86
How to do it... 87
How it works... 89
Initializing the database with Spring JPA and Hibernate 90
Initializing the database with Spring JDBC 90
Creating tests using an in-memory database 91
How to do it... 92
How it works... 95
Creating tests using mock objects 96
How to do it... 97
How it works... 98
Creating a JPA component test 99
How to do it... 100
How it works... 101
Creating a WebMvc component test 101

How to do it...	102
How it works...	103
Writing tests using Cucumber	**104**
How to do it...	105
How it works...	111
Writing tests using Spock	**114**
How to do it...	115
How it works...	121
Chapter 6: Application Packaging and Deployment	**125**
Introduction	**125**
Creating a Spring Boot executable JAR	**126**
How to do it...	127
How it works...	128
Creating Docker images	**130**
How to do it...	130
How it works...	134
Building self-executing binaries	**137**
Getting ready	137
How to do it...	137
How it works...	140
Spring Boot environment configuration, hierarchy, and precedence	**142**
How to do it...	142
How it works...	143
Adding a custom PropertySource to the environment using EnvironmentPostProcessor	**145**
How to do it...	146
How it works...	149
Externalizing environmental config using property files	**150**
How to do it...	151
How it works...	152
Externalizing environmental configuration using environment variables	**154**
How to do it...	154
How it works...	155

Externalizing environmental configuration using Java system properties   156
    How to do it...   157
    How it works...   157
Externalizing environmental config using JSON   158
    How to do it...   159
    How it works...   159
Setting up Consul   160
    How to do it...   160
    How it works...   163
Externalizing environmental config using Consul and envconsul   163
    Getting ready   164
    How to do it...   164
    How it works...   166
Chapter 7: Health Monitoring and Data Visualization   169
Introduction   169
Writing custom health indicators   170
    How to do it...   171
    How it works...   176
Configuring management context   179
    How to do it...   179
    How it works...   181
Emitting metrics   183
    Getting ready   183
    How to do it...   185
    How it works...   188
Monitoring Spring Boot via JMX   192
    Getting ready   192
    How to do it...   193
    How it works...   194
Managing Spring Boot via SSHd Shell and writing custom remote Shell commands   195
    How to do it...   195
    How it works...   199
Integrating Micrometer metrics with Graphite   203

Getting ready	203
How to do it...	207
How it works...	211
Integrating Micrometer metrics with Dashing	**213**
Getting ready	214
How to do it...	215
How it works...	219
Chapter 8: Spring Boot DevTools	**223**
Introduction	**223**
Adding Spring Boot DevTools to a project	**224**
How to do it...	224
How it works...	225
Configuring LiveReload	**225**
How to do it...	226
How it works...	226
Configuring dynamic application restart triggers	**227**
How to do it...	227
How it works...	228
Using Remote Update	**230**
How to do it...	231
How it works...	234
Chapter 9: Spring Cloud	**237**
Introduction	**237**
Getting started with Spring Cloud	**238**
How to do it...	238
How it works...	240
Service discovery using Spring Cloud Consul	**242**
How to do it...	243
How it works...	245
Using Spring Cloud Netflix – Feign	**247**
How to do it...	248
How it works...	251
Service discovery using Spring Cloud Netflix – Eureka	**253**
How to do it...	254
How it works...	255

Using Spring Cloud Netflix – Hystrix   256
    How to do it...   257
    How it works...   259
Other Books You May Enjoy   263
Index   267

Preface

The Spring Framework provides great flexibility for Java development, which also results in tedious configuration work. Spring Boot addresses the configuration difficulties of Spring and makes it easy to create standalone, production-grade Spring-based applications. This practical guide makes the existing development process more efficient. *Spring Boot Cookbook 2.0, Second Edition* smartly combines all the skills and expertise to efficiently develop, test, deploy, and monitor applications using Spring Boot on-premises and in the cloud. We start with an overview of the important Spring Boot features you will learn to create a web application for a RESTful service. You will also learn how to fine-tune the behavior of a web application by learning about custom routes and asset paths and how to modify routing patterns along with addressing the requirements of a complex enterprise application and understanding the creation of custom Spring Boot starters.

This book also includes examples of the new and improved facilities available to create the various kinds of tests introduced in Spring Boot 1.4 and 2.0 and gain insights into Spring Boot DevTools. We will explore the basics of Spring Boot Cloud modules and various cloud starters to make cloud-native applications and take advantage of service discovery and circuit breakers.

Who this book is for

This book is targeted at Java Developers who have a good knowledge and understanding of Spring and Java application development, are familiar with the notions of the Software Development Life Cycle (SDLC), and understand the need of different kinds of testing strategies, general monitoring, and deployment concerns. This book will help you learn efficient Spring Boot development techniques and integration and extension capabilities in order to make the existing development process more efficient.

What this book covers

Chapter 1, *Getting Started with Spring Boot*, provides an overview of the important and useful Spring Boot starters that are included in the framework. You will learn how to use spring.io resources, how to get started with a simple project, and how to configure the build file to contain their desired starters. The chapter will finish with creating a simple command-line application configured to execute some scheduled tasks.

Chapter 2, *Configuring Web Applications*, provides examples of how to create and add custom servlet filters, interceptors, converters, formatters, and PropertyEditors to a Spring Boot web application. It will start by creating a new web application and use it as a base to customize with the components we discuss earlier in the chapter.

Chapter 3, *Web Framework Behavior Tuning*, delves into fine-tuning the behavior of a web application. It will cover configuring custom routing rules and patterns, adding additional static asset paths, and adding and modifying servlet container connectors and other properties, such as enabling SSL.

Chapter 4, *Writing Custom Spring Boot Starters*, shows how to create custom Spring Boot starters to provide additional behaviors and functionality that might be required for complex enterprise applications. You will learn about how the autoconfiguration mechanics works under the hood and how to use them to selectively enable/disable default functionality and conditionally load your own.

Chapter 5, *Application Testing*, explores different techniques for testing Spring Boot applications. It will start by introducing you to testing MVC applications, then proceed with some tips on how to use in-memory databases with pre-populated data to mimic real DB interactions during tests, and conclude with examples of BDD via testing tools such as Cucumber and Spock.

Chapter 6, *Application Packaging and Deployment*, will cover examples of configuring your build to produce Docker images and self-executing binary files for Linux/OSX environments. We will explore the options for external application configuration using Consul and delve into the details of Spring Boot environment and configuration functionality.

Chapter 7, *Health Monitoring and Data Visualization*, explores the various mechanisms that Spring Boot provides to help us see data relating to application's health. We will start by learning how to write and expose custom health metrics and see the data using HTTP endpoints and JMX. It will then proceed with the overview and creation of management commands for SSHd and finish with integration of monitoring data with Graphite and Dashing using the Micrometer metrics framework.

Chapter 8, *Spring Boot DevTools*, provides an insight into how to use Spring Boot DevTools during application development to simplify common tasks of dynamic code recompiling/restarting and remote code updating. We will learn how to add DevTools to the project, followed by exploring how DevTools helps speed up the development process by automatically restarting a running application when code changes take place.

Chapter 9, *Spring Cloud*, provides examples of various features in Spring Boot Cloud modules. You will learn how to use different cloud modules for service discovery, such as Consul or Netflix Eureka. Later, we will look at how to incorporate Netflix libraries such as the Hystrix circuit breaker and the Feign interface-based REST client.

To get the most out of this book

For this book, you need to have JDK 1.8 installed on your favorite operating system, Linux, Windows, or OS X. It is assumed that readers have reasonable familiarity with Java, including the latest features added by JDK 1.8, as well as basic knowledge of Spring Framework and its operating concepts, such as dependency injection, inversion of control, and MVC.

The rest of the software, such as the Gradle build tool, all the necessary Java libraries, such as Spring Boot, Spring Framework, and its dependencies, as well as Docker, Consul, Graphite, Grafana, and Dashing will be all installed throughout the recipes.

Download the example code files

You can download the example code files for this book from your account at www.packtpub.com. If you purchased this book elsewhere, you can visit www.packtpub.com/support and register to have the files emailed directly to you.

You can download the code files by following these steps:

1. Log in or register at www.packtpub.com.
2. Select the **SUPPORT** tab.
3. Click on **Code Downloads & Errata**.
4. Enter the name of the book in the **Search** box and follow the onscreen instructions.

Once the file is downloaded, please make sure that you unzip or extract the folder using the latest version of:

- WinRAR/7-Zip for Windows
- Zipeg/iZip/UnRarX for Mac
- 7-Zip/PeaZip for Linux

The code bundle for the book is also hosted on GitHub at `https://github.com/PacktPublishing/Spring-Boot-2.0-Cookbook-Second-Edition`. In case there's an update to the code, it will be updated on the existing GitHub repository.

We also have other code bundles from our rich catalog of books and videos available at `https://github.com/PacktPublishing/`. Check them out!

Conventions used

There are a number of text conventions used throughout this book.

`CodeInText`: Indicates code words in text, database table names, folder names, filenames, file extensions, pathnames, dummy URLs, user input, and Twitter handles. Here is an example: "Now we will add a `@Bean` declaration for `LocaleChangeInterceptor`."

A block of code is set as follows:

```
@Override
public void addInterceptors(InterceptorRegistry registry) {
    registry.addInterceptor(localeChangeInterceptor());
}
```

When we wish to draw your attention to a particular part of a code block, the relevant lines or items are set in bold:

```
[default]
exten => s,1,Dial(Zap/1|30)
exten => s,2,Voicemail(u100)
exten => s,102,Voicemail(b100)
exten => i,1,Voicemail(s0)
```

Any command-line input or output is written as follows:

```
$ ./gradlew clean bootRun
```

Bold: Indicates a new term, an important word, or words that you see onscreen. For example, words in menus or dialog boxes appear in the text like this. Here is an example: "Select the **Actuator** option under **Search for dependencies**."

Warnings or important notes appear like this.

 Tips and tricks appear like this.

Sections

In this book, you will find several headings that appear frequently (*Getting ready, How to do it..., How it works..., There's more...,* and *See also*).

To give clear instructions on how to complete a recipe, use these sections as follows:

Getting ready

This section tells you what to expect in the recipe and describes how to set up any software or any preliminary settings required for the recipe.

How to do it...

This section contains the steps required to follow the recipe.

How it works...

This section usually consists of a detailed explanation of what happened in the previous section.

There's more...

This section consists of additional information about the recipe in order to make you more knowledgeable about the recipe.

See also

This section provides helpful links to other useful information for the recipe.

Get in touch

Feedback from our readers is always welcome.

General feedback: Email feedback@packtpub.com and mention the book title in the subject of your message. If you have questions about any aspect of this book, please email us at questions@packtpub.com.

Errata: Although we have taken every care to ensure the accuracy of our content, mistakes do happen. If you have found a mistake in this book, we would be grateful if you would report this to us. Please visit www.packtpub.com/submit-errata, selecting your book, clicking on the Errata Submission Form link, and entering the details.

Piracy: If you come across any illegal copies of our works in any form on the internet, we would be grateful if you would provide us with the location address or website name. Please contact us at copyright@packtpub.com with a link to the material.

If you are interested in becoming an author: If there is a topic that you have expertise in and you are interested in either writing or contributing to a book, please visit authors.packtpub.com.

Reviews

Please leave a review. Once you have read and used this book, why not leave a review on the site that you purchased it from? Potential readers can then see and use your unbiased opinion to make purchase decisions, we at Packt can understand what you think about our products, and our authors can see your feedback on their book. Thank you!

For more information about Packt, please visit packtpub.com.

1

Getting Started with Spring Boot

Spring Boot has a lot of starters that are already a part of the Spring Boot family. This chapter will provide you with an overview of `http://start.spring.io/`, available starter modules, and will also show you how to make a project Bootiful, as Josh Long likes to call it.

In this chapter, we will learn about the following topics:

- Using a Spring Boot template and starter
- Creating a simple application
- Launching an application using Gradle
- Using the command-line runners
- Setting up a database connection
- Setting up a data repository service
- Scheduling executors

Introduction

In the fast-paced world of today's software development, the speed of application creation and the need for rapid prototyping are becoming more and more important. If you are developing a software using a JVM language, Spring Boot is exactly the kind of framework that will give you the power combined with the flexibility that will enable you to produce high-quality software at a rapid pace. So, let's take a look at how Spring Boot can help you to make your application Bootiful.

Using a Spring Boot template and starter

Spring Boot comes with over 40 different starter modules, which provide ready-to-use integration libraries for many different frameworks, such as database connections that are both relational and NoSQL, web services, social network integration, monitoring libraries, logging, template rendering, and the list just keeps going on. While it is not practically feasible to cover every single one of these components, we will go over the important and popular ones to get an idea of the possibilities and the ease of application development that Spring Boot provides us with.

How to do it...

We will start by creating a basic simple project skeleton, and Spring Boot will help us achieve this:

1. Head over to `http://start.spring.io`
2. Fill out a simple form with the details about our project
3. Click on **Generate Project alt +** a premade project skeleton will download; this is where we begin

How it works...

You will see the **Project Dependencies** section, where we can choose the kind of functionalities that our application will perform: Will it connect to a database? Will it have a web interface? Do we plan to integrate with any of the social networks bake in operational support? and so on. By selecting the desired technologies, the appropriate starter libraries will be added automatically to the dependency list of our pregenerated project template.

Before we proceed with the generation of our project, let's go over what exactly a Spring Boot starter is and the benefits it provides us with.

Spring Boot aims to make it easy to get started with creating an application. Spring Boot starters are bootstrap libraries that contain a collection of all the relevant transitive dependencies that are needed to start a particular functionality. Each starter has a special file, which contains the list of all the provided dependencies Spring provides. Let's take a look at the following link for a `spring-boot-starter-test` definition as an example:

```
https://github.com/spring-projects/spring-boot/blob/master/spring-boot-project/
spring-boot-starters/spring-boot-starter-test/src/main/resources/META-INF/
spring.provides
```

Here we will see the following code:

```
provides: spring-test, spring-boot, junit, mockito, hamcrest-library,
jsonassert, json-path
```

This tells us that by including `spring-boot-starter-test` in our build as a dependency, we will automatically get `spring-test`, `spring-boot`, `junit`, `mockito`, `hamcrest-library`,`jsonassert`, and `json-path`. These libraries will provide us with all the necessary things in order to start writing application tests for the software that we will develop, without needing to manually add these dependencies to the build file individually.

With more than 100 starters provided, and with the ongoing community additions increasing the list, it is very likely that unless, we find ourselves with the need to integrate with a fairly common or popular framework, there is already a starter out there that we can use.

The following table shows you the most notable ones so as to give you an idea of what is available:

Starter	Description
`spring-boot-starter`	This is the core Spring Boot starter that provides you with all the foundational functionalities. It is depended upon by all other starters, so no need to declare it explicitly.
`spring-boot-starter-actuator`	This starter provides you with a functionality to monitor, manage an application, and audit.
`spring-boot-starter-jdbc`	This starter provides you with a support to connect and use JDBC databases, connection pools, and so on.

`spring-boot-starter-data-jpa` `spring-boot-starter-data-*`	The JPA starter provides you with needed libraries so you can use **Java Persistence API** (**JPA**): Hibernate, and others. Various `data-*` `family` starters provide support for a number of datastores, such as MongoDB, Data REST, or Solr.
`spring-boot-starter-security`	This brings in all the needed dependencies for Spring Security.
`spring-boot-starter-social-*`	This allows you to integrate with Facebook, Twitter, and LinkedIn.
`spring-boot-starter-test`	This is a starter that contains the dependencies for `spring-test` and assorted testing frameworks: JUnit and Mockito, among others.
`spring-boot-starter-web`	This gives you all the needed dependencies for web application development. It can be enhanced with `spring-boot-starter-hateoas`, `spring-boot-starter-websocket`, `spring-boot-starter-mobile`, or `spring-boot-starter-ws`, and assorted template-rendering starters: `sping-boot-starter-thymeleaf` or `spring-boot-starter-mustache`.
`spring-cloud-starter-*`	Various `cloud-*` family starters providing support for a number of frameworks, such as Netflix OSS, Consul, or AWS.

Creating a simple application

Now that we have a basic idea of the starters that are available to us, let's go ahead and create our application template at `http://start.spring.io`.

How to do it...

The application that we are going to create is a book catalog management system. It will keep a record of books that were published, who the authors were, the reviewers, publishing houses, and so forth. We will name our project BookPub, and apply the following steps:

1. First let's switch to the full version by clicking the link below the **Generate Project alt +** button
2. Choose **Gradle Project** at the top
3. Use **Spring Boot** version **2.0.0(SNAPSHOT)**
4. Use the default proposed **Group** name: com.example
5. Enter bookpub for an **Artifact** field
6. Provide BookPub as a **Name** for the application
7. Specify com.example.bookpub as our **Package Name**
8. Select **Jar** as **Packaging**
9. Use **Java Version** as **8**
10. Select the **H2**, **JDBC**, and **JPA** starters from the **Search for dependencies** selection so that we can get the needed artifacts in our build file to connect to an H2 database
11. Click on **Generate Project alt +** to download the project archive

How it works...

Clicking on the **Generate Project alt +** button will download the bookpub.zip archive, which we will extract from our working directory. In the newly created bookpub directory, we will see a build.gradle file that defines our build. It already comes preconfigured with the right version of a Spring Boot plugin and libraries, and even includes the extra starters, which we have chosen. The following is the code of the build.gradle file:

```
dependencies {
  compile("org.springframework.boot:spring-boot-starter-data-jpa")
  compile("org.springframework.boot:spring-boot-starter-jdbc")
  runtime("com.h2database:h2")
  testCompile("org.springframework.boot:spring-boot-starter-test")
}
```

We have selected the following starters:

- `org.springframework.boot:spring-boot-starter-data-jpa`: This starter pulls in the JPA dependency.
- `org.springframework.boot:spring-boot-starter-jdbc`: This starter pulls in the JDBC supporting libraries.
- `com.h2database`: H2 is a particular type of database implementation, namely H2.
- `org.springframework.boot:spring-boot-starter-test`: This starter pulls all the necessary dependencies for running tests. It is only being used during the test phase of the build, and it is not included during the regular application compile time and runtime.

As you can see, the `runtime("com.h2database:h2")` dependency is a runtime one. This is because we don't really need, and probably don't even want to know, the exact type of database to which we will connect at the compile time. Spring Boot will autoconfigure the needed settings and create appropriate beans once it detects the presence of the `org.h2.Driver` class in the classpath when the application is launched. We will look into the inner workings of how and where this happens later in this chapter.

The `data-jpa` and `jdbc` are Spring Boot starter artifacts. If we look in these dependency JARs once they are downloaded, or using Maven Central, we will find that they don't contain any actual classes, only the various metadata. The two containing files that are of interest are `pom.xml` and `spring.provides`. Let's first look at the `spring.provides` file in the `spring-boot-starter-jdbc` JAR artifact, as follows:

```
provides: spring-jdbc, spring-tx, tomcat-jdbc
```

This tells us that, by having this starter as our dependency, we will transitively get the `spring-jdbc`, `spring-tx`, and `tomcat-jdbc` dependency libraries in our build. The `pom.xml` file contains the proper dependency declarations that will be used by Gradle or Maven to resolve the needed dependencies during the build time. This also applies to our second starter: `spring-boot-starter-data-jpa`. This starter will transitively provide us with the `spring-orm`, `hibernate-entity-manager`, and the `spring-data-jpa` libraries.

At this point, we have enough libraries/classes in our application classpath so as to give Spring Boot an idea of what kind of application we are trying to run and what type of facilities and frameworks need to be configured automatically by Spring Boot to stitch things together.

Earlier, we mentioned that the presence of the `org.h2.Driver` class in the classpath will trigger Spring Boot to automatically configure the H2 database connection for our application. To see exactly how this will happen, let's start by looking at our newly created application template, specifically at `BookPubApplication.java`, which is located in the `src/main/java/com/example/bookpub` directory in the root of the project. We do this as follows:

```
package com.example.bookpub;

import org.springframework.boot.SpringApplication;
import org.springframework.boot.autoconfigure.
SpringBootApplication;

@SpringBootApplication
public class BookPubApplication {

  public static void main(String[] args) {
    SpringApplication.run(BookPubApplication.class, args);
  }
}
```

This is effectively our entire and fully runnable application. There's not a whole lot of code here and definitely no mention of configuration or databases anywhere. The key to making magic is the `@SpringBootApplication` meta-annotation. In this, we will find the real annotations that will direct Spring Boot to set things up automatically:

```
@SpringBootConfiguration
@EnableAutoConfiguration
@ComponentScan (excludeFilters = @Filter(type =
                                FilterType.CUSTOM,
              classes = TypeExcludeFilter.class))
public @interface SpringBootApplication {...}
```

Let's go through the following list of annotations mentioned in the preceding code snippet:

- `@SpringBootConfiguration`: This annotation is in itself a meta-annotation; it tells Spring Boot that the annotated class contains Spring Boot configuration definitions, such as the `@Bean`, `@Component`, and `@Service` declarations, and so on. Inside, it uses the `@Configuration` annotation, which is a Spring annotation, and not just Spring Boot, as it is a Spring Framework core annotation, used to mark classes containing Spring configuration definitions.

It is important to note that using `@SpringBootConfiguration` over `@Configuration` is helpful when executing tests with Spring Boot Test framework, as this configuration will automatically be loaded by the Test framework when the test is annotated with `@SpringBootTest`. As it is noted in the Javadoc, an application should only ever include one `@SpringApplicationConfiguration`, and most idiomatic Spring Boot applications will inherit it from `@SpringBootApplication`.

- `@ComponentScan`: This annotation tells Spring that we want to scan our application packages starting from the package of our annotated class as a default package root for the other classes that may be annotated with `@Configuration`, `@Controller`, and other applicable annotations, which Spring will automatically include as part of the context configuration. The applied `TypeExcludeFilter` class provides filtering out for various classes to be excluded from `ApplicationContext`. It is mostly used by `spring-boot-test` to exclude classes that should be used only during tests; however, it is possible to add your own beans that extend from `TypeExcludeFilter` and provide filtering for other types that are deemed necessary.

- `@EnableAutoConfiguration`: This annotation is a part of the Spring Boot annotation, which is a meta-annotation on its own (you will find that Spring libraries rely very heavily on the meta-annotations so they can group and compose configurations together). It imports the `EnableAutoConfigurationImportSelector` and `AutoConfigurationPackages.Registrar` classes that effectively instruct Spring to automatically configure the conditional beans depending on the classes available in the classpath. (We will cover the inner workings of autoconfiguration in detail in Chapter 4, *Writing Custom Spring Boot Starters*.)

The `SpringApplication.run(BookPubApplication.class, args);` code line in the main method basically creates a Spring application context that reads the annotations in `BookPubApplication.class` and instantiates a context, which is similar to how it would have been done had we not used Spring Boot and stuck with just a regular Spring Framework.

Launching an application using Gradle

Typically, the very first step of creating any application is to have a basic startable skeleton. As the Spring Boot starter has created the application template for us already, all we have to do is extract the code, build, and execute it. Now let's go to the console and launch the application with Gradle.

How to do it...

Change the location of our directory to where the `bookpub.zip` archive was extracted from and execute the following command from the command line:

```
$ ./gradlew clean bootRun
```

If you don't have `gradlew` in the directory, then download a version of Gradle from `https://gradle.org/downloads` or install it via Homebrew by executing `brew install gradle`. After Gradle is installed, run `wrapper` in the `gradle` folder to get the Gradle `wrapper` files generated. Another way is to invoke `$gradleclean bootRun`.

The output of the preceding command will be as follows:

```
  .   ____          _            __ _ _
 /\\ / ___'_ __ _ _(_)_ __  __ _ \ \ \ \
( ( )\___ | '_ | '_| | '_ \/ _` | \ \ \ \
 \\/  ___)| |_)| | | | | || (_| |  ) ) ) )
  '  |____| .__|_| |_|_| |_\__, | / / / /
 =========|_|==============|___/=/_/_/_/
 :: Spring Boot ::    (v2.0.0.BUILD-SNAPSHOT)
2017-12-16 23:18:53.721 : Starting BookPubApplication on mbp with
PID 43850
2017-12-16 23:18:53.781 : Refreshing org.springframework.context.
annotation.Annotatio
2017-12-16 23:18:55.544 : Building JPA container
EntityManagerFactory for persistence
2017-12-16 23:18:55.565 : HHH000204: Processing
PersistenceUnitInfo [name: default
2017-12-16 23:18:55.624 : HHH000412: Hibernate Core
{5.2.12.Final}
2017-12-16 23:18:55.625 : HHH000206: hibernate.properties not
found
2017-12-16 23:18:55.627 : HHH000021: Bytecode provider name :
javassist
```

```
2017-12-16 23:18:55.774 : HCANN000001: Hibernate Commons
Annotations {5.0.1.Final
2017-12-16 23:18:55.850 : HHH000400: Using dialect:
org.hibernate.dialect.H2Dialect
2017-12-16 23:18:55.902 : HHH000397: Using
ASTQueryTranslatorFactory
2017-12-16 23:18:56.094 : HHH000227: Running hbm2ddl schema
export
2017-12-16 23:18:56.096 : HHH000230: Schema export complete
2017-12-16 23:18:56.337 : Registering beans for JMX exposure on
startup
2017-12-16 23:18:56.345 : Started BookPubApplication in 3.024
seconds (JVM running...
2017-12-16 23:18:56.346 : Closing
org.springframework.context.annotation.AnnotationC..
2017-12-16 23:18:56.347 : Unregistering JMX-exposed beans on
shutdown
2017-12-16 23:18:56.349 : Closing JPA EntityManagerFactory for
persistence unit 'def...
2017-12-16 23:18:56.349 : HHH000227: Running hbm2ddl schema
export
2017-12-16 23:18:56.350 : HHH000230: Schema export complete
BUILD SUCCESSFUL
Total time: 52.323 secs
```

How it works...

As we can see, the application started just fine, but as we didn't add any functionality or configure any services, it existed straight away. From the startup log, however, we do see that the autoconfiguration did take place. Let's take a look at the following lines:

```
Building JPA container EntityManagerFactory for persistence unit
'default'
HHH000412: Hibernate Core {5.2.12.Final}
HHH000400: Using dialect: org.hibernate.dialect.H2Dialect
```

This information tells us that, because we added the jdbc and data-jpa starters, the JPA container was created and will use Hibernate 5.2.12.Final to manage the persistence using H2Dialect. This was possible because we had the right classes in the classpath.

Using the command-line runners

With our basic application skeleton ready, let's add some meat to the bones by making our application do something.

Let's start by first creating a class named `StartupRunner`. This will implement the `CommandLineRunner` interface, which basically provides just one method: `public void run(String... args)` --that will get called by Spring Boot only once after the application has started.

How to do it...

1. Create the file named `StartupRunner.java` under the `src/main/java/com/example/bookpub/` directory from the root of our project with the following content:

```
package com.example.bookpub;

import com.example.bookpub.repository.BookRepository;
import org.apache.commons.logging.Log;
import org.apache.commons.logging.LogFactory;
import org.springframework.beans.factory.annotation.Autowired;
import org.springframework.boot.CommandLineRunner;
import org.springframework.scheduling.annotation.Scheduled;

public class StartupRunner implements CommandLineRunner {
    protected final Log logger = LogFactory.getLog(getClass());
    @Override
    public void run(String... args) throws Exception {
        logger.info("Hello");
    }
}
```

2. After we have defined the class, let's proceed by defining it as `@Bean` in the `BookPubApplication.java` application configuration, which is located in the same folder as our newly created `StartupRunner.java` file as follows:

```
@Bean
public StartupRunner schedulerRunner() {
    return new StartupRunner();
}
```

How it works...

If we run our application again, by executing $ ./gradlew clean bootRun, we will get an output that is similar to the previous one. However, we will see our Hello message in the logs as well, which is as follows:

```
2017-12-16 21:57:51.048  INFO ---
com.example.bookpub.StartupRunner        : Hello
```

Even though the program will get terminated on execution, at least we made it do something!

Command-line runners are a useful functionality to execute the various types of code that only have to be run once, after startup. Some also use this as a place to start various executor threads, but Spring Boot provides a better solution for this task, which will be discussed at the end of this chapter. The command-line runner interface is used by Spring Boot to scan all of its implementations and invoke each instance's run method with the startup arguments. We can also use an @Order annotation or implement an Ordered interface so as to define the exact order in which we want Spring Boot to execute them. For example, **Spring Batch** relies on the runners to trigger the execution of the jobs.

As the command-line runners are instantiated and executed after the application has started, we can use the dependency injection to our advantage to wire in whatever dependencies we need, such as datasources, services, and other components. These can be utilized later while implementing run.

It is important to note that if any exception is thrown in the run(String... args) method, this will cause the context to close and an application to shut down. Wrapping the risky code blocks with try/catch is recommended to prevent this from happening.

Setting up a database connection

In every application, there is a need to access some data and conduct some operations on it. Most frequently, this source of data is a datastore of some kind, namely a database. Spring Boot makes it very easy to get started in order to connect to the database and start consuming the data via the JPA, among others.

Getting ready

In our previous example, we created the basic application that will execute a command-line runner by printing a message in the logs. Let's enhance this application by adding a connection to a database.

Earlier, we already added the necessary `jdbc` and `data-jpa` starters as well as an H2 database dependency to our `build` file. Now we will configure an in-memory instance of the H2 database.

 In the case of an embedded database, such as H2, **Hyper SQL Database (HSQLDB)**, or Derby, no actual configuration is required besides including the dependency on one of these in the `build` file. When one of these databases is detected in the classpath and a `DataSource` bean dependency is declared in the code, Spring Boot will automatically create one for you.

To demonstrate the fact that just by including the H2 dependency in the classpath, we will automatically get a default database, let's modify our `StartupRunner.java` file to look as follows:

```
public class StartupRunner implements CommandLineRunner {
    protected final Log logger = LogFactory.getLog(getClass());
    @Autowired
    private DataSource ds;
    @Override
    public void run(String... args) throws Exception {
        logger.info("DataSource: "+ds.toString());
    }
}
```

Now, if we proceed with the running of our application, we will see the name of the datasource printed in the log, as follows:

```
2017-12-16 21:46:22.067 com.example.bookpub.StartupRunner
:DataSource: org.apache.tomcat.jdbc.pool.DataSource@4...
{...driverClassName=org.h2.Driver; ... }
```

So, under the hood, Spring Boot recognized that we've autowired a `DataSource` bean dependency and automatically created one initializing the in-memory H2 datastore. This is all well and good, but probably not all too useful beyond an early prototyping phase or for the purpose of testing. Who would want a database that goes away with all the data as soon as your application shuts down and you have to start with a clean slate every time you restart the application?

How to do it...

Let's change the defaults in order to create an embedded H2 database that will not store data in-memory, but rather use a file to persist the data among application restarts, by performing the following steps:

1. Open the file named `application.properties` under the `src/main/resources` directory from the root of our project and add the following content:

   ```
   spring.datasource.url =
   jdbc:h2:~/test;DB_CLOSE_DELAY=-1;DB_CLOSE_ON_EXIT=FALSE
   spring.datasource.username = sa
   spring.datasource.password =
   ```

2. Start the application by executing `./gradlew clean bootRun` from the command line
3. Check your home directory, and you should see the following file in there: `test.mv.db`

 The user home directory is located under `/home/<username>` on Linux and under `/Users/<username>` on macOS X.

How it works...

Even though, by default, Spring Boot makes certain assumptions about the database configuration by examining the classpath for the presence of supported database drivers, it provides you with easy configuration options to tweak the database access via a set of exposed properties grouped under `spring.datasource`.

The things that we can configure are `url`, `username`, `password`, `driver-class-name`, and so on. If you want to consume the datasource from a JNDI location, where an outside container creates it, you can configure this using the `spring.datasource.jndi-name` property. The complete set of possible properties is fairly large, so we will not go into all of them. However, we will cover more options in `Chapter` 5, *Application Testing*, where we will talk about mocking data for application tests using a database.

By looking at various blogs and examples, you may notice that some places use dashes in property names like `driver-class-name`, while others use camel-cased variants: `driverClassName`. In Spring Boot, these are actually two equally supported ways of naming the same property, and they get translated into the same thing internally.

If you want to connect to a regular (non-embedded) database, besides just having the appropriate driver library in the classpath, we need to specify the driver of our choice in the configuration. The following code snippet is what the configuration to connect to MySQL would resemble:

```
spring.datasource.driver-class-name: com.mysql.jdbc.Driver
spring.datasource.url:
jdbc:mysql://localhost:3306/springbootcookbook
spring.datasource.username: root
spring.datasource.password:
```

If we wanted Hibernate to create the schema automatically, based on our entity classes, we would need to add the following line to the configuration:

```
spring.jpa.hibernate.ddl-auto=create-drop
```

 Don't do it in the production environment, otherwise, on startup, all the table schemas and data will be deleted! Use the update or validate values instead, where needed.

You can go even further in the abstraction layer and, instead of autowiring a `DataSource` object, you could go straight for `JdbcTemplate`. This would instruct Spring Boot to automatically create a DataSource and then create a `JdbcTemplate` wrapping the datasource, thus providing you with a more convenient way of interacting with a database in a safe way. The code for `JdbcTemplate` is as follows:

```
@Autowired
private JdbcTemplate jdbcTemplate;
```

You can also look in the `spring-boot-autoconfigure` source at an `org.springframework.boot.autoconfigure.jdbc.DataSourceAutoConfiguration` file to see the code behind the datasource creation magic.

Setting up a data repository service

Connecting to a database and then executing good old SQL, though simplistic and straightforward, is not the most convenient way to operate on the data, map it in a set of domain objects, and manipulate the relational content. This is why multiple frameworks emerged to aid you with mapping the data from tables to objects, better known as **object-relational mapping (ORM)**. The most notable example of such a framework is Hibernate.

In the previous example, we covered how to set up a connection to a database and configure the settings for the username and password, and we also discussed which driver to use, and so on. In this recipe, we will enhance our application by adding a few entity objects that define the structure of the data in the database and a CrudRepository interface to access the data.

As our application is a book-tracking catalogue, the obvious domain objects would be Book, Author, Reviewers, and Publisher.

How to do it...

1. Create a new package folder named entity under the src/main/java/com/example/bookpub directory from the root of our project.

2. In this newly created package, create a new class named Book with the following content:

```
@Entity
public class Book {
  @Id
  @GeneratedValue
  private Long id;
  private String isbn;
  private String title;
  private String description;

  @ManyToOne
  private Author author;
  @ManyToOne
  private Publisher publisher;

  @ManyToMany
  private List<Reviewers> reviewers;

  protected Book() {}
```

```
public Book(String isbn, String title, Author author,
    Publisher publisher) {
  this.isbn = isbn;
  this.title = title;
  this.author = author;
  this.publisher = publisher;
}
//Skipping getters and setters to save space, but we do need
them
}
```

3. As any book should have an author and a publisher, and ideally some reviewers, we need to create these entity objects as well. Let's start by creating an `Author` entity class, under the same directory as our `Book`, as follows:

```
@Entity
public class Author {
  @Id
  @GeneratedValue
  private Long id;
  private String firstName;
  private String lastName;
  @OneToMany(mappedBy = "author")
  private List<Book> books;

  protected Author() {}

  public Author(String firstName, String lastName) {...}
    //Skipping implementation to save space, but we do need
      it all
}
```

4. Similarly, we will create the `Publisher` and `Reviewer` classes, as shown in the following code:

```
@Entity
public class Publisher {
  @Id
  @GeneratedValue
  private Long id;
  private String name;
  @OneToMany(mappedBy = "publisher")
  private List<Book> books;

  protected Publisher() {}

  public Publisher(String name) {...}
```

```
     }

     @Entity
     public class Reviewer {
       @Id
       @GeneratedValue
       private Long id;
       private String firstName;
       private String lastName;

       protected Reviewer() {}

       public Reviewer(String firstName, String lastName)
         {...}
     }
```

5. Now we will create our `BookRepository` interface by extending Spring's `CrudRepository` interface under the `src/main/java/com/example/bookpub/repository` package, as follows:

```
     @Repository
     public interface BookRepository
             extends CrudRepository<Book, Long> {
       public Book findBookByIsbn(String isbn);
     }
```

6. Finally, let's modify our `StartupRunner` class in order to print the number of books in our collection, instead of some random datasource string, by autowiring a newly created `BookRepository` and printing the result of a `.count()` call to the log, as follows:

```
     public class StartupRunner implements CommandLineRunner {
       @Autowired private BookRepository bookRepository;

       public void run(String... args) throws Exception {
         logger.info("Number of books: " +
           bookRepository.count());
       }
     }
```

How it works...

As you have probably noticed, we didn't write a single line of SQL, or even mention anything about database connections, building queries, or things like that. The only hint about the fact that we are dealing with the database-backed data in our code is the presence of class and field annotations: `@Entity`, `@Repository`, `@Id`, `@GeneratedValue`, and `@ManyToOne`, along with `@ManyToMany` and `@OneToMany`. These annotations, which are a part of the JPA, along with the extension of the `CrudRepository` interface, are our ways of communicating with Spring about the need to map our objects to the appropriate tables and fields in the database and provide us with the programmatic ability to interact with this data.

Let's go through the following annotations:

- `@Entity` indicates that the annotated class should be mapped to a database table. The name of the table will be derived from the name of the class, but it can be configured, if needed. It is important to note that every entity class should have a default `protected` constructor, which is needed for automated instantiation and Hibernate interactions.

- `@Repository` indicates that the interface is intended to provide you with the access and manipulation of data for a database. It also serves as an indication to Spring during the component scan that this instance should be created as a bean that will be available for use and injection into other beans in the application.

- The `CrudRepository` interface defines the basic common methods to read, create, update, and delete data from a data repository. The extra methods that we will define in our `BookRepository` extension, `public Book findBookByIsbn(String isbn)`, indicate that Spring JPA should map the call to this method to a SQL query selecting a book by its ISBN field. This is a convention-named mapping that translates the method name into a SQL query. It can be a very powerful ally, allowing you to build queries, such as `findByNameIgnoringCase(String name)` and others.

- The `@Id` and `@GeneratedValue` annotations provide you with an indication that an annotated field should be mapped to a primary key column in the database and that the value for this field should be generated, instead of being explicitly entered.

- The `@ManyToOne` and `@ManyToMany` annotations define the relational field associations that refer to the data stored in the other tables. In our case, multiple books belong to one author, and many reviewers review multiple books.

- The `mappedBy` attribute in the `@OneToMay` annotation defines a reverse association mapping. It indicates to Hibernate that the mapping source of truth is defined in the `Book` class, in the `author` or `publisher` fields.

 For more information about all the vast capabilities of Spring Data, visit `http://docs.spring.io/spring-data/data-commons/docs/current/refe rence/html/`.

Scheduling executors

Earlier in this chapter, we discussed how the command-line runners can be used as a place to start the scheduled executor thread pools to run the worker threads in intervals. While that is certainly a possibility, Spring provides you with a more concise configuration to achieve the same goal: `@EnableScheduling`.

Getting ready

We will enhance our application so that it will print a count of books in our repository every 10 seconds. To achieve this, we will make the necessary modifications to the `BookPubApplication` and `StartupRunner` classes.

How to do it...

1. Let's add an `@EnableScheduling` annotation to the `BookPubApplication` class, as follows:

```
@SpringBootApplication
@EnableScheduling
public class BookPubApplication {...}
```

2. As a `@Scheduled` annotation can be placed only on methods without arguments, let's add a new `run()` method to the `StartupRunner` class and annotate it with the `@Scheduled` annotation, as shown in the following line:

```
@Scheduled(initialDelay = 1000, fixedRate = 10000)
public void run() {
    logger.info("Number of books: " +
        bookRepository.count());
}
```

3. Start the application by executing `./gradlew clean bootRun` from the command line so as to observe the `Number of books: 0` message that shows in the logs every 10 seconds.

How it works...

`@EnableScheduling`, as many other annotations that we have discussed and will discuss in this book, is not a Spring Boot; it is a Spring Context module annotation. Similar to the `@SpringBootApplication` and `@EnableAutoConfiguration` annotations, this is a meta-annotation and internally imports `SchedulingConfiguration` via the `@Import(SchedulingConfiguration.class)` instruction, which can be found inside `ScheduledAnnotationBeanPostProcessor` that will be created by the imported configuration and will scan the declared Spring beans for the presence of the `@Scheduled` annotations. For every annotated method without arguments, the appropriate executor thread pool will be created. It will manage the scheduled invocation of the annotated method.

2
Configuring Web Applications

In the previous chapter, we learned about how to create a starting application template, add some basic functionalities, and set up a connection to a database. In this chapter, we will continue to evolve our BookPub application and give it a web presence.

In this chapter, we will learn about the following topics:

- Creating a basic RESTful application
- Creating Spring Data REST service
- Configuring custom servlet filters
- Configuring custom interceptors
- Configuring custom HttpMessageConverters
- Configuring custom PropertyEditors
- Configuring custom type formatters

Creating a basic RESTful application

While the command-line applications do have their place and use, most of today's application development is centered around web, REST, and data services. Let's start with enhancing our `BookPub` application by providing it with a web-based API in order to get access to the book catalogs.

We will start where we left off in the previous chapter, so there should already be an application skeleton with the entity objects and a repository service defined and a connection to the database configured.

How to do it...

1. The very first thing that we will need to do is add a new dependency to build.gradle with the spring-boot-starter-web starter to get us all the necessary libraries for web-based functionality. The following code snippet is what it will look like:

```
dependencies {
    compile("org.springframework.boot:spring-boot-starter-data-jpa")
    compile("org.springframework.boot:spring-boot-starter-jdbc")
    compile("org.springframework.boot:spring-boot-starter-web")
    runtime("com.h2database:h2")
    runtime("mysql:mysql-connector-java")
    testCompile("org.springframework.boot:spring-boot-starter-test")
}
```

2. Next, we will need to create a Spring controller that will be used to handle the web requests for the catalog data in our application. Let's start by creating a new package structure to house our controllers so that we have our code nicely grouped by its appropriate purposes. Create a package folder called controllers in the src/main/java/com/example/bookpub directory from the root of our project.

3. As we will be exposing the book data, let's create the controller class file called BookController in our newly created package with the following content:

```
@RestController
@RequestMapping("/books")
public class BookController {
    @Autowired
    private BookRepository bookRepository;

    @RequestMapping(value = "", method = RequestMethod.GET)
    public Iterable<Book> getAllBooks() {
        return bookRepository.findAll();
    }

    @RequestMapping(value = "/{isbn}", method =
        RequestMethod.GET)
    public Book getBook(@PathVariable String isbn) {
```

```
        return bookRepository.findBookByIsbn(isbn);
    }
}
```

4. Start the application by running `./gradlew clean bootRun`.
5. After the application has started, open the browser and go to `http://localhost:8080/books` and you should see a response: `[]`.

How it works...

The key to getting the service exposed to web requests is the `@RestController` annotation. This is yet another example of a meta-annotation or a convenience annotation, as the Spring documentation refers to it at times, which we have seen in previous recipes. In `@RestController`, two annotations are defined: `@Controller` and `@ResponseBody`. So we could just as easily annotate `BookController`, as follows:

```
@Controller
@ResponseBody
@RequestMapping("/books")
public class BookController {...}
```

Let's take a look at the following annotations from the preceding code snippet:

- `@Controller`: This is a Spring stereotype annotation that is similar to `@Bean` and `@Repository` and declares the annotated class as an MVC
- `@ResponseBody`: This is a Spring MVC annotation indicating that responses from the web-request-mapped methods constitute the entire content of the HTTP response body payload, which is typical for the RESTful applications
- `@RequestMapping`: This is a Spring MVC annotation indicating that requests to `/books/*` URL will be routed to this controller.

Creating Spring Data REST service

In the previous example, we fronted our `BookRepository` interface with a REST controller in order to expose the data behind it via a web RESTful API. While this is definitely a quick and easy way to make the data accessible, it does require us to manually create a controller and define the mappings for all the desired operations. To minimize the boilerplate code, Spring provides us with a more convenient way: `spring-boot-starter-data-rest`. This allows us to simply add an annotation to the repository interface and Spring will do the rest to expose it to the web.

We will continue from where we finished in the previous recipe, and so the entity models and the `BookRepository` interface should already exist.

How to do it...

1. We will start by adding another dependency to our `build.gradle` file in order to add the `spring-boot-starter-data-rest` artifact:

   ```
   dependencies {
     ...
     compile("org.springframework.boot:spring-boot-starter-data-rest")
     ...
   }
   ```

2. Now, let's create a new interface to define `AuthorRepository` in the `src/main/java/com/example/bookpub/repository` directory from the root of our project with the following content:

   ```
   @RepositoryRestResource
   public interface AuthorRepository extends
     PagingAndSortingRepository<Author, Long> {
   }
   ```

3. While we are at it—given how little code it takes—let's create the repository interfaces for the remaining entity models, `PublisherRepository` and `ReviewerRepository` by placing the files in the same package directory as `AuthorRepository` with the following content:

```
@RepositoryRestResource
public interface PublisherRepository extends
    PagingAndSortingRepository<Publisher, Long> {
}
```

Otherwise, you can use the following code instead of the preceding code:

```
@RepositoryRestResource
public interface ReviewerRepository extends
    PagingAndSortingRepository<Reviewer, Long> {
}
```

4. Start the application by running `./gradlew clean bootRun`
5. After the application has started, open the browser and go to `http://localhost:8080/authors` and you should see the following response:

How it works...

As is evidenced from the browser view, we will get significantly more information than we got when we wrote the books controller. This is in part due to us extending not a `CrudRepository` interface, but a `PagingAndSortingRepository` one, which in turn is an extension of `CrudRepository`. The reason that we've decided to do this is to get the extra benefits provided by `PagingAndSortingRepository`. This will add the extra functionality to retrieve entities using the pagination and being able to sort them.

The `@RepositoryRestResource` annotation, while optional, provides us with the ability to have finer control over the exposure of the repository as a web data service. For example, if we wanted to change the URL `path` or `rel` value, to `writers` instead of `authors`, we could have tuned the annotation as follows:

```
@RepositoryRestResource(collectionResourceRel = "writers", path =
"writers")
```

As we included `spring-boot-starter-data-rest` in our build dependencies, we will also get the `spring-hateoas` library support, which gives us nice ALPS metadata, such as a `_links` object. This can be very helpful when building an API-driven UI, which can deduce the navigational capabilities from the metadata and present them appropriately.

Configuring custom servlet filters

In a real-world web application, we almost always find a need to add facades or wrappers to service requests, to log them, filter out bad characters for XSS, perform authentication, and so on. Out of the box, Spring Boot automatically adds `OrderedCharacterEncodingFilter` and `HiddenHttpMethodFilter`, but we can always add more. Let's see how Spring Boot helps us achieve this task.

Among the various assortments of Spring Boot, Spring Web, Spring MVC, and others, there is already a vast variety of different servlet filters that are available and all we have to do is define them as beans in the configuration. Let's say that our application will be running behind a load balancer proxy and we would like to translate the real request IP that is used by the users instead of the IP from the proxy when our application instance receives the request. Luckily, Apache Tomcat 8 already provides us with an implementation: `RemoteIpFilter`. All we will need to do is add it to our filter chain.

How to do it...

1. It is a good idea to separate and group the configurations into different classes in order to provide more clarity about what kind of things are being configured. So, let's create a separate configuration class called WebConfiguration in the src/main/java/com/example/bookpub directory from the root of our project with the following content:

```
@Configuration
public class WebConfiguration {
    @Bean
    public RemoteIpFilter remoteIpFilter() {
        return new RemoteIpFilter();
    }
}
```

2. Start the application by running ./gradlew clean bootRun.

3. In the startup log, we should see the following line, indicating that our filter has been added:

```
...FilterRegistrationBean : Mapping filter: 'remoteIpFilter' to:
[/*]
```

How it works...

The magic behind this functionality is actually very simple. Let's start from the separate configuration class and work our way to the filter bean detection.

If we look in our main class, BookPubApplication, we will see that it is annotated with @SpringBootApplication, which in turn is a convenience meta-annotation that declares @ComponentScan among others. We discussed this in detail in one of our earlier recipes. The presence of @ComponentScan instructs Spring Boot to detect WebConfiguration as a @Configuration class and add its definitions to the context. So, anything that we will declare in WebConfiguration is as good as if we were to put it right in BookPubApplication itself.

The `@BeanpublicRemoteIpFilterremoteIpFilter() {...}` declaration simply creates a Spring bean for the `RemoteIpFilter` class. When Spring Boot detects all the beans of `javax.servlet.Filter`, it will add them to the filter chain automatically. So, all we have to do, if we want to add more filters, is to just declare them as `@Bean` configurations. For example, for a more advanced filter configuration, if we want a particular filter to apply only to specific URL patterns, we can create a `@Bean` configuration of a `FilterRegistrationBean` type and use it to configure the precise settings.

> To make supporting this use-case easier Spring Boot provides us with configuration properties that can be used instead of manually configuring the `RemoteIpFilter` bean for occasions when Tomcat servlet container is being used. Use `server.use-forward-headers=true` to indicate to Spring Boot that it needs to automatically configure support for proxy headers, to provide proper request obfuscation. Specifically for Tomcat, one can also use `server.tomcat.remote_ip_header=x-forwarded-for` and `server.tomcat.protocol_header=x-forwarded-proto` properties to configure what specific header names should be used to retrieve the values.

Configuring custom interceptors

While servlet filters are a part of the Servlet API and have nothing to do with Spring besides being automatically added in the filter chain --Spring MVC provides us with another way of wrapping web requests: `HandlerInterceptor`. According to the documentation, `HandlerInterceptor` is just like a filter. Instead of wrapping a request in a nested chain, an interceptor gives us cutaway points at different phases, such as before the request gets handled, after the request has been processed, before the view has been rendered, and at the very end, after the request has been fully completed. It does not let us change anything about the request, but it does let us stop the execution by throwing an exception or returning false if the interceptor logic determines so.

Similar to using filters, Spring MVC comes with a number of premade `HandlerInterceptors`. The commonly used ones are `LocaleChangeInterceptor` and `ThemeChangeInterceptor`; but there are certainly others that provide great value. So let's add `LocaleChangeInterceptor` to our application in order to see how it is done.

How to do it...

Despite what you might think, after seeing the previous recipe, adding an interceptor is not as straightforward as just declaring it as a bean. We actually need to do it via WebMvcConfigurer or by overriding WebMvcConfigurationSupport. Let's take a look at the following steps:

1. Let's enhance our WebConfiguration class to implement WebMvcConfigurer:

   ```
   public class WebConfiguration implements WebMvcConfigurer {...}
   ```

2. Now we will add a @Bean declaration for LocaleChangeInterceptor:

   ```
   @Bean
   public LocaleChangeInterceptor localeChangeInterceptor() {
     return new LocaleChangeInterceptor();
   }
   ```

3. This will actually create the interceptor Spring bean, but will not add it to the request handling chain. For this to happen, we will need to override the addInterceptors method and add our interceptor to the provided registry:

   ```
   @Override
   public void addInterceptors(InterceptorRegistry registry) {
     registry.addInterceptor(localeChangeInterceptor());
   }
   ```

4. Start the application by running ./gradlew clean bootRun

5. In the browser, go to http://localhost:8080/books?locale=foo

6. Now, if you look at the console logs, you will see a bunch of stack trace errors basically saying the following:

   ```
   Caused by: java.lang.UnsupportedOperationException: Cannot change
   HTTP accept header - use a different locale resolution strategy
   ```

While the error is not because we entered an invalid locale, but because the default locale resolution strategy does not allow the resetting of the locale that is requested by the browser, the fact that we got an error shows that our interceptor is working.

How it works...

When it comes to configuring the Spring MVC internals, it is not as simple as just defining a bunch of beans at least not always. This is due to the need to provide a more fine-tuned mapping of the MVC components to requests. To make things easier, Spring provides us with a collection of default methods in WebMvcConfigurer interface that we can extend and override the settings of that we need.

In the particular case of configuring interceptors, we are overriding the addInterceptors(InterceptorRegistry registry) method. This is a typical callback method where we are given a registry in order to register as many additional interceptors as we need. During the MVC autoconfiguration phase, Spring Boot, just like in the case of filters, detects instances of WebMvcConfigurer and sequentially calls the callback methods on all of them. It means that we can have more than one implementation of the WebMvcConfigurer class if we want to have some logical separation.

Configuring custom HttpMessageConverters

While we were building our RESTful web data service, we defined the controllers, repositories, and put some annotations on them; but nowhere did we do any kind of object translation from the Java entity beans to the HTTP data stream output. However, behind the scenes, Spring Boot automatically configured HttpMessageConverters so as to translate our entity beans into a JSON representation written to HTTP response using the Jackson library. When multiple converters are available, the most applicable one gets selected based on the message object class and the requested content type.

The purpose of `HttpMessageConverters` is to translate various object types into their corresponding HTTP output formats. A converter can either support a range of multiple data types or multiple output formats, or a combination of both. For example, `MappingJackson2HttpMessageConverter` can translate any Java object into `application/json`, whereas `ProtobufHttpMessageConverter` can only operate on instances of `com.google.protobuf.Message` but can write them to the wire as `application/json`, `application/xml`, `text/plain`, or `application/x-protobuf`. `HttpMessageConverters` support not only writing out to the HTTP stream but also converting HTTP requests to appropriate Java objects as well.

How to do it...

There are a number of ways in which we can configure converters. It all depends on which one you prefer or how much control you want to achieve.

1. Let's add `ByteArrayHttpMessageConverter` as `@Bean` to our `WebConfiguration` class in the following manner:

```
@Bean
public
  ByteArrayHttpMessageConverter
    byteArrayHttpMessageConverter() {
  return new ByteArrayHttpMessageConverter();
}
```

2. Another way to achieve this is to override the `configureMessageConverters` method in the `WebConfiguration` class, which extends `WebMvcConfigurerAdapter`, defining such a method as follows:

```
@Override
public void configureMessageConverters
            (List<HttpMessageConverter<?>> converters) {
  converters.add(new ByteArrayHttpMessageConverter());
}
```

3. If you want to have a bit more control, we can override the
   `extendMessageConverters` method in the following way:

```
@Override
public void extendMessageConverters
                (List<HttpMessageConverter<?>> converters) {
  converters.clear();
  converters.add(new ByteArrayHttpMessageConverter());
}
```

How it works...

As you can see, Spring gives us multiple ways of achieving the same thing and it all depends on our preference or particular details of the implementation.

We covered three different ways of adding `HttpMessageConverter` to our application. So what is the difference, one might ask?

Declaring `HttpMessageConverter` as `@Bean` is the quickest and simplest way of adding a custom converter to the application. It is similar to how we added servlet filters in an earlier example. If Spring detects a bean of the `HttpMessageConverter` type, it will add it to the list automatically. If we did not have a `WebConfiguration` class that implements `WebMvcConfigurer`, it would have been the preferred approach.

When the application needs to define a more precise control over the settings, like interceptors, mappings, etc, it is best to use `WebMvcConfigurer` implementation to configure those, as it would be more consistent to override the `configureMessageConverters` method and add our converter to the list. As there can be multiple instances of `WebMvcConfigurers`, which could be either added by us or via the auto-configuration settings from various Spring Boot starters, there is no guarantee that our method can get called in any particular order.

If we need to do something even more drastic such as removing all the other converters from the list or clearing it of duplicate converters, this is where overriding `extendMessageConverters` comes into play. This method gets invoked after all the `WebMvcConfigurers` get called for `configureMessageConverters` and the list of converters is fully populated. Of course, it is entirely possible that some other instance of `WebMvcConfigurer` could override `extendMessageConverters` as well; but the chances of this are very low so you have a high degree of having the desired impact.

Configuring custom PropertyEditors

In the previous example, we learned how to configure converters for an HTTP request and response data. There are other kinds of conversions that take place, especially in regards to dynamically converting parameters to various objects, such as Strings to Date or an Integer.

When we declare a mapping method in a controller, Spring allows us to freely define the method signature with the exact object types that we require. The way in which this is achieved is via the use of the PropertyEditor implementations. PropertyEditor is a default concept defined as part of the JDK and designed to allow the transformation of a textual value to a given type. It was initially intended to be used to build Java Swing / **Abstract Window Toolkit (AWT)** GUI and later proved to be a good fit for Spring's need to convert web parameters to method argument types.

Spring MVC already provides you with a lot of PropertyEditor implementations for most of the common types, such as Boolean, Currency, and Class. Let's say that we want to create a proper Isbn class object and use this in our controller instead of a plain String.

How to do it...

1. First, we will need to remove the extendMessageConverters method from our WebConfiguration class as the converters.clear() call will break the rendering because we removed all of the supported type converters

2. Let's create a new package called model under the src/main/java/com/example/bookpub directory from the root of our project

3. Next we create a class named Isbn under our newly created package directory from the root of our project with the following content:

```
package com.example.bookpub.model;

import org.springframework.util.Assert;

public class Isbn {
    private String eanPrefix;
    private String registrationGroup;
    private String registrant;
    private String publication;
    private String checkDigit;

    public Isbn(String eanPrefix, String registrationGroup,
```

```
                 String registrant, String publication,
                 String checkDigit) {

    this.eanPrefix = eanPrefix;
    this.registrationGroup = registrationGroup;
    this.registrant = registrant;
    this.publication = publication;
    this.checkDigit = checkDigit;
}

public String getEanPrefix() {
    return eanPrefix;
}

public void setEanPrefix(String eanPrefix) {
    this.eanPrefix = eanPrefix;
}

public String getRegistrationGroup() {
    return registrationGroup;
}

public void setRegistrationGroup
            (String registrationGroup)  {
    this.registrationGroup = registrationGroup;
}

public String getRegistrant() {
    return registrant;
}

public void setRegistrant(String registrant) {
    this.registrant = registrant;
}

public String getPublication() {
    return publication;
}

public void setPublication(String publication) {
    this.publication = publication;
}

public String getCheckDigit() {
    return checkDigit;
}

public void setCheckDigit(String checkDigit) {
```

```
            this.checkDigit = checkDigit;
        }

        public static Isbn parseFrom(String isbn) {
            Assert.notNull(isbn);
            String[] parts = isbn.split("-");
            Assert.state(parts.length == 5);
            Assert.noNullElements(parts);
            return new Isbn(parts[0], parts[1], parts[2],
                parts[3], parts[4]);
        }

        @Override
        public String toString() {
            return eanPrefix + '-'
                + registrationGroup + '-'
                + registrant + '-'
                + publication + '-'
                + checkDigit;
        }
    }
```

4. Let's create a new package called editors under
    the src/main/java/com/example/bookpub directory from the root of our
    project
5. Let's create a class named IsbnEditor under our newly created package
    directory from the root of our project with the following content:

```
package com.example.bookpub.editors;

import org.springframework.util.StringUtils;
import com.example.bookpub.model.Isbn;

import java.beans.PropertyEditorSupport;

public class IsbnEditor extends PropertyEditorSupport {
    @Override
    public void setAsText(String text) {
        if (text == null) {
            setValue(null);
        }
        else {
            String value = text.trim();
            if (!StringUtils.isEmpty(value)) {
                setValue(Isbn.parseFrom(value));
            } else {
```

```
                    setValue(null);
            }
        }
    }

    @Override
    public String getAsText() {
        Object value = getValue();
        return (value != null ? value.toString() : "");
    }
}
```

6. Next, we will add a method, `initBinder`, to `BookController` where we will configure the `IsbnEditor` method with the following content:

```
@InitBinder
public void initBinder(WebDataBinder binder) {
  binder.registerCustomEditor(Isbn.class, new
    IsbnEditor());
}
```

7. Our `getBook` method in `BookController` will also change in order to accept the `Isbn` object, in the following way:

```
@RequestMapping(value = "/{isbn}", method =
  RequestMethod.GET)
public Book getBook(@PathVariable Isbn isbn) {
    return bookRepository.findBookByIsbn(isbn.toString());
}
```

8. Start the application by running `./gradlew clean bootRun`

9. In the browser, go to `http://localhost:8080/books/978-1-78528-415-1`

10. While we will not observe any visible changes, `IsbnEditor` is indeed at work, creating an instance of an `Isbn` class object from the `{isbn}` parameter

How it works...

Spring automatically configures a large number of default editors; but for custom types, we have to explicitly instantiate new editors for every web request. This is done in the controller in a method that is annotated with `@InitBinder`. This annotation is scanned and all the detected methods should have a signature of accepting `WebDataBinder` as an argument. Among other things, `WebDataBinder` provides us with an ability to register as many custom editors as we require for the controller methods to be bound properly.

 It is very important to know that `PropertyEditor` is not thread-safe! For this reason, we have to create a new instance of our custom editors for every web request and register them with `WebDataBinder`.

In case a new `PropertyEditor` is needed, it is best to create one by extending `PropertyEditorSupport` and overriding the desired methods with custom implementation.

Configuring custom type formatters

Mostly because of its statefulness and lack of thread safety, since version 3, Spring has added a `Formatter` interface as a replacement for `PropertyEditor`. The formatters are intended to provide a similar functionality but in a completely thread-safe manner and focusing on a very specific task of parsing a String in an object type and converting an object to its String representation.

Let's suppose that for our application, we would like to have a formatter that would take the ISBN number of a book in a String form and convert it to a book entity object. This way, we can define the controller request methods with a `Book` argument when the request URL signature only contains an ISBN number or a database ID.

How to do it...

1. First, let's create a new package called `formatters` in the `src/main/java/com/example/bookpub` directory from the root of our project

2. Next, we will create the `Formatter` implementation called `BookFormatter` in our newly created package directory from the root of our project with the following content:

```
public class BookFormatter implements Formatter<Book> {
  private BookRepository repository;
  public BookFormatter(BookRepository repository) {
    this.repository= repository;
  }
  @Override
  public Book parse(String bookIdentifier, Locale locale)
      throws ParseException {
    Book book = repository.findBookByIsbn(bookIdentifier);
    return book != null ? book :
        repository.findById(Long.valueOf(bookIdentifier))
          .get();
  }
  @Override
  public String print(Book book, Locale locale) {
    return book.getIsbn();
  }
}
```

3. Now that we have our formatter, we will add it to the registry by overriding an `addFormatters(FormatterRegistry registry)` method in the `WebConfiguration` class:

```
@Autowired
private BookRepository bookRepository;
@Override
public void addFormatters(FormatterRegistry registry) {
  registry.addFormatter(new BookFormatter(bookRepository));
}
```

4. Finally, let's add a new request method to our `BookController` class located in the `src/main/java/com/example/bookpub/controllers` directory from the root of our project that will display the reviewers for a given ISBN of a book:

```
@RequestMapping(value = "/{isbn}/reviewers", method =
    RequestMethod.GET)
public List<Reviewer> getReviewers(@PathVariable("isbn")
    Book book) {
  return book.getReviewers();
}
```

5. Just so we can have some data to play with, let's manually (for now) populate our database with some test data by adding two more autowired repositories to the `StartupRunner` class:

```
@Autowired
private AuthorRepository authorRepository;
@Autowired
private PublisherRepository publisherRepository;
```

6. The following code snippet is destined for the `run(...)` method of `StartupRunner`:

```
Author author = new Author("Alex", "Antonov");
author = authorRepository.save(author);
Publisher publisher = new Publisher("Packt");
publisher = publisherRepository.save(publisher);
Book book = new Book("978-1-78528-415-1",
    "Spring Boot Recipes", author, publisher);
bookRepository.save(book);
```

7. Start the application by running `./gradlew clean bootRun`

8. Let's open `http://localhost:8080/books/978-1-78528-415-1/reviewers` in the browser and you should be able to see the following results:

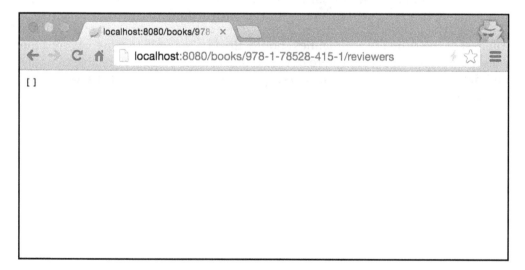

How it works...

The formatter facility is aims to provide a similar functionality to `PropertyEditors`. By registering our formatter with `FormatterRegistry` in the overridden `addFormatters` method, we are instructing Spring to use our formatter to translate a textual representation of our book into an entity object and back. As formatters are stateless, we don't need to do the registration in our controller for every call; we have to do it only once and this will ensure Spring uses it for every web request.

It is also good to remember that if you want to define a conversion of a common type, such as String or Boolean, for example trimming text, it is best to do this via `PropertyEditors` in controller's `InitBinder` because such a change is probably not globally desired and is only needed for a particular functionality.

You have probably noticed that we also autowired `BookRepository` to a `WebConfiguration` class, as this was needed to create `BookFormatter`. This is one of the cool parts about Spring --it lets us combine the configuration classes and make them dependent on the other beans at the same time. As we indicated that in order for a `WebConfiguration` class to be created we need `BookRepository`, Spring ensured that `BookRepository` will be created first and then automatically injected as a dependency during the creation of the `WebConfiguration` class. After `WebConfiguration` is instantiated, it is processed for configuration instructions.

The rest of the added functionalities should already be familiar as we covered them in our previous recipes. We will explore how to automatically populate databases with schemas and data in Chapter 5, *Application Testing*, in detail, where we will also talk about application testing.

3
Web Framework Behavior Tuning

In this chapter, we will learn about the following topics:

- Configuring route matching patterns
- Configuring custom static path mappings
- Tuning Tomcat via ServletWebServerFactory
- Choosing embedded servlet containers
- Adding custom connectors

Introduction

In Chapter 2, *Configuring Web Applications*, we explored how to configure web applications in Spring Boot with our custom filters, interceptors, and so on. We will continue to look further into enhancing our web application by doing behavior tuning, configuring the custom routing rules and patterns, adding additional static asset paths, adding and modifying servlet container connectors, and other properties such as enabling SSL.

Configuring route matching patterns

When we build web applications, it is not always the case that a default out-of-the-box mapping configuration is applicable. At times, we want to create RESTful URLs that contain characters such as dot (`.`), which Spring treats as a delimiter-defining format, like `path.xml`; or we might not want to recognize a trailing slash, and so on. Conveniently, Spring provides us with a way to accomplish this with ease.

In `Chapter 2`, *Configuring Web Applications*, we introduced a `WebConfiguration` class, which extends from `WebMvcConfigurerAdapter`. This extension allows us to override methods that are geared toward adding filters, formatters, and many more. It also has methods that can be overridden in order to configure the path match, among other things.

Let's imagine that the ISBN format does allow the use of dots to separate the book number from the revision with a pattern looking like `[isbn-number].[revision]`.

How to do it...

We will configure our application to not use the suffix pattern match of `.*` and to not strip the values after the dot when parsing the parameters. Let's perform the following steps:

1. Let's add the necessary configuration to our `WebConfiguration` class with the following content:

```
@Override
public void
  configurePathMatch(PathMatchConfigurer configurer) {
    configurer.setUseSuffixPatternMatch(false).
      setUseTrailingSlashMatch(true);
}
```

2. Start the application by running `./gradlew clean bootRun`.

3. Let's open `http://localhost:8080/books/978-1-78528-415-1.1` in the browser to see the following results:

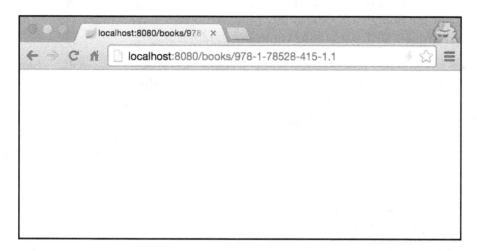

4. If we enter the correct ISBN, we will see a different result, as follows:

How it works...

Let's look at what we did in detail. The `configurePathMatch(PathMatchConfigurer configurer)` method gives us the ability to set our own behavior in how we want Spring to match the request URL path to the controller parameters:

- `configurer.setUseSuffixPatternMatch(false)`: This method indicates that we don't want to use the `.*` suffix, so as to strip the trailing characters after the last dot. This means that Spring parses out the entire `978-1-78528-415-1.1` ISBN as an `{isbn}` parameter for `BookController`.
  So, `http://localhost:8080/books/978-1-78528-415-1.1` and `http://localhost:8080/books/978-1-78528-415-1` will become different URLs.
- `configurer.setUseTrailingSlashMatch(true)`: This method indicates that we want to use the trailing `/` symbol in the URL as a match as if it were not there. This effectively makes `http://localhost:8080/books/978-1-78528-415-1` the same as `http://localhost:8080/books/978-1-78528-415-1/`.

If you want to do further configuration of how the path matching takes place, you can provide your own implementation of `PathMatcher` and `UrlPathHelper`, but these would be required in the most extreme and custom-tailored situations and are not generally recommended.

Configuring custom static path mappings

In the previous recipe, we looked at how to tune the URL path mapping for requests and translate them into controller methods. It is also possible to control how our web application deals with static assets and the files that exist on the filesystem or are bundled in the deployable archive.

Let's say that we want to expose our internal `application.properties` file via the static web URL of `http://localhost:8080/internal/application.properties` from our application. To get started with this, proceed with the steps in the next section.

How to do it...

1. Let's add a new method, `addResourceHandlers`, to the `WebConfiguration` class with the following content:

```
@Override
public void addResourceHandlers(ResourceHandlerRegistry registry) {
    registry.addResourceHandler("/internal/**")
            .addResourceLocations("classpath:/");
}
```

2. Start the application by running `./gradlew clean bootRun`

3. Let's open `http://localhost:8080/internal/application.properties` in the browser to see the following results:

How it works...

The method that we overrode, `addResourceHandlers(ResourceHandlerRegistry registry)`, is another configuration method from `WebMvcConfigurer`, which gives us the ability to define custom mappings for static resource URLs and connect them with the resources on the filesystem or application classpath. In our case, we defined a mapping of anything that is being accessed via the `/ internal` URL to be looked for in the `classpath:/` path of our application (for the production environment, you probably don't want to expose the entire classpath as a static resource!).

So let's look at what we did in detail, as follows:

- The `registry.addResourceHandler("/internal/**")` method adds a resource handler to the registry to handle our static resources, and returns `ResourceHandlerRegistration` to us, which can be used to further configure the mapping in a chained fashion. The `/internal/**` is a path pattern that will be used to match against the request URL using `PathMatcher`. We have seen how `PathMatcher` can be configured in the previous example, but by default an `AntPathMatcher` implementation is used. We can configure more than one URL pattern to be matched to a particular resource location.
- The `addResourceLocations("classpath:/")` method is called on the newly created instance of `ResourceHandlerRegistration`, and it defines the directories where the resources should be loaded from. These should be valid filesystems or classpath directories, and more than one can be entered. If multiple locations are provided, they will be checked in the order in which they were entered.

We can also configure a caching interval for the given resource using the `setCachePeriod(Integer cachePeriod)` method.

Tuning Tomcat via ServletWebServerFactory

Spring Boot exposes many of the server properties that can be used to configure things such as PORT, SSL, and others by simply setting the values in `application.properties`. However, if we need to do any more complex tuning, Spring Boot provides us with a `ServletWebServerFactory` interface to programmatically define our configuration.

Even though the session timeout can be easily configured by setting the `server.session.timeout` property in `application.properties` to our desired value in seconds, we will do it using `ServletWebServerFactory` to demonstrate how it is done.

How to do it...

1. Let's say that we want our session to be for one minute. To make this happen, we will ad a `ServletWebServerFactory` bean to our `WebConfiguration` class with the following content:

```
@Bean
public ServletWebServerFactory servletContainer() {
    TomcatServletWebServerFactory tomcat =
            new TomcatServletWebServerFactory();
    tomcat.getSession().setTimeout(Duration.ofMinutes(1));
    return tomcat;
}
```

2. Just for the purpose of demonstration, we will get the session from the request to force its creation. To do this, we will add a new request mapping to our `BookController` class with the following content:

```
@RequestMapping(value = "/session", method =
    RequestMethod.GET)
public String getSessionId(HttpServletRequest request) {
    return request.getSession().getId();
}
```

3. Start the application by running `./gradlew clean bootRun`.

4. Let's open `http://localhost:8080/books/session` in the browser to see the following results:

If we wait for more than a minute and then reload this page, the session ID will change to a different one.

How it works...

The `ServletWebServerFactory` interface defines the `WebServer`
`getWebServer(ServletContextInitializer... initializers)` method. Out of the
box, Spring Boot provides concrete factory implementations for the
`TomcatServletWebServerFactory`, `JettyServletWebServerFactory`, and
`UndertowServletWebServerFactory` application servers. Since we are using Tomcat in
our example, we will be using the provided `TomcatServletWebServerFactory` class to
configure the behavior of the session.

During application startup, Spring Boot autoconfiguration detects the presence of the
factory and invokes the `getWebServer(...)` method, passing the reference to a collection
of `ServletContextInitializer` beans. Typically, those initializers are created and
managed by Spring Boot internally, but we can always create some custom
`ServletContextInitializer` beans to add custom behavior that should be executed
during the startup life cycle of the application server.

Choosing embedded servlet containers

If we decide that we want to use Jetty as our servlet container, we will need to add a Jetty
starter to our `build` file.

How to do it...

1. As Tomcat already comes as a transitive dependency of Spring Boot, we will need
   to exclude it from our `build` dependency tree by adding the following to
   `build.gradle`:

   ```
   configurations {
     compile.exclude module: "spring-boot-starter-tomcat"
   }
   ```

2. We will also need to add a `compile` dependency to our `build` dependencies on
   Jetty:

   ```
   compile("org.springframework.boot:spring-boot-starter-jetty")
   ```

3. To fix the compiler errors, we will need to remove the bean declaration of Tomcat's `RemoteIpFilter` from our `WebConfiguration` class, as the Tomcat dependency has been removed.

4. Start the application by running `./gradlew clean bootRun`

5. If we now look at the console logs, we will see that our application is running in Jetty:

```
2017-12-16 --- o.eclipse.jetty.server.AbstractConnector
 : Started ServerConnector...
2017-12-16 ---.o.s.b.web.embedded.jetty.JettyWebServer
 : Jetty started on port(s) 8080 (http/1.1)...
```

How it works...

The reason that this works is because of Spring Boot's autoconfiguration magic. We had to remove the Tomcat dependency from the `build` file in order to prevent a dependency collision between Tomcat and Jetty. Spring Boot does a conditional scan of the classes in the classpath and depending on what it detects, it determines which servlet container will be used.

If we look in the `ServletWebServerFactoryAutoConfiguration` class, we will see the following conditional code that checks this:

```
/**
 * Nested configuration if Jetty is being used.
 */
@Configuration
@ConditionalOnClass({ Servlet.class, Server.class, Loader.class})
@ConditionalOnMissingBean(value = ServletWebServerFactory.class,
                     search = SearchStrategy.CURRENT)
public static class EmbeddedJetty {

  @Bean
  public JettyServletWebServerFactory
      JettyServletWebServerFactory() {
          return new JettyServletWebServerFactory();
  }

}
```

The `@ConditionalOnClass` annotation tells Spring Boot to use only the `EmbeddedJetty` configuration if the classes of Jetty, namely `org.eclipse.jetty.server.Server` and `org.eclipse.jetty.util.Loader`, are present in the classpath.

Adding custom connectors

Another very common scenario in the enterprise application development and deployment is to run the application with two separate HTTP port connectors: one for HTTP and the other for HTTPS

Getting ready

We will start by going back to using Tomcat; so for this recipe, we will undo the changes that we implemented in the previous example.

In order to create an HTTPS connector, we will need a few things; but most importantly, we will need to generate the certificate keystore that is used to encrypt and decrypt the SSL communication with the browser.

If you are using Unix or macOS, you can do it by running the following command:

```
$JAVA_HOME/bin/keytool -genkey -alias tomcat -keyalg RSA
```

On Windows, this can be achieved via the following command:

```
"%JAVA_HOME%binkeytool" -genkey -alias tomcat -keyalg RSA
```

During the creation of the keystore, you should enter the information that is appropriate to you, including passwords, name, and so on. For the purpose of this book, we will use the default password: `changeit`. Once the execution is complete, a newly generated keystore file will appear in your home directory under the name: `keystore`.

 You can find more information about preparing the certificate keystore at `https://tomcat.apache.org/tomcat-8.0-doc/ssl-howto.html#Prepare_ the_Certificate_Keystore`.

How to do it...

With the keystore creation complete, we will need to create a separate `properties` file in order to store our configuration for the HTTPS connectors, such as port. After that, we will create a configuration property binding object and use it to configure our new connector. Perform the following steps:

1. First, we will create a new properties file named `tomcat.https.properties` in the `src/main/resources` directory from the root of our project with the following content:

    ```
    custom.tomcat.https.port=8443
    custom.tomcat.https.secure=true
    custom.tomcat.https.scheme=https
    custom.tomcat.https.ssl=true
    custom.tomcat.https.keystore=${user.home}/.keystore
    custom.tomcat.https.keystore-password=changeit
    ```

2. Next, we will create a nested static class named `TomcatSslConnectorProperties` in our `WebConfiguration` class with the following content:

    ```
    @ConfigurationProperties(prefix = "custom.tomcat.https")
    public static class TomcatSslConnectorProperties {
      private Integer port;
      private Boolean ssl = true;
      private Boolean secure = true;
      private String scheme = "https";
      private File keystore;
      private String keystorePassword;
      //Skipping getters and setters to save space, but we do need them

      public void configureConnector(Connector connector) {
        if (port != null)
          connector.setPort(port);
        if (secure != null)
          connector.setSecure(secure);
        if (scheme != null)
          connector.setScheme(scheme);
        if (ssl!= null)
          connector.setProperty("SSLEnabled", ssl.toString());
        if (keystore!= null &&keystore.exists()) {
          connector.setProperty("keystoreFile",
            keystore.getAbsolutePath());
          connector.setProperty("keystorePassword",
            keystorePassword);
    ```

```
        }
    }
}
```

3. Now, we will need to add our newly created `tomcat.http.properties` file as a Spring Boot property source and enable `TomcatSslConnectorProperties` to be bound. This can be done by adding the following code right prior to the class declaration of the `WebConfiguration` class:

```
@Configuration
@PropertySource("classpath:/tomcat.https.properties")
@EnableConfigurationProperties(WebConfiguration.TomcatSslConnectorP
roperties.class)
public class WebConfiguration extends WebMvcConfigurerAdapter {...}
```

4. Finally, we will need to modify a `ServletWebServerFactory` Spring bean, where we will add our HTTPS connector. We will do that by changing the following code in the `WebConfiguration` class:

```
@Bean
public ServletWebServerFactory servletContainer
            (TomcatSslConnectorProperties properties) {
    TomcatServletWebServerFactory tomcat =
        new TomcatServletWebServerFactory();
    tomcat.addAdditionalTomcatConnectors
        (createSslConnector(properties));
    tomcat.getSession().setTimeout(Duration.ofMinutes(1));
    return tomcat;
}
private Connector createSslConnector
            (TomcatSslConnectorProperties properties) {
    Connector connector = new Connector();
    properties.configureConnector(connector);
    return connector;
}
```

5. Start the application by running `./gradlew clean bootRun`.

6. Let's open `https://localhost:8443/internal/tomcat.https.properties` in the browser to see the following results:

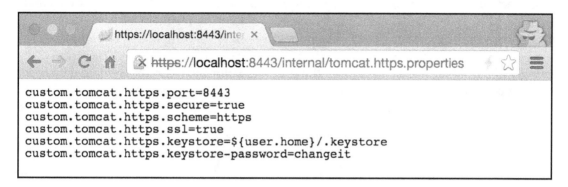

```
custom.tomcat.https.port=8443
custom.tomcat.https.secure=true
custom.tomcat.https.scheme=https
custom.tomcat.https.ssl=true
custom.tomcat.https.keystore=${user.home}/.keystore
custom.tomcat.https.keystore-password=changeit
```

How it works...

In this recipe, we did a number of things; so let's break them down one change at a time.

The first change, ignoring the need to create the keystore, was the creation of the `tomcat.https.properties` and `TomcatSslConnectorProperties` objects to bind them to. Previously, we already dealt with making changes to the various settings in `application.properties` when configuring our datasource. At that time, though, we did not have to create any binding objects because Spring Boot already had them defined.

As we learned earlier, Spring Boot already exposes many properties to configure the application settings, including a whole set of settings for the `server` section. These values get bound to an internal Spring Boot class: `ServerProperties`

A complete list of the common application properties can be found in the Spring Boot reference documentation at `http://docs.spring.io/spring-boot/docs/current/reference/html/common-application-properties.html`.

What we did with our addition was simply mimic Spring Boot and create our own configuration group with a binding object behind it. The reason that we didn't use the already existing `server.tomcat.` prefix, and instead opt for `custom.tomcat`, was mostly governed by the need to separate our config values from the default ones. Since we are adding a second connector, we want to have a clean separation between the default configuration properties and our custom ones.

The @ConfigurationProperties(prefix = "custom.tomcat.https") method is an important annotation for our TomcatSslConnectorProperties object. It tells Spring Boot to automatically bind the properties with the custom.tomcat.https prefix to fields that are declared in TomcatSslConnectorProperties. In order for the binding to take place—in addition to defining the fields in the class—it is very important to define the getters and setters as well. It is also worth mentioning that during the binding process, Spring will automatically try to convert the property values to their appropriate data types. For example, the value of custom.tomcat.https.keystore gets automatically bound to a private file keystore field object.

 The converters, which we learned about earlier, will also be used during the process of converting to custom-defined data types.

The next step is to tell Spring Boot to include the properties that are defined in tomcat.https.properties in the list of properties. This is achieved by adding @PropertySource("classpath:/tomcat.https.properties") next to @Configuration in the WebConfiguration class.

After the values are imported, we will need to tell Spring Boot to automatically create an instance of TomcatSslConnectorProperties for us to use. This is done by adding the following annotation next to @Configuration:

```
@EnableConfigurationProperties(WebConfiguration.TomcatSslConnectorPropertie
s.class)
```

This will instruct Spring Boot to automatically create a bean of type TomcatSslConnectorProperties and bind it with the values from the specified classpath:/tomcat.https.properties file. This bean can later be used for autowiring into different places, such as when we create a ServletWebServerFactory bean.

After all the property support is set and done, we will proceed with the actual code to create a second connector. The creation of the ServletWebServerFactory bean provides Spring Boot with a factory to use in order to create WebServer. The convenient configureConnector(Connector connector) method, which we added to TomcatSslConnectorProperties, gives us a good place to encapsulate and consolidate all the settings that are needed to configure the newly created Connector instance.

4

Writing Custom Spring Boot Starters

In this chapter, we will cover the following topics:

- Understanding Spring Boot autoconfiguration
- Creating a custom Spring Boot autoconfiguration starter
- Configuring custom conditional bean instantiations
- Using custom @Enable annotations to toggle configurations

Introduction

In the previous chapters, we did a lot of configuration, and even more autoconfiguration, while developing our Spring Boot application. Now, it is time to take a look behind the scenes to find out the magic behind Spring Boot autoconfiguration and write some starters of our own as well.

This is a very useful capability to possess, especially for large software enterprises where the presence of a proprietary code is inevitable. It is very helpful to be able to create internal custom starters that would automatically add some of the configuration or functionalities to the applications. Some likely candidates would be custom configuration systems, libraries, and configurations that deal with connecting to databases, using custom connection pools, HTTP clients, servers, and more. We will go through the internals of Spring Boot autoconfiguration, take a look at how new starters are created, explore conditional initialization and wiring of beans based on various rules, and see that annotations can be a powerful tool, providing the consumers of the starters with more control over dictating what configurations should be used and where.

Understanding Spring Boot autoconfiguration

Spring Boot has a lot of power when it comes to bootstrapping an application and configuring it with exactly the things that are needed, all without much of the glue code that is required of us, the developers. The secret behind this power actually comes from Spring itself, or rather from the Java Configuration functionality that it provides. As we add more starters as dependencies, more and more classes will appear in our classpath. Spring Boot detects the presence or absence of specific classes and based on this information, makes some decisions, which are fairly complicated at times, and automatically creates and wires the necessary beans to the application context.

Sounds simple, right?

In the previous recipes, we added a number of Spring Boot starters such as `spring-boot-starter-data-jpa`, `spring-boot-starter-web`, `spring-boot-starter-data-test`, and so on. We will use the same code that we finished in the previous chapter, in order to see what actually happens during the application startup and the decisions that Spring Boot will make while wiring our application together.

How to do it...

1. Conveniently, Spring Boot provides us with an ability to get the `CONDITIONS EVALUATION REPORT` by simply starting the application with the `debug` flag. This can be passed to the application either as an environment variable, `DEBUG`, as a system property, `-Ddebug`, or as an application property, `--debug`.

2. Start the application by running `DEBUG=true ./gradlew clean bootRun`.

3. Now, if you look at the console logs, you will see a lot more information printed there that is marked with the `DEBUG` level log. At the end of the startup log sequence, we will see the `CONDITIONS EVALUATION REPORT` as follows:

```
=========================
CONDITIONS EVALUATION REPORT
=========================
Positive matches:
-----------------

...

DataSourceAutoConfiguration
      - @ConditionalOnClass classes found:
```

```
javax.sql.DataSource,org.springframework.jdbc.
datasource.embedded.EmbeddedDatabaseType
(OnClassCondition)
      . . .
Negative matches:
-----------------

. . .

GsonAutoConfiguration
      - required @ConditionalOnClass classes not found:
      com.google.gson.Gson (OnClassCondition)
      . . .
```

How it works...

As you can see, the amount of information that is printed in the debug mode can be somewhat overwhelming, so I've selected only one example of positive and negative matches each.

For each line of the report, Spring Boot tells us why certain configurations have been selected to be included, what they have been positively matched on, or, for the negative matches, what was missing that prevented a particular configuration being included in the mix. Let's look at the positive match for DataSourceAutoConfiguration:

- The @ConditionalOnClass classes found tells us that Spring Boot has detected the presence of a particular class, specifically two classes in our case: javax.sql.DataSource and org.springframework.jdbc.datasource.embedded.EmbeddedDatabaseType.
- The OnClassCondition indicates the kind of matching that was used. This is supported by the @ConditionalOnClass and @ConditionalOnMissingClass annotations.

While OnClassCondition is the most common kind of detection, Spring Boot also uses many other conditions. For example, OnBeanCondition is used to check the presence or absence of specific bean instances, OnPropertyCondition is used to check the presence, absence, or specific value of a property, as well as any number of the custom conditions that can be defined using the @Conditional annotation and Condition interface implementations.

The negative matches show us a list of configurations that Spring Boot has evaluated, which means that they do exist in the classpath and were scanned by Spring Boot but didn't pass the conditions required for their inclusion. GsonAutoConfiguration, while available in the classpath as it is a part of the imported spring-boot-autoconfigure artifact, was not included because the required com.google.gson.Gson class was not detected as present in the classpath, thus failing the OnClassCondition.

The implementation of the GsonAutoConfiguration file looks as follows:

```
@Configuration
@ConditionalOnClass(Gson.class)
public class GsonAutoConfiguration {

  @Bean
  @ConditionalOnMissingBean
  public Gson gson() {
    return new Gson();
  }

}
```

After looking at the code, it is very easy to make the connection between the conditional annotations and report information that is provided by Spring Boot at the start time.

Creating a custom Spring Boot autoconfiguration starter

We have a high-level idea of the process by which Spring Boot decides which configurations to include in the formation of the application context. Now, let's take a stab at creating our own Spring Boot starter artifact, which we can include as an autoconfigurable dependency in our build.

In Chapter 2, *Configuring Web Applications*, you learned how to create database Repository objects. So, let's build a simple starter that will create another CommandLineRunner that will take the collection of all the Repository instances and print out the count of the total entries for each.

We will start by adding a child Gradle project to our existing project that will house the codebase for the starter artifact. We will call it db-count-starter.

How to do it...

1. We will start by creating a new directory named db-count-starter in the root of our project.
2. As our project has now become what is known as a multiproject build, we will need to create a settings.gradle configuration file in the root of our project with the following content:

```
include 'db-count-starter'
```

3. We should also create a separate build.gradle configuration file for our subproject in the db-count-starter directory in the root of our project, with the following content:

```
apply plugin: 'java'

repositories {
  mavenCentral()
  maven { url "https://repo.spring.io/snapshot" }
  maven { url "https://repo.spring.io/milestone" }

}

dependencies {
  compile("org.springframework.boot:spring-boot:2.0.0.BUILD-SNAPSHOT")
  compile("org.springframework.data:spring-data-commons:2.0.2.RELEASE")
}
```

4. Now we are ready to start coding. So, the first thing is to create the directory structure, src/main/java/com/example/bookpubstarter/dbcount, in the db-count-starter directory in the root of our project.
5. In the newly created directory, let's add our implementation of the CommandLineRunner file named DbCountRunner.java with the following content:

```
public class DbCountRunner implements CommandLineRunner {
    protected final Log logger = LogFactory.getLog(getClass());
```

```
    private Collection<CrudRepository> repositories;

    public DbCountRunner(Collection<CrudRepository> repositories) {
        this.repositories = repositories;
    }

    @Override
    public void run(String... args) throws Exception {
        repositories.forEach(crudRepository ->
            logger.info(String.format("%s has %s entries",
                getRepositoryName(crudRepository.getClass()),
                crudRepository.count()))));

    }

    private static String
            getRepositoryName(Class crudRepositoryClass) {
        for(Class repositoryInterface :
                crudRepositoryClass.getInterfaces()) {
            if (repositoryInterface.getName().
                    startsWith("com.example.bookpub.repository")) {
                return repositoryInterface.getSimpleName();
            }
        }
        return "UnknownRepository";
    }
}
```

6. With the actual implementation of DbCountRunner in place, we will now need to create the configuration object that will declaratively create an instance during the configuration phase. So, let's create a new class file called DbCountAutoConfiguration.java with the following content:

```
@Configuration
public class DbCountAutoConfiguration {
    @Bean
    public DbCountRunner dbCountRunner
            (Collection<CrudRepository> repositories) {
        return new DbCountRunner(repositories);
    }
}
```

7. We will also need to tell Spring Boot that our newly created JAR artifact contains the autoconfiguration classes. For this, we will need to create a resources/META-INF directory in the db-count-starter/src/main directory in the root of our project.

8. In this newly created directory, we will place the file named `spring.factories` with the following content:

```
org.springframework.boot.autoconfigure.EnableAutoConfiguration=\
com.example.bookpubstarter.dbcount.DbCountAutoConfiguration
```

9. For the purpose of our demo, we will add the dependency to our starter artifact in the main project's `build.gradle` by adding the following entry in the dependencies section:

```
compile project(':db-count-starter')
```

10. Start the application by running `./gradlew clean bootRun`.

11. Once the application is compiled and has started, we should see the following in the console logs:

```
    2017-12-16 INFO com.example.bookpub.StartupRunner         :
Welcome to the Book Catalog System!
    2017-12-16 INFO c.e.b.dbcount.DbCountRunner               :
AuthorRepository has 1 entries
    2017-12-16 INFO c.e.b.dbcount.DbCountRunner               :
PublisherRepository has 1 entries
    2017-12-16 INFO c.e.b.dbcount.DbCountRunner               :
BookRepository has 1 entries
    2017-12-16 INFO c.e.b.dbcount.DbCountRunner               :
ReviewerRepository has 0 entries
    2017-12-16 INFO com.example.bookpub.BookPubApplication    :
Started BookPubApplication in 8.528 seconds (JVM running for 9.002)
    2017-12-16 INFO com.example.bookpub.StartupRunner         :
Number of books: 1
```

How it works...

Congratulations! You have now built your very own Spring Boot autoconfiguration starter.

First, let's quickly walk through the changes that we made to our Gradle build configuration and then we will examine the starter setup in detail.

As the Spring Boot starter is a separate, independent artifact, just adding more classes to our existing project source tree would not really demonstrate much. To make this separate artifact, we have a couple of choices: making a separate Gradle configuration in our existing project, or creating a completely separate project altogether. The most ideal solution, however, was to just convert our build to Gradle Multi-Project Build by adding a nested project directory and subproject dependency to the `build.gradle` file of the root project. By doing this, Gradle actually creates a separate JAR artifact for us but we don't have to publish it anywhere, only include it as a compile `project(':db-count-starter')` dependency.

 For more information about Gradle multi-project builds, you can check out the manual at `http://gradle.org/docs/current/userguide/multi_project_builds.ht ml`.

The Spring Boot Auto-Configuration starter is nothing more than a regular Spring Java Configuration class annotated with the `@Configuration` annotation and the presence of `spring.factories` in the classpath in the `META-INF` directory with the appropriate configuration entries.

During the application startup, Spring Boot uses `SpringFactoriesLoader`, which is a part of Spring Core, in order to get a list of the Spring Java Configurations that are configured for the `org.springframework.boot.autoconfigure.EnableAutoConfiguration` property key. Under the hood, this call collects all the `spring.factories` files located in the `META-INF` directory from all the jars or other entries in the classpath, and builds a composite list to be added as application context configurations. In addition to the `EnableAutoConfiguration` key, we can declare the following automatically initializable startup implementations in a similar fashion:

- `org.springframework.context.ApplicationContextInitializer`
- `org.springframework.context.ApplicationListener`
- `org.springframework.boot.autoconfigure.AutoConfigurationImportListener`
- `org.springframework.boot.autoconfigure.AutoConfigurationImportFilter`
- `org.springframework.boot.autoconfigure.template.TemplateAvailabilityProvider`

- `org.springframework.boot.SpringBootExceptionReporter`
- `org.springframework.boot.SpringApplicationRunListener`
- `org.springframework.boot.env.PropertySourceLoader`
- `org.springframework.boot.env.EnvironmentPostProcessor`
- `org.springframework.boot.diagnostics.FailureAnalyzer`
- `org.springframework.boot.diagnostics.FailureAnalysisReporter`
- `org.springframework.test.contex.TestExecutionListener`

Ironically enough, a Spring Boot Starter does not need to depend on the Spring Boot library as its compile time dependency. If we look at the list of class imports in the `DbCountAutoConfiguration` class, we will not see anything from the `org.springframework.boot` package. The only reason that we have a dependency declared on Spring Boot is because our implementation of `DbCountRunner` implements the `org.springframework.boot.CommandLineRunner` interface.

Configuring custom conditional bean instantiations

In the previous example, you learned how to get the basic Spring Boot Starter going. On the inclusion of the jar in the application classpath, the `DbCountRunner` bean will be created automatically and added to the application context. In the very first recipe of this chapter, we have also seen that Spring Boot has an ability to do conditional configurations depending on a few conditions, such as the presence of specific classes in the classpath, existence of a bean, and others.

For this recipe, we will enhance our starter with a conditional check. This will create the instance of `DbCountRunner` only if no other bean instance of this class has already been created and added to the application context.

How to do it...

1. In the `DbCountAutoConfiguration` class, we will add an `@ConditionalOnMissingBean` annotation to the `dbCountRunner(...)` method, as follows:

```
@Bean
@ConditionalOnMissingBean
public DbCountRunner
    dbCountRunner(Collection<CrudRepository> repositories) {
  return new DbCountRunner(repositories);
}
```

2. We will also need to add a dependency on the `spring-boot-autoconfigure` artifact to the dependencies section of the `db-count-starter/build.gradle` file:

```
compile("org.springframework.boot:spring-boot-
autoconfigure:2.0.0.BUILD-SNAPSHOT")
```

3. Now, let's start the application by running `./gradlew clean bootRun` in order to verify that we will still see the same output in the console logs as we did in the previous recipe

4. If we start the application with the DEBUG switch so as to see the Auto-Configuration Report, which we already learned in the first recipe of this chapter, we will see that our autoconfiguration is in the Positive Matches group, as follows:

```
DbCountAutoConfiguration#dbCountRunner
        - @ConditionalOnMissingBean (types:
com.example.bookpubstarter.dbcount.DbCountRunner; SearchStrategy:
all) found no beans (OnBeanCondition)
```

5. Let's explicitly/manually create an instance of `DbCountRunner` in our main
   `BookPubApplication` configuration class, and we will also override its
   `run(...)` method, just so we can see the difference in the logs:

```
protected final Log logger = LogFactory.getLog(getClass());
@Bean
public DbCountRunner dbCountRunner
                    (Collection<CrudRepository> repositories) {
  return new DbCountRunner(repositories) {
    @Override
    public void run(String... args) throws Exception {
      logger.info("Manually Declared DbCountRunner");
    }
  };
}
```

6. Start the application by running `DEBUG=true ./gradlew clean bootRun`.

7. If we look at the console logs, we will see two things: the Auto-Configuration
   Report will print our autoconfiguration in the Negative Matches group and,
   instead of the count output for each repository, we will see `Manually Declared
   DbCountRunner` text to appear:

```
DbCountAutoConfiguration#dbCountRunner
        - @ConditionalOnMissingBean (types:
com.example.bookpubstarter.dbcount.DbCountRunner; SearchStrategy:
all) found the following [dbCountRunner] (OnBeanCondition)
2017-12-16 INFO com.example.bookpub.BookPubApplication$1    :
Manually Declared DbCountRunner
```

How it works...

As we learned from the previous recipe, Spring Boot will automatically process all the
configuration class entries from `spring.factories` during the application context
creation. Without any extra guidance, everything that is annotated with an `@Bean`
annotation will be used to create a Spring Bean. This functionality is actually a part of the
plain old Spring Framework Java Configuration. What Spring Boot adds on top is the ability
to conditionally control the rules for when certain `@Configuration` or `@Bean` annotations
should be executed and when it is best to ignore them.

In our case, we used the `@ConditionalOnMissingBean` annotation to instruct Spring Boot to create our `DbCountRunner` bean only if there was no other bean matching either the class type or bean name already declared elsewhere. As we explicitly created an `@Bean` entry for `DbCountRunner` in the `BookPubApplication` configuration, this took precedence and caused `OnBeanCondition` to detect the existence of the bean; thus instructing Spring Boot not to use `DbCountAutoConfiguration` during the application context setup.

Using custom @Enable annotations to toggle configuration

Allowing Spring Boot to automatically evaluate the classpath and detected configurations that are found there makes it very quick and easy to get a simple application going. However, there are times when we want to provide the configuration classes but require consumers of the starter library to explicitly enable such a configuration, rather than relying on Spring Boot to decide automatically if it should be included or not.

We will modify our previous recipe to make the starter be enabled via a meta-annotation rather than using the `spring.factories` route.

How to do it...

1. First, we will comment out the content of the `spring.factories` file located in `db-count-starter/src/main/resources` in the root of our project, as follows:

```
#org.springframework.boot.autoconfigure.EnableAutoConfiguration=\
#com.example.bookpubstarter.dbcount.DbCountAutoConfiguration
```

2. Next, we will need to create the meta-annotation. We will create a new file named `EnableDbCounting.java` in the `db-count-starter/src/main/java/com/example/bookpubstarter/dbcount` directory in the root of our project with the following content:

```
@Target(ElementType.TYPE)
@Retention(RetentionPolicy.RUNTIME)
@Import(DbCountAutoConfiguration.class)
@Documented
public @interface EnableDbCounting {
}
```

3. We will now add the `@EnableDbCounting` annotation to our `BookPubApplication` class and also remove the `dbCountRunner(...)` method from it, as shown in the following snippet:

```
@SpringBootApplication
@EnableScheduling
@EnableDbCounting
public class BookPubApplication {

    public static void main(String[] args) {
        SpringApplication.run(BookPubApplication.class, args);
    }

    @Bean
    public StartupRunner schedulerRunner() {
        return new StartupRunner();
    }
}
```

4. Start the application by running `./gradlew clean bootRun`.

How it works...

After running the application, the first thing that you might have noticed is that the printed counts all showed 0, even though `StartupRunner` had printed `Number of books: 1` to the console, as shown in the following output:

```
c.e.b.dbcount.DbCountRunner        : AuthorRepository has 0 entries
c.e.b.dbcount.DbCountRunner        : BookRepository has 0 entries
c.e.b.dbcount.DbCountRunner        : PublisherRepository has 0 entries
c.e.b.dbcount.DbCountRunner        : ReviewerRepository has 0 entries
com.example.bookpub.StartupRunner  : Welcome to the Book Catalog System!
com.example.bookpub.StartupRunner  : Number of books: 1
```

This is because Spring Boot is randomly executing `CommandLineRunners` and, as we changed the configuration to use the `@EnableDbCounting` annotation, it gets processed before the configuration in the `BookPubApplication` class itself. As the database population is done by us in the `StartupRunner.run(...)` method and the execution of `DbCountRunner.run(...)` happens before this, the database tables have no data and so report the 0 count.

If we want to enforce the order, Spring provides us with this ability using the `@Order` annotation. Let's annotate the `StartupRunner` class with `@Order(Ordered.LOWEST_PRECEDENCE - 15)`. As `LOWEST_PRECEDENCE` is the default order that is assigned, we will ensure that `StartupRunner` will be executed after `DbCountRunner` by slightly reducing the order number. Let's run the app again and now we will see that the counts are properly displayed.

Now that this little ordering issue is behind us, let's examine what we did with the `@EnableDbCounting` annotation in a bit more detail.

Without `spring.factories` containing the configuration, Spring Boot does not really know that the `DbCountAutoConfiguration` class should be included during the application context creation. By default, the configuration component scan will look only from the `BookPubApplication` package and below. As the packages are different—`com.example.bookpub` versus `com.example.bookpubstarter.dbcount`—the scanner won't pick it up.

This is where our newly created meta-annotation comes into play. In the `@EnableDbCounting` annotation, there is a key-nested annotation, `@Import(DbCountAutoConfiguration.class)`, which makes things happen. This is an annotation that is provided by Spring, which can be used to annotate other annotations with declarations of which configuration classes should be imported in the process. By annotating our `BookPubApplication` class with `@EnableDbCounting`, we transitively tell Spring that it should include `DbCountAutoConfiguration` as a part of the application context as well.

Using the convenience meta-annotations, `spring.factories`, and conditional bean annotations, we can now create sophisticated and elaborate custom autoconfiguration Spring Boot starters in order to solve the needs of our enterprises.

5
Application Testing

In this chapter, we will cover the following topics:

- Creating tests for MVC controllers
- Configuring a database schema and populating it
- Creating tests using an in-memory database
- Creating tests using mock objects
- Creating a JPA component test
- Creating a WebMvc component test
- Writing tests using Cucumber
- Writing tests using Spock

Introduction

In the previous chapters, we did a lot of coding. We created a new Spring Boot application from scratch, added an MVC component and some database services to it, made a few tweaks to the application behavior, and even wrote our very own Spring Boot starter. It is now time to take the next step and learn what kind of tools and capabilities Spring Boot offers when it comes to testing all this code, and how well it integrates with the other popular testing frameworks.

We will see how to use Spring JUnit integration to create unit tests. Next, we will explore the options of setting up the database with test data to test against it. We will then look to the **behavior-driven development** (**BDD**) tools Cucumber and Spock and see how they integrate with Spring Boot.

Creating tests for MVC controllers

In the previous chapters, we made a lot of progress in gradually creating our application, but how do we know that it actually does what we want it to do? More importantly, how do we know for sure that after six months, or even a year from now, it will still continue to do what we expected it to do at the very beginning? This question is best answered by creating a set of tests, preferably automated, that run a suite of assertions against our code. This ensures that we constantly get the same and expected output given the specific input. Tests give us the much-needed peace of mind that our application not only elegantly is coded and looks beautiful, but that it also performs reliably and is as error-free as possible.

In Chapter 4, *Writing Custom Spring Boot Starters*, we left off with our web application fitted with a custom-written Spring Boot starter. We will now create some basic tests to test our web application and to ensure that all the controllers expose the expected RESTful URLs, which we can rely on as the service API. This type of testing is a bit beyond what is commonly known as **unit testing** as it tests the entire web application, it requires the application context to be fully initialized, and all the beans should be wired together in order to work. This kind of testing is sometimes referred to as **integration** or **service testing**.

How to do it...

1. Spring Boot gets us going by creating a placeholder test file, BookPubApplicationTests.java, in the src/test/java/com/example/bookpub directory at the root of our project with the following content:

```
@RunWith(SpringRunner.class)
@SpringApplicationConfiguration(classes =
    BookPubApplication.class)
public class BookPubApplicationTests {
  @Test
  public void contextLoads() {
  }
}
```

2. In build.gradle, we also get a test dependency on spring-boot-starter-test, as follows:

```
testCompile("org.springframework.boot:spring-boot-starter-test")
```

3. We will go ahead and extend the basic template test to contain the following code:

```
import static org.hamcrest.Matchers.containsString;
import static org.junit.Assert.assertEquals;
import static org.junit.Assert.assertNotNull;
import static
org.springframework.test.web.servlet.setup.MockMvcBuilders.webAppCo
ntextSetup;
import static
org.springframework.test.web.servlet.request.MockMvcRequestBuilders
.get;
import static
org.springframework.test.web.servlet.result.MockMvcResultMatchers.c
ontent;
import static
org.springframework.test.web.servlet.result.MockMvcResultMatchers.j
sonPath;
import static
org.springframework.test.web.servlet.result.MockMvcResultMatchers.s
tatus;

@RunWith(SpringRunner.class)
@SpringBootTest(webEnvironment =
SpringBootTest.WebEnvironment.RANDOM_PORT)
public class BookPubApplicationTests {
    @Autowired
    private WebApplicationContext context;
    @Autowired
    private TestRestTemplate restTemplate;
    @Autowired
    private BookRepository repository;

    @LocalServerPort
    private int port;

    private MockMvc mockMvc;

    @Before
    public void setupMockMvc() {
        mockMvc = webAppContextSetup(context).build();
    }

    @Test
    public void contextLoads() {
        assertEquals(1, repository.count());
    }
```

```
@Test
public void webappBookIsbnApi() {
    Book book =
      restTemplate.getForObject("http://localhost:" +
        port + "/books/978-1-78528-415-1", Book.class);
    assertNotNull(book);
    assertEquals("Packt", book.getPublisher().getName());
}

@Test
public void webappPublisherApi() throws Exception {
    mockMvc.perform(get("/publishers/1")).
            andExpect(status().isOk()).andExpect(content().
              contentType(MediaType.parseMediaType
                ("application/hal+json;charset=UTF-8"))).
            andExpect(content().
                          string(containsString("Packt"))).
            andExpect(jsonPath("$.name").value("Packt"));
    }
}
```

4. Execute the tests by running `./gradlew clean test`.

5. By looking at the console output, we can tell that our tests have succeeded and are running, but we don't really see much information besides the following lines (truncated for brevity):

```
:compileJava
:compileTestJava
:testClasses
:test
2016-10-13 21:40:44.694  INFO 25739 --- [        Thread-4]
ationConfigEmbeddedWebApplicationContext : Closing
org.springframework.boot.context.embedded.AnnotationConfigEmbeddedW
ebApplicationContext@206f4aa6: startup date [Mon Apr 13 21:40:36
CDT 2015]; root of context hierarchy
2016-10-13 21:40:44.704  INFO 25739 --- [        Thread-4]
j.LocalContainerEntityManagerFactoryBean : Closing JPA
EntityManagerFactory for persistence unit 'default'
2016-10-13 21:40:44.705  INFO 25739 --- [        Thread-4]
org.hibernate.tool.hbm2ddl.SchemaExport   : HHH000227: Running
hbm2ddl schema export
2016-10-13 21:40:44.780  INFO 25739 --- [        Thread-4]
org.hibernate.tool.hbm2ddl.SchemaExport   : HHH000230: Schema export
complete
BUILD SUCCESSFUL
Total time: 24.635 secs
```

6. Better insight can be gathered by viewing the HTML reports that are generated by Gradle, which can be opened in the browser and reside in `build/reports/tests/index.html`, as shown in the following screenshot:

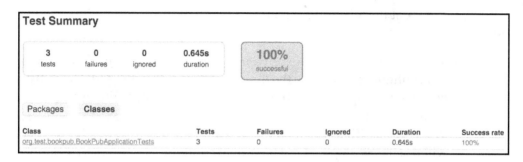

7. Clicking on `com.example.bookpub.BookPubApplicationTests` will take us to the individual test case breakdown, which shows the status of each test and how long it took to get executed, as follows:

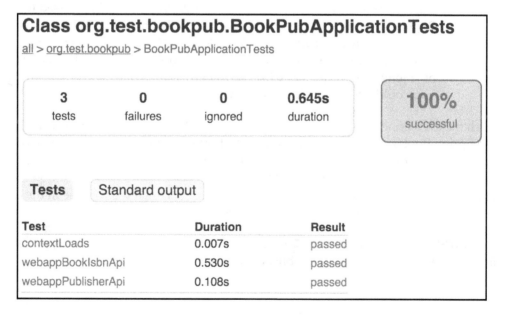

8. The more curious minds can also click on the **Standard output** button in order to see the runtime application logs that are produced during the execution of the test.

How it works...

Now that we have created our first test, let's examine the code in detail.

We will first look at the following annotations that have been declared for the `BookPubApplicationTests` class:

- `@RunWith(SpringRunner.class)`: This is a standard JUnit annotation that we can configure so as to use the `SpringRunner`, providing functionality to bootstrap the Spring Boot framework to the standard JUnit tests.

- `@SpringBootTest(webEnvironment=SpringBootTest.WebEnvironment.RANDOM_PORT)`: This is an annotation that marks the class as a Spring Boot test. It will use the Spring Boot framework to configure the test class instance, provide appropriate configuration, autowiring, and so on. The `webEnvironment=SpringBootTest.WebEnvironment.RANDOM_PORT` attribute means that the current test is going to use a real, running service instance and will require a complete context initialization and application startup, as if it were the real deal. The `RANDOM_PORT` value is used to tell Spring Boot to start the Tomcat server on a randomly-chosen HTTP port, which we will later obtain by declaring the `@LocalServerPortprivate int port;` value field. This ability to select a random HTTP port is very handy when running tests on a Jenkins or any other CI server where, if multiple jobs are running in parallel, you could encounter port collision.

With the class annotations magic dispelled, let's look at the content of the class itself. As this is a Spring Boot test, we can declare any objects that are managed by Spring to be `@Autowired` during the execution or set to a specific environment value using a `@Value` annotation. In our test, we autowired the `WebApplicationContext` and `BookRepository` objects, as well as an instance of `TestRestTemplate`, which we will use in the execution of the standard JUnit `@Test` annotated test cases.

In the first test case, the `contextLoads()` method, we will just assert that we have the `BookRepository` connection established and that it contains one book entry.

Our second test will ensure that our web application responds to a RESTful URL for a `Book` lookup via `ISBN` - `"/books/{isbn}"`. For this test, we will use the instance of `TestRestTemplate` and make a RESTful call to the running instance on a randomly-selected port. Spring Boot provides the value of the `port` field.

In the `webappBookIsbnApi` test, we are using a full URL with the starting part being `"http://localhost:" + port`, which is technically not required if `TestRestTemplate` was autowired and injected by Spring Boot. In this case, it is possible to use a relative URL, looking like `Book book = restTemplate.getForObject("/books/978-1-78528-415-1", Book.class);`, and `TestRestTemplate` will automatically determine the port of the running test server instance.

Alternatively, we can execute the same flavor of tests by going through the `MockMvc` object. This is provided by the Spring Test Framework and allows you to perform MVC testing without actually doing client-side-based testing through `RestTemplate`, but instead doing it fully on the server side where the controller requests are executed from the same context as the tested application.

In order to use `MockMvc`, we will use the `MockMvcBuilders` utility to build an instance using `@Autowired WebApplicationContext`. We will do this in the setup method so that we don't have to do it in every test explicitly.

It is also possible to get Spring Boot to automatically create an instance of `MockMvc`, if we annotate our test using `WebEnvironment.MOCK` instead of `RANDOM_PORT`. That configuration will only make the test run in the mock context, and no real server will be started. Our example shows how to combine having a real server instance and `MockMVC` in the same test class.

`MockMvc` provides us with a very extensive set of capabilities in order to execute assertions on practically all the things that are related to a web request. It is designed to be used in a method-chained fashion, allowing us to link the various tests together and forming a nice, continuous logical chain:

- `perform(get(...))`: This method sets up the web request. In our particular case, we perform a GET request but the `MockMvcRequestBuilders` class provides us with static helper functions for all the common method calls.
- `andExpect(...)`: This method can be invoked multiple times, where each call represents an evaluation of a condition against the result of the `perform(...)` call. The argument of this call is any implementation of the `ResultMatcher` interface along with many stock ones that are provided by the `MockMvcResultMatchers` static utility class. This really opens up the possibility of having an infinite number of different checks such as verifying the response status, content type, values stored in a session, flash scope, verify redirects, contents of the rendering model or headers, and much more. We will use a third-party `json-path` add-on library (which is automatically brought as a `spring-boot-test` dependency) to test the JSON response data in order to ensure that it contains the right elements in the right tree hierarchy. `andExpect(jsonPath("$.name").value("Packt"))` validates that we have a name element at the root of the JSON document with a value of `Packt`.

 To learn more about the various possibilities that are available in MockMvc, you can refer to `https://github.com/spring-projects/ spring-mvc-showcase/tree/master/src/test/java/org/ springframework/samples/mvc`.

Configuring a database schema and populating it

Earlier in the book, in `Chapter 2`, *Configuring Web Applications*, we manually added a few entries to the database in the `StartupRunner's run(...)` method. While doing so programmatically can be a quick and easy way to get something going very quickly, in the long run, it is not really a good idea to do so, especially when you are dealing with a large amount of data. It is also good practice to separate the database preparations, changes, and other configurations from the rest of the running application code, even if it is setting up the test cases. Thankfully, Spring has provided you with the support to make this task fairly easy and straightforward.

We will continue with the state of the application as we left it in the previous recipe. Spring provides us with a couple of ways to define how both the structure and data should be populated in the database. The first way relies on using Hibernate to automatically create the table structure by inferring it from our defined @Entity objects and using the import.sql file to populate the data. The second approach is to use the plain old Spring JDBC capability, which relies on using the schema.sql file that contains the database table definition and a corresponding data.sql file that contains the data.

How to do it...

1. First, we will remove the programmatic database population which we created in Chapter 2, *Configuring Web Applications*. So let's comment out the following code from the StartupRunner's run(...) method:

```
Author author = new Author("Alex", "Antonov");
author = authorRepository.save(author);
Publisher publisher = new Publisher("Packt");
publisher = publisherRepository.save(publisher);
Book book = new Book("978-1-78528-415-1", "Spring Boot Recipes",
author, publisher);
bookRepository.save(book);
```

2. If we were to run our tests, they might fail if the test.h2.db file is missing because they expect the data to be in the database. We will populate the database by creating a Hibernate import.sql file in the src/main/resources directory at the root of our project with the following content:

```
INSERT INTO author (id, first_name, last_name) VALUES (1, 'Alex',
'Antonov')
INSERT INTO publisher (id, name) VALUES (1, 'Packt')
INSERT INTO book (isbn, title, author_id, publisher_id) VALUES
('978-1-78528-415-1', 'Spring Boot Recipes', 1, 1)
```

3. On running the tests again by running ./gradlew clean test, they are magically started and get passed again.

4. Another way to do this is to use the Spring JDBC support for schema.sql and data.sql. Let's rename the newly-created import.sql file to data.sql and create a schema.sql file in the same directory with the following content:

```
-- Create syntax for TABLE 'author'
DROP TABLE IF EXISTS `author`;
```

```
CREATE TABLE `author` (
  `id` bigint(20) NOT NULL AUTO_INCREMENT,
  `first_name` varchar(255) DEFAULT NULL,
  `last_name` varchar(255) DEFAULT NULL,
  PRIMARY KEY (`id`)
);
-- Create syntax for TABLE 'publisher'
DROP TABLE IF EXISTS `publisher`;
CREATE TABLE `publisher` (
  `id` bigint(20) NOT NULL AUTO_INCREMENT,
  `name` varchar(255) DEFAULT NULL,
  PRIMARY KEY (`id`)
);
-- Create syntax for TABLE 'reviewer'
DROP TABLE IF EXISTS `reviewer`;
CREATE TABLE `reviewer` (
  `id` bigint(20) NOT NULL AUTO_INCREMENT,
  `first_name` varchar(255) DEFAULT NULL,
  `last_name` varchar(255) DEFAULT NULL,
  PRIMARY KEY (`id`)
);
-- Create syntax for TABLE 'book'
DROP TABLE IF EXISTS `book`;
CREATE TABLE `book` (
  `id` bigint(20) NOT NULL AUTO_INCREMENT,
  `description` varchar(255) DEFAULT NULL,
  `isbn` varchar(255) DEFAULT NULL,
  `title` varchar(255) DEFAULT NULL,
  `author_id` bigint(20) DEFAULT NULL,
  `publisher_id` bigint(20) DEFAULT NULL,
  PRIMARY KEY (`id`),
  CONSTRAINT `FK_publisher` FOREIGN KEY (`publisher_id`) REFERENCES
`publisher` (`id`),
  CONSTRAINT `FK_author` FOREIGN KEY (`author_id`) REFERENCES
`author` (`id`)
);
-- Create syntax for TABLE 'book_reviewers'
DROP TABLE IF EXISTS `book_reviewers`;
CREATE TABLE `book_reviewers` (
  `book_id` bigint(20) NOT NULL,
  `reviewers_id` bigint(20) NOT NULL,
  CONSTRAINT `FK_book` FOREIGN KEY (`book_id`) REFERENCES `book`
(`id`),
  CONSTRAINT `FK_reviewer` FOREIGN KEY (`reviewers_id`) REFERENCES
`reviewer` (`id`)
);
```

5. As we are now manually creating the database schema, we will need to tell the Hibernate mapper not to automatically derive one from the entities and populate the database with it. So, let's set the `spring.jpa.hibernate.ddl-auto=none` property in the `application.properties` file in the `src/main/resources` directory at the root of our project.

6. Execute the tests by running `./gradlew clean test` and they should get passed.

How it works...

In this recipe, we actually explored two ways of achieving the same thing, and this is quite common when you are living in the Spring ecosystem. Depending on the components that are used, whether it's a plain Spring JDBC, Spring JPA with Hibernate, or the Flyway or Liquibase migrations, the approach of populating and initializing the database differs but the end result remains pretty much the same.

Both Flyway and Liquibase are frameworks that provide incremental database migration capabilities. This comes in very handy when one wants to maintain the incremental log of the database changes in a programmatic, describable fashion with the ability to quickly put the database in a desired state for a particular version. While these frameworks differ in their approach in terms of providing such support, they are similar in their purpose. More detailed information can be obtained at their respective sites, `http://flywaydb.org` and `http://www.liquibase.org`.

In the preceding example, we explored two different ways of populating and initializing the database.

Initializing the database with Spring JPA and Hibernate

In this approach, most of the work is actually done by the `Hibernate` library and we merely set up the appropriate configurations and create conventionally expected files that are needed for Hibernate to do the work:

- The `spring.jpa.hibernate.ddl-auto=create-drop` setting instructs Hibernate to use the `@Entity` models and, based on their structure, automatically deduces the database schema. Upon starting the application, the calculated schema will be used to preinitialize the database table structure; when the application is shut down, it will all be destroyed. Even in the event that the application was forcefully terminated or it abruptly crashed, upon startup, if the existing tables are detected, they will be dropped and recreated from scratch. So it's probably not a good idea to rely on this for a production environment.

> If the `spring.jpa.hibernate.ddl-auto` property is not explicitly configured, Spring Boot uses create-drop for embedded databases such as H2 by default, so be careful and set it appropriately.

- Hibernate expects that the `import.sql` file is residing in the root of the classpath. This is used to execute the declared SQL statements upon application startup. While any valid SQL statement can go in the file, it is recommended that you put in the data-importing statements such as `INSERT` or `UPDATE` and steer clear of table structure mutations, as the schema definition is already taken care of by Hibernate.

Initializing the database with Spring JDBC

If the application does not use JPA, or you don't want to depend on the Hibernate functionality explicitly, Spring offers you another way of getting the database set up, as long as the `spring-boot-starter-jdbc` dependency is present. So let's take a look at what we did to get it to work, as shown in the following list:

- The `spring.jpa.hibernate.ddl-auto=none` setting tells Hibernate not to do any automatic handling of the database if the Hibernate dependency also exists, as it does in our case. This setting is good practice for a production environment as you probably don't want to get all of your database tables wiped clean inadvertently. That would be one hell of a disaster, that's for sure!

- The `schema.sql` file is expected to exist in the root of the classpath. It is executed by Spring during the schema creation of the database upon every startup of the application. However, unlike Hibernate, this will not drop any of the existing tables automatically, so it might be a good idea to either use `DROP TABLE IF EXISTS` to delete an existing table before creating the new one, or use `CREATE TABLE IF NOT EXISTS` as part of the table creation SQL if you only want to create new tables when they don't already exist. This makes it a lot more flexible to declare the database structure evolution logic, thus making it safer to be used in production as well.
- The `data.sql` file is expected to exist in the root of the classpath. This is used to execute the data population SQL, so this is where all the `INSERT INTO` statements go.

Given that this is a Spring native functionality, we will also get the ability to define the schema and data files not only globally, but also as per the specific database platform. For example, we can have one set of files that we can use for Oracle, `schema-oracle.sql`, and a different one for MySQL, `schema-mysql.sql`. The same applies to the `data.sql` variants as well; however, they don't have to be defined per platform, so while you might have platform-specific schema files, there could be a shared data file. The `spring.datasource.platform` configuration value can be explicitly set if you want to override Spring Boot's automatically deduced value.

 In case one wants to override the default names of `schema.sql` and `data.sql`, Spring Boot provides the configuration properties, which we can use to control `spring.datasource.schema` and `spring.datasource.data`.

Creating tests using an in-memory database

In the previous recipe, we explored how to get our databases set up with the desired tables and populated with the required data. When it comes to testing, one of the typical challenges is to get the environment set up correctly and predictably so that when the tests are executed, we can safely assert the behavior in a deterministic fashion. In an application that connects to a database, making sure that the database contains a deterministic dataset on which the assertions can be evaluated is extremely important. For an elaborate test suite, it is also necessary to be able to refresh or change that dataset based on the tests. Thankfully, Spring has some nice facilities that aid you in accomplishing this task.

We will pick up from the state of our BookPub application as we left it in the previous recipe. At this point, we have the schema.sql file defining all the tables, and we also need the database with some starting data that is defined in data.sql. In this recipe, we will extend our tests to use the specific data fixture files that are tailored to a particular test suite.

How to do it...

1. Our first step will be to create a resources directory in the src/test directory at the root of our project.

2. In this directory, we will start placing our fixture SQL data files. Let's create a new file named test-data.sql in the resources directory with the following content:

```
INSERT INTO author (id, first_name, last_name) VALUES (2, 'Greg',
'Turnquist')
INSERT INTO book (isbn, title, author_id, publisher_id) VALUES
('978-1-78439-302-1', 'Learning Spring Boot', 2, 1)
```

3. We now need a way to load this file when our test runs. We will modify our BookPubApplicationTests class in the following way:

```
public class BookPubApplicationTests {
    ...
    @Autowired
    private BookRepository repository;
    @Autowired
    private RestTemplate restTemplate;
    @Autowired
    private DataSource ds;
    @LocalServerPort
    private int port;

    private MockMvc mockMvc;
    private static boolean loadDataFixtures = true;

    @Before
    public void setupMockMvc() {
        ...
    }

    @Before
    public void loadDataFixtures() {
        if (loadDataFixtures) {
```

```
        ResourceDatabasePopulator populator =
          new ResourceDatabasePopulator(
              context.getResource("classpath:/test-data.sql"));
        DatabasePopulatorUtils.execute(populator, ds);
        loadDataFixtures = false;
    }
}

@Test
public void contextLoads() {
    assertEquals(2, repository.count());
}

@Test
public void webappBookIsbnApi() {
    ...
}

@Test
public void webappPublisherApi() throws Exception {
    ...
}
}
```

4. Execute the tests by running `./gradlew clean test`, and they should continue to get passed despite us adding another book and its author to the database.

5. We can also use the method of populating the database that we learned in the previous recipe. As the test code has its own `resources` directory, it is possible to add another `data.sql` file to it, and Spring Boot will use both the files to populate the database. Let's go ahead and create the `data.sql` file in the `src/test/resources` directory at the root of our project with the following content:

```
INSERT INTO author (id, first_name, last_name) VALUES (3,
'William', 'Shakespeare')
INSERT INTO publisher (id, name) VALUES (2, 'Classical Books')
INSERT INTO book (isbn, title, author_id, publisher_id) VALUES
('978-1-23456-789-1', 'Romeo and Juliet', 3, 2)
```

As Spring Boot collects all the occurrences of the data files from the classpath, it is possible to place the data files in JARs or different physical locations that all end up being at the root of the classpath. It is also important to remember that the loading order of these scripts is not deterministic, and if you rely on certain referential IDs, it is better if you use selects to get them instead of making assumptions.

6. As we added another book to the database and we now have three of them, we should fix the assertion in our `contextLoads()` test method:

```
assertEquals(3, repository.count());
```

7. Execute the tests by running `./gradlew clean test` and they should continue to get passed.

8. It would be a fair statement to say that when running unit tests, an in-memory database is probably more suitable for the role than a persistent one. Let's create a dedicated test configuration instance of the `application.properties` file in the `src/test/resources` directory at the root of our project with the following content:

```
spring.datasource.url =
jdbc:h2:mem:testdb;DB_CLOSE_DELAY=-1;DB_CLOSE_ON_EXIT=FALSE
spring.jpa.hibernate.ddl-auto=update
```

It is important to know that Spring Boot loads only one `application.properties` file from the classpath. When we created another `application.properties` in `src/test/resources`, the previous one from `src/main/resources` was no longer loaded and thus none of the properties defined in it were merged in the environment. For this reason, you should configure all of the property values that are required. In our case, we had to redefine the `spring.jpa.hibernate.dll-auto` property, even though it was already declared in the `src/main/resources/application.properties` location.

9. Execute the tests by running `./gradlew clean test` and the tests should continue to get passed.

How it works...

In this recipe, we relied on the facility that is provided by Spring to initialize and populate the database in order to get our database populated with the data required to run the tests and assert on them. However, we also wanted to be able to use some data that was only relevant to a particular test suite. For this, we turned to the `ResourceDatabasePopulator` and `DatabasePopulatorUtils` classes to insert the desired data right before the test got executed. These are exactly the same classes that are used internally by Spring in order to handle the `schema.sql` and `data.sql` files, except now, we are explicitly defining the script files that we want to execute.

So, let's break up what we did step by step, as follows:

- We created a setup method named `loadDataFixtures()`, which we annotated with a `@Before` annotation to tell JUnit to run it before every test.

- In this method, we obtained a resource handle to the `classpath:/test-data.sql` data file that resides in our application's classpath and where we store our test data and execute it against `@Autowired DataSource ds`.

- As Spring can only autowire dependencies in the instances of the class, and the `@Before` annotated setup methods get executed for every test, we had to get a little creative in order to avoid repopulating our database with the duplicate data for every test instead of once per test suite/class. To achieve this, we created a `static boolean loadDataFixtures` variable that retained its state for every instance of the `BookPubApplicationTests` class, thus ensuring that we executed `DatabasePopulatorUtils` only once. The reason that the variable has to be static is as a new instance of the test class gets created for every test method that it runs in the class; having the `boolean` flag at the instance level will not do the trick.

 Alternatively, we could have used the `@Sql` annotation instead of the `loadDataFixtures()` method and marked our `BookPubApplicationTests` class as `@Transactional` to make sure that the `test-data.sql` file got populated before every test method was run. Then we could have rolled back to the pre-execution state of the database.

This makes test setup a bit simpler and the transactional part allows for having tests that mutate the data in the database without worrying about race conditions, but this has the downside of executing the SQL population before every test, which adds a bit of extra latency.

To make this work, we need to remove the `loadDataFixtures()` method and add the following annotations to the `BookPubApplicationTests` class:

```
@Transactional
@Sql(scripts = "classpath:/test-data.sql")
```

- For the finishing touch, we decided to have a separate `application.properties` file to be used for testing purposes. We added this to our `src/test/resources` classpath with a testing configuration of the in-memory database instead of using the file-based persistent one.

- Unlike `application.properties`, where only one file can be loaded from the classpath, Spring supports a number of profile configurations which will be merged together. So, instead of declaring a completely separate `application.properties` file, we could create an `application-test.properties` file and set an active profile to test while running the tests.

Creating tests using mock objects

In the previous recipe, we used a data fixture file to populate an in-memory database in order to run our tests on predictable and static sets of data. While this makes the tests consistent and deterministic, we are still paying the price of having to create a database, populate it with data, and initialize all the JPA and connectivity components, which could be viewed as an excessive step for a test. Luckily, Spring Boot provides internal support for being able to mock beans and inject them as components in the tests for setup and further use as dependencies within an application context.

Let's examine how we can use the power of Mockito so that we don't need to rely on the database at all. We will learn how to elegantly mock the `Repository` instance objects using the Mockito framework and some `@MockBean` annotation cleverness.

How to do it...

1. First, we will create a new `MockPublisherRepositoryTests` test class in the `src/test/java/com/example/bookpub` directory at the root of our project with the following content:

```java
import static org.assertj.core.api.Assertions.assertThat;
import static org.mockito.BDDMockito.given;
import static org.mockito.BDDMockito.reset;

@RunWith(SpringRunner.class)
@SpringBootTest(webEnvironment =
SpringBootTest.WebEnvironment.NONE)
public class MockPublisherRepositoryTests {
    @MockBean
    private PublisherRepository repository;

    @Before
    public void setupPublisherRepositoryMock() {
        given(repository.count()).willReturn(5L);
    }

    @Test
    public void publishersExist() {
        assertThat(repository.count()).isEqualTo(5L);
    }

    @After
    public void resetPublisherRepositoryMock() {
        reset(repository);
    }
}
```

2. Execute the tests by running `./gradlew clean test` and the tests should get passed

How it works...

There are a few magical things happening here. Let's start with the annotations that we put into the MockPublisherRepositoryTests class:

- The @SpringBootTest annotation's webEnvironment attribute was replaced with WebEnvironment.NONE. This is to inform Spring Boot that we don't want a full application web server to be initialized for this test, since we will only be interacting with the repository object, without making calls to controllers or using any part of the WebMvc stack. We did this to save test startup time, and if one is curious to see the difference, just simply switching it back to the WebEnvironment.RANDOM_PORT value and rerunning the test would show that the time has almost doubled. (On my beefy MacBook Pro, it increased from 5 seconds to almost 9.)

With the application changes examined, let's now look at what we did in the MockPublisherRepositoryTests class itself:

- The @MockBean annotation instructs Spring that this dependency is not a real instance, but a mock object currently backed by the Mockito framework. This has an interesting effect in that it actually replaces our PublisherRepository bean instance in the context with the mock one, so, everywhere within the context, all dependencies for PublisherRepository get wired with the mocked version instead of a real, database-backed one.

Now that we know how the mocked instance of PublisherRepository gets injected into our tests, let's take a look at the newly-created test setup methods. The two methods of particular interest are setupPublisherRepositoryMock() and resetPublisherRepositoryMock(). They are described as follows:

- The setupPublisherRepositoryMock() method is annotated with @Before, which tells JUnit to execute this method before running every @Test method in the class. We will use the Mockito framework in order to configure the behavior of our mocked instance. We configure it such, that when the repository.count() method is called, it will return 5 as a result. The Mockito, Junit, and Hamcrest libraries provide us with many convenient DLS-like methods, which we can use to define such rules with an English-like, easy-to-read style.

- The `resetPublisherRepositoryMock()` method is annotated with `@After`, which tells JUnit to execute this method after running every `@Test` method in the class. At the end of every test, we will need to reset the mocked behavior, so we will use the `reset(...)` method call to clear out all of our settings and get the mock ready for the next test, which can be used in another test suite altogether.

 Ideally, there is no need to reset the `mock` object at the end of the test run, as each test class gets its own context spawned up, so between test classes the instance of a mock is not shared. It is considered good practice to create many smaller tests instead of a single large one. There are, however, some use cases that warrant resetting the mock when it is being managed by a container injection, so I thought it was worth mentioning. For the best practices on using `reset(...)`, see `https://github.com/mockito/mockito/wiki/FAQ#can-i-reset-a-mock`.

Creating a JPA component test

Most of our previous test examples had to start up the entire application and configure all the beans in order to execute. While that is not a big issue for our simple application, which has little code, it might prove an expensive and lengthy process for some larger, more complex enterprise-grade services. Considering that one of the key aspects of having good test coverage is a low execution time, we might want to opt out of having to bootstrap the entire application in order to test just one component, or *slice*, as Spring Boot refers to it.

In this recipe, we will try to create a similar test to our previous `PublisherRepository` one, but without starting the entire container and initializing all the beans. Conveniently, Spring Boot provides us with the `@DataJpaTest` annotation, which we can put on our test class, and it will automatically configure all the components necessary for the JPA functionality, but not the entire context. So beans like controllers, services, and so on, will be missing. This test is very good at quickly testing the validity of entity domain object bindings, to make sure the field names, associations, and so on, have been configured correctly.

How to do it...

1. Let's create a new `JpaAuthorRepositoryTests` test class in the `src/test/java/com/example/bookpub` directory at the root of our project with the following content:

```java
import static org.assertj.core.api.Assertions.assertThat;

@RunWith(SpringRunner.class)
@DataJpaTest
public class JpaAuthorRepositoryTests {
    @Autowired
    private TestEntityManager mgr;

    @Autowired
    private AuthorRepository repository;

    @Test
    public void testAuthorEntityBinding() {
        Long id = mgr.persistAndGetId(createAuthor(),
                                Long.class);

        Author author = repository.findById(id).get();
        assertThat(author.getFirstName()).
                isEqualTo("Mark");
        assertThat(author.getLastName()).
                isEqualTo("Twain");
    }

    private Author createAuthor() {
        return new Author("Mark", "Twain");
    }
}
```

2. Execute the tests by running `./gradlew clean test` and the tests should continue to pass

How it works...

The key difference from our previous test is the absence of the `@SpringBootTest` annotation, which has been replaced with the `@DataJpaTest` annotation. The apparent simplicity of the test class itself is possible thanks to the `@DataJpaTest` annotation doing the bulk of the declarations and workload to configure the test environment. If we look inside the annotation definition, we will see a myriad of different internal annotations configuring all the necessary components. The important ones are the `@AutoConfigure*` annotations, such as `@AutoConfigureDataJpa` or `@AutoConfigureTestDatabase`. Those annotations essentially instruct Spring Boot to import the necessary component configurations when bootstrapping the test. For example, in `@DataJpaTest`, only `Cache`, `DataJpa`, `TestDatabase`, and `TestEntityManager` components would be configured and made available, which significantly reduces the test footprint, both memory-wise as well as startup and execution times. The specific configuration classes are then loaded, as we've seen before, from the `META-INF/spring.factories` descriptors provided by various artifacts.

With the right components initialized, we can take advantage of some preconfigured beans, such as `TestEntityManager`, which gives us the ability to interact with the test instance of the database, pre-initialize the desired state of its content, and manipulate test data. This gives us the guarantee that after each test suite is done executing, we will get a clean slate for the next set without the need of an explicit cleanup. This makes it easier to write tests, without having to worry about the order of execution and potential over stepping of changes from test suite to test suite, avoiding the inadvertent dirty state that makes tests inconsistent.

Creating a WebMvc component test

Another one of the collection of `*Test` slices is `@WebMvcTest`, which allows us to create tests for the WebMvc part of the application, quickly testing controllers, filters, and so on, while providing ability to use `@MockBean` to configure the necessary dependencies such as services, data repositories, and so on.

This is another very useful testing slice provided by the Spring Boot Test Framework, and we will explore its use in this recipe, taking a look at how we can create an Mvc layer test for our `BookController` file, mocking the `BookRepository` service with a predefined dataset and making sure the returned JSON document is what we would expect based on that data.

How to do it...

1. First, we will create a new `WebMvcBookControllerTests` test class in the `src/test/java/com/example/bookpub` directory at the root of our project with the following content:

```
import static org.hamcrest.Matchers.containsString;
import static org.mockito.BDDMockito.given;
import static
org.springframework.test.web.servlet.request.MockMvcRequestBuilders
.get;
import static
org.springframework.test.web.servlet.result.MockMvcResultMatchers.c
ontent;
import static
org.springframework.test.web.servlet.result.MockMvcResultMatchers.j
sonPath;
import static
org.springframework.test.web.servlet.result.MockMvcResultMatchers.s
tatus;

@RunWith(SpringRunner.class)
@WebMvcTest
public class WebMvcBookControllerTests {
    @Autowired
    private MockMvc mockMvc;

    @MockBean
    private BookRepository repository;

    // The 2 repositories below are needed to
    //successfully initialize StartupRunner
    @MockBean
    private AuthorRepository authorRepository;
    @MockBean
    private PublisherRepository publisherRepository;

    @Test
    public void webappBookApi() throws Exception {
        given(repository.findBookByIsbn("978-1-78528-415-1"))
            .willReturn(new Book("978-1-78528-415-1",
                                "Spring Boot Recipes",
                                new Author("Alex", "Antonov"),
                                new Publisher("Packt")));

        mockMvc.perform(get("/books/978-1-78528-415-1")).
```

```
                        andExpect(status().isOk()).
                        andExpect(content().
                                contentType(MediaType.parseMediaType
                                ("application/json;charset=UTF-8"))).
                        andExpect(content().
                                string(containsString("Spring Boot
        Recipes"))).
                        andExpect(jsonPath("$.isbn").
                                value("978-1-78528-415-1"));
                }
        }
```

2. Execute the tests by running `./gradlew clean test` and the tests should continue to pass

How it works...

The functionality of `@WebMvcTest` is very similar to the `@DataJpaTest` annotation we have seen in the previous recipe. The difference is really just a set of components that get initialized during the test bootstrap. Unlike `@DataJpaTest`, this time there are no database components that are provided for us, but instead we get the `WebMvc` and `MockMvc` configurations, which bring all the necessary foundations for initializing controllers, filters, interceptors, and so on. For that reason, we had to add `AuthorRepository` and `PublisherRepository` as mock beans into our test code, because otherwise the test would fail to start because Spring Boot would be unable to satisfy the bean dependency that the `StartupRunner` class has on those two repositories.

 Another solution to this problem could be removing the dependency on those two repositories from the `StartupRunner` class, since we've commented out the code that uses them earlier in this chapter, in the *Configuring database schema and populating it* recipe. If that was not possible, I wanted to demonstrate how to handle the situation where you have bean dependencies in other classes, unrelated directly to the test, but causing startup failures during initialization and execution.

As one can see, unlike our previous recipe test, where we did not use any bean mocking since it was testing a lower-layer component without further dependencies, this time we need to provide a `BookRepository` mock, which is being used by our `BookController` class, the functionality of which we are testing.

We have already seen how to use the `@Before` annotation to preconfigure mock objects in the `MockPublisherRepositoryTests` class, so this time we are doing the configuration directly in the `webappBookApi` test method, similar to the style you will see when we learn about writing tests using the Spock framework.

Inside the `given(...)` call, we pre-configure the behavior of the `BookRepository` mock object, instructing it to return a specific `Book` instance when its `findBookByIsbn` method gets called with `"978-1-78528-415-1"` as an argument.

Our next call to `mockMvc.perform` with `/books/978-1-78528-415-1` triggers the invocation of the `BookController` `getBook` method, which delegates the pre-wired mocked instance of `bookRepository` and uses our pre-configured `Book` object instance to run validation logic upon.

As evident from the log, we can see that only the WebMvc layer has been bootstrapped. No database or other components have been initialized, which has resulted in significant savings in runtime, taking only 3 seconds compared to the 9 seconds it took for a complete application bootstrap test earlier.

Writing tests using Cucumber

Unit testing has been an expected part of the software development life cycle for quite some time now, and one can hardly imagine writing code without having unit tests along with it. The art of testing does not stay the same, and advances in testing philosophies have extended the concept of unit testing even further, introducing things such as service testing, integration testing, and, lastly, what is known as BDD that proposes to create the test suites describing the application behavior at large without getting down to the minute implementation details at the lower levels of the code. One such framework, which has gained a lot of popularity first in the Ruby world and later expanding to other languages including Java, is the Cucumber BDD.

For the purpose of this recipe, we will pick up on our previous example and continue enhancing the testing suite by adding the Cucumber-JVM implementation, which will provide us with the Java-based version of the original Ruby Cucumber framework, and create a few tests in order to demonstrate the capabilities and integration points with the Spring Boot application.

This recipe is by no means intended to cover the entire set of functionalities provided by the Cucumber testing framework and is mostly focused on the integration points of Cucumber and Spring Boot. To learn more about Cucumber-JVM, you can go to `https://cukes.info/docs#cucumber-implementations` or `https://github.com/cucumber/cucumber-jvm` for details.

How to do it...

1. The first thing that we need to do is add the necessary dependencies for the Cucumber libraries to our `build.gradle` file, as follows:

```
dependencies {
    compile("org.springframework.boot:spring-boot-starter-data-jpa")
    compile("org.springframework.boot:spring-boot-starter-jdbc")
    compile("org.springframework.boot:spring-boot-starter-web")
    compile("org.springframework.boot:spring-boot-starter-data-rest")
    compile project(":db-count-starter")
    runtime("com.h2database:h2")
    runtime("mysql:mysql-connector-java")
    testCompile("org.springframework.boot:spring-boot-starter-test")
    testCompile("info.cukes:cucumber-spring:1.2.5")
    testCompile("info.cukes:cucumber-java8:1.2.5")
    testCompile("info.cukes:cucumber-junit:1.2.5")
}
```

2. Next, we will need to create a test driver class to run Cucumber tests. Let's create a `RunCukeTests.java` file in the `src/test/java/com/example/bookpub` directory at the root of our project with the following content:

```
@RunWith(Cucumber.class)
@CucumberOptions(plugin={"pretty", "html:build/reports/cucumber"},
                glue = {"cucumber.api.spring",
                        "classpath:com.example.bookpub"},
                monochrome = true)
public class RunCukeTests {
}
```

3. With the driver class created, we are ready to start writing what Cucumber refers to as Step Definitions. I will talk briefly about what these are in the *How it works...* section of this recipe. For now, let's create a `RepositoryStepdefs.java` file in the `src/test/java/com/example/bookpub` directory at the root of our project with the following content:

```java
@WebAppConfiguration
@ContextConfiguration(classes = BookPubApplication.class,
                  loader = SpringBootContextLoader.class)
public class RepositoryStepdefs {
    @Autowired
    private WebApplicationContext context;
    @Autowired
    private DataSource ds;
    @Autowired
    private BookRepository bookRepository;

    private Book loadedBook;

    @Given("^([^\"]*) fixture is loaded$")
    public void data_fixture_is_loaded(String fixtureName)
      throws Throwable {
        ResourceDatabasePopulator populator
          = new ResourceDatabasePopulator
              (context.getResource("classpath:/" + fixtureName +
".sql"));
        DatabasePopulatorUtils.execute(populator, ds);
    }

    @Given("^(\d+) books available in the catalogue$")
    public void books_available_in_the_catalogue(int bookCount)
      throws Throwable {
        assertEquals(bookCount, bookRepository.count());
    }

    @When("^searching for book by isbn ([\d-]+)$")
    public void searching_for_book_by_isbn(String isbn)
      throws Throwable {
        loadedBook = bookRepository.findBookByIsbn(isbn);
        assertNotNull(loadedBook);
        assertEquals(isbn, loadedBook.getIsbn());
    }

    @Then("^book title will be ([^"]*)$")
    public void book_title_will_be(String bookTitle)
      throws Throwable {
        assertNotNull(loadedBook);
```

```
        assertEquals(bookTitle, loadedBook.getTitle());
    }
}
```

4. Now, we will need to create a corresponding testing feature definition file named `repositories.feature` in the `src/test/resources/com/example/bookpub` directory at the root of our project with the following content:

```
@txn
Feature: Finding a book by ISBN
  Background: Preload DB Mock Data
    Given packt-books fixture is loaded

  Scenario: Load one book
    Given 3 books available in the catalogue
    When searching for book by isbn 978-1-78398-478-7
    Then book title will be Orchestrating Docker
```

5. Lastly, we will create one more data SQL file named `packt-books.sql` in the `src/test/resources` directory at the root of our project with the following content:

```
INSERT INTO author (id, first_name, last_name) VALUES (5,
'Shrikrishna', 'Holla')
INSERT INTO book (isbn, title, author_id, publisher_id) VALUES
('978-1-78398-478-7', 'Orchestrating Docker', 5, 1)
```

6. Execute the tests by running `./gradlew clean test` and the tests should get passed.

7. With the addition of Cucumber, we also get the results of the tests in both the JUnit report and Cucumber-specific report HTML files. If we open `build/reports/tests/index.html` in the browser and click on the **Classes** button, we will see our scenario in the table, as shown in the following screenshot:

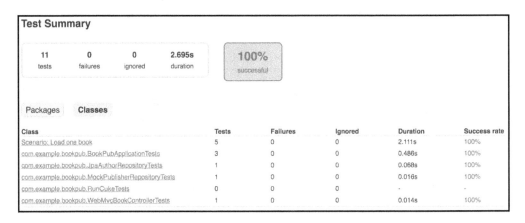

Class	Tests	Failures	Ignored	Duration	Success rate
Scenario: Load one book	5	0	0	2.111s	100%
com.example.bookpub.BookPubApplicationTests	3	0	0	0.486s	100%
com.example.bookpub.JpaAuthorRepositoryTests	1	0	0	0.068s	100%
com.example.bookpub.MockPublisherRepositoryTests	1	0	0	0.016s	100%
com.example.bookpub.RunCukeTests	0	0	0	-	-
com.example.bookpub.WebMvcBookControllerTests	1	0	0	0.014s	100%

8. Selecting the **Scenario: Load one book** link will take us to the detailed report page, as shown in the following screenshot:

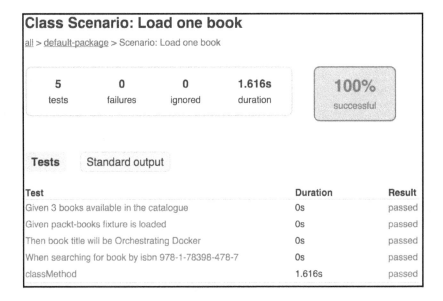

Test	Duration	Result
Given 3 books available in the catalogue	0s	passed
Given packt-books fixture is loaded	0s	passed
Then book title will be Orchestrating Docker	0s	passed
When searching for book by isbn 978-1-78398-478-7	0s	passed
classMethod	1.616s	passed

9. As we can see, the descriptions are nicer than the class and method names that we saw in the original JUnit-based test cases.

10. Cucumber also generates its own report, which can be viewed by opening `build/reports/cucumber/index.html` in the browser.

11. Being a behavior-driven testing framework, the feature files allow us not only to define individual conditions, but also to declare entire scenario outlines, which make the defining of multiple assertions of similar data easier. Let's create another feature file named `restful.feature` in the `src/test/resources/com/example/bookpub` directory at the root of our project with the following content:

```
@txn
Feature: Finding a book via REST API
  Background:
    Given packt-books fixture is loaded

  Scenario Outline: Using RESTful API to lookup books by ISBN
    Given catalogue with books
    When requesting url /books/<isbn>
    Then status code will be 200
    And response content contains <title>

  Examples:
    |isbn             |title               |
    |978-1-78398-478-7|Orchestrating Docker|
    |978-1-78528-415-1|Spring Boot Recipes |
```

12. We will also create a corresponding `RestfulStepdefs.java` file in the `src/test/java/com/example/bookpub` directory at the root of our project with the following content:

```
import cucumber.api.java.Before;
import cucumber.api.java.en.Given;
import cucumber.api.java.en.Then;
import cucumber.api.java.en.When;

import static org.hamcrest.CoreMatchers.containsString;
import static org.junit.Assert.assertTrue;
import static org.junit.Assert.assertNotNull;
import static
org.springframework.test.web.servlet.request.MockMvcRequestBuilders
.get;
import static
org.springframework.test.web.servlet.result.MockMvcResultMatchers.s
tatus;
```

```
import static
org.springframework.test.web.servlet.result.MockMvcResultMatchers.c
ontent;

@WebAppConfiguration
@ContextConfiguration(classes = BookPubApplication.class, loader =
SpringBootContextLoader.class)
public class RestfulStepdefs {
  @Autowired
  private WebApplicationContext context;
  @Autowired
  private BookRepository bookRepository;

  private MockMvc mockMvc;
  private ResultActions result;

  @Before
  public void setup() throws IOException {
    mockMvc =
        MockMvcBuilders.webAppContextSetup(context).build();
  }

  @Given("^catalogue with books$")
  public void catalogue_with_books() {
    assertTrue(bookRepository.count() > 0);
  }

  @When("^requesting url ([^"]*)$")
  public void requesting_url(String url) throws Exception {
    result = mockMvc.perform(get(url));
  }

  @Then("^status code will be ([\d]*)$")
  public void status_code_will_be(int code) throws
    Throwable {
    assertNotNull(result);
    result.andExpect(status().is(code));
  }

  @Then("^response content contains ([^"]*)$")
  public void response_content_contains(String content)
    throws Throwable {

    assertNotNull(result);
    result.andExpect(
      content().string(containsString(content))
    );
  }
```

```
}
```

13. Execute the tests by running `./gradlew clean test` and the tests should continue to get passed.

How it works...

If you feel a bit lost after looking at all this code and following along without having a full understanding of what exactly is going on, here you will find a detailed breakdown of everything that we did.

Let's start with a quick overview of what **Step Definitions** are. As the Cucumber framework uses the **Gherkin** feature document files in order to describe the business rules that are to be tested, which are represented in the form of English-like sentence statements, these need to be translated into executable code. This is the job of the Step Definition classes. Every step in a defined feature scenario needs to be matched to a method in a Step Definition class that will execute it. This matching is done by declaring a regular expression in the step annotations above the methods. The regex contains the matching groups that Cucumber uses so as to extract the method arguments and pass them to the executing method.

In `RepositoryStepdefs`, we can see this in the following method:

```
@Given("^([^\"]*) fixture is loaded$")
public void data_fixture_is_loaded(String fixtureName) {...}
```

The `@Given` annotation contains the regular expression that matches the `Given packt-books fixture is loaded` text, loaded from `repositories.feature` file, and extracts the `packt-books` text from the pattern, which is then passed as a `fixtureName` argument to the method. The `@When` and `@Then` annotations work on exactly the same principle. So, in effect, what the Cucumber framework does is it matches the English-like worded rules from the feature files to the matched patterns of the executing methods and extracts parts of the rules as arguments to the matched methods.

 More information on Gherkin and how to use it can be found at `https://cukes.info/docs/reference#gherkin`.

With the basic Cucumber overview explained, let's shift our focus to how the tests integrate with Spring Boot and are configured.

It all starts with the driver harness class, which in our case is `RunCukeTests`. This class itself does not contain any tests, but it has two important annotations that stitch things together, `@RunWith(Cucumber.class)` and `@CucumberOptions`:

- `@RunWith(Cucumber.class)`: This is a JUnit annotation that indicates that JUnit runner should use the Cucumber feature files to execute the tests.

`@CucumberOptions`: This provides additional configuration for Cucumber:

- `plugin={"pretty", "html:build/reports/cucumber"}`: This tells Cucumber to generate its reports in HTML format in the `build/reports/cucumber` directory.
- `glue = {"cucumber.api.spring", "classpath:com.example.bookpub"}`: This is a very important setting, as it tells Cucumber which packages to load and from where to load them during the execution of the tests. The `cucumber.api.spring` package needs to be present in order to take advantage of the `cucumber-spring` integration library, and the `com.example.bookpub` package is the location of our Step Definition implementation classes.
- `monochrome = true`: This tells Cucumber not to print the output with the ANSI color as we integrate with JUnit, as it will not look correct in the saved console output files.

> A complete list of the options can be found at `https://cukes.info/docs/reference/jvm#list-all-options`.

Now let's look at the `RepositoryStepdefs` class. It starts with the following annotations at the class level:

- `@WebAppConfiguration` instructs Spring that this class needs `WebApplicationContext` to be initialized, and it will be used for testing purposes during the execution
- `@ContextConfiguration(classes = BookPubApplication.class and loader = SpringBootContextLoader.class)` instruct Spring to use the `BookPubApplication` class as a configuration for the Spring application context, as well as to use the `SpringBootContextLoader` class from Spring Boot in order to bootstrap the testing harness

It is important to note that these annotations have to match all the Step Definition classes, or only one of the classes will be annotated with the `@ContextConfiguration` annotation to wire in the Spring support for the Cucumber test.

As the `cucumber-spring` integration does not know about Spring Boot but only about Spring, we can't use the `@SpringBootTest` meta-annotation. We have to resort to using only the annotations from Spring in order to stitch things together. Thankfully, we don't have to go through many hoops, but just declare the exact annotation that `SpringBootTest` facades by passing the desired configuration classes and loader.

Once the proper annotations are in place, Spring and Spring Boot will take over and provide us with the same convenience of autowiring beans as dependencies of our Step Definition classes.

One interesting characteristic of the Cucumber tests is the instantiation of a new instance of the Step Definition class for every execution of a **Scenario**. Even though the method namespace is global—meaning that we can use the methods that are declared in the different Step Definition classes—they operate on states defined in them and are not directly shared. It is, however, possible to `@Autowire` an instance of another Step Definition in a different Step Definition instance and rely on public methods or fields to access and mutate the data.

As a new instance gets created per scenario, the definition classes are stateful and rely on internal variables to keep a state among transitions from assertion to assertion. For example, in the `@When` annotated method, a particular state gets set, and in the `@Then` annotated method, a set of assertions on that state get evaluated. In our example of the `RepositoryStepdefs` class, we will internally set the state of the `loadedBook` class variable in its `searching_for_book_by_isbn(...)` method, which later gets used to assert on so as to verify the match of the book's title in the `book_title_will_be(...)` method afterwards. Due to this, if we mix the rules from the different definition classes in our feature files, the internal states would not be accessible among the multiple classes.

When integrating with Spring, one can use the injection of the mocked objects—as we have seen in `MockPublisherRepositoryTests` from one of our previous examples—and can have the shared `@Given` annotated method be used to set up the particular behavior of the mock for the given test. Then we can use the same dependency instance and inject it into another definition class that can be used in order to evaluate the `@Then` annotated assertion methods.

Another approach is the one that we saw in the second definition class, `RestfulStepdefs`, where we injected `BookRepository`. However, in `restful.feature`, we will be using the `Given packt-books fixture is loaded` behavior declaration that translates to the invocation of `data_fixture_is_loaded` method from the `RepositoryStepdefs` class, which shares the same instance of the injected `BookRepository` object, inserting the `packt-books.sql` data into it.

If we were to have a need to access the value of the `loadedBook` field from the `RepositoryStepdefs` instance inside the `RestfulStepdefs` class, we could declare the `@Autowired RepositoryStepdefs` field inside `RestfulStepdefs` and make the `loadedBook` field `public` instead of `private` to make it accessible to the outside world.

Another neat feature of the Cucumber and Spring integration is the use of the `@txn` annotation in the feature files. This tells Spring to execute the tests in a transaction wrapper, reset the database between the test executions, and guarantee a clean database state for every test.

Due to the global method namespace among all the Step Definition classes and test behavior defining feature files, we can use the power of Spring injection to our advantage so as to reuse the testing models and have a common setup logic for all of the tests. This makes the tests behave similarly to how our application would function in a real production environment.

Writing tests using Spock

Another no-less-popular testing framework is Spock, which was written in Groovy by Peter Niederwieser. Being a Groovy-based framework, it is ideally suited to create testing suites for a majority of the JVM-based languages, especially for Java and Groovy itself. The dynamic language traits of Groovy make it well suited to write elegant, efficient, and expressive specifications in the Groovy language without the need for translations. It is done in Cucumber with the help of the Gherkin library. Being based on top of JUnit, and integrating with it through the JUnit's `@RunWith` facility, just like Cucumber does, it is an easy enhancement to the traditional unit tests and works well with all the existing tools, which have built-in support or integration with JUnit.

In this recipe, we will pick up from where the previous recipe left off and enhance our test collection with a couple of Spock-based tests. In these tests, we will see how to set up MockMVC using the Spring dependency injection and testing harnesses. These will be used by the Spock test specifications in order to validate the fact that our data repository services will return the data as expected.

How to do it...

1. In order to add the Spock tests to our application, we will need to make a few changes to our `build.gradle` file first. As Spock tests are written in Groovy, the first thing to do is add a `groovy` plugin to our `build.gradle` file, as follows:

```
apply plugin: 'java'
apply plugin: 'eclipse'
apply plugin: 'groovy'
apply plugin: 'spring-boot'
```

2. We will also need to add the necessary Spock framework dependencies to the `build.gradle` dependencies block:

```
dependencies {
   ...
   testCompile('org.spockframework:spock-core:1.1-groovy-2.4-rc-2')
   testCompile('org.spockframework:spock-spring:1.1-groovy-2.4-
rc-2')
   ...
}
```

3. As the tests will be in Groovy, we will need to create a new source directory for the files. Let's create the `src/test/groovy/com/example/bookpub` directory in the root of our project.

4. Now we are ready to write our first test. Create a `SpockBookRepositorySpecification.groovy` file in the `src/test/groovy/com/example/bookpub` directory at the root of our project with the following content:

```
package com.example.bookpub;

import com.example.bookpub.entity.Author;
import com.example.bookpub.entity.Book
import com.example.bookpub.entity.Publisher
import com.example.bookpub.repository.BookRepository
import com.example.bookpub.repository.PublisherRepository
import org.mockito.Mockito
import org.springframework.beans.factory.annotation.Autowired
import
org.springframework.boot.test.autoconfigure.web.servlet.AutoConfigu
reMockMvc
import org.springframework.boot.test.context.SpringBootTest
```

```
import org.springframework.boot.test.mock.mockito.MockBean
import
org.springframework.jdbc.datasource.init.DatabasePopulatorUtils
import
org.springframework.jdbc.datasource.init.ResourceDatabasePopulator
import org.springframework.test.web.servlet.MockMvc
import org.springframework.transaction.annotation.Transactional
import
org.springframework.web.context.ConfigurableWebApplicationContext
import spock.lang.Specification

import javax.sql.DataSource

import static org.hamcrest.CoreMatchers.containsString
import static
org.springframework.test.web.servlet.request.MockMvcRequestBuilders
.get
import static
org.springframework.test.web.servlet.result.MockMvcResultMatchers.c
ontent
import static
org.springframework.test.web.servlet.result.MockMvcResultMatchers.s
tatus;

@SpringBootTest
@AutoConfigureMockMvc
class SpockBookRepositorySpecification extends Specification {
  @Autowired
  private ConfigurableWebApplicationContext context

  @Autowired
  private DataSource ds;

  @Autowired
  private BookRepository repository;

  @Autowired
  private MockMvc mockMvc;

  void setup() {
    ResourceDatabasePopulator populator =
      new ResourceDatabasePopulator(
        context.getResource("classpath:/packt-books.sql"));
    DatabasePopulatorUtils.execute(populator, ds);
  }

  @Transactional
  def "Test RESTful GET"() {
```

```
    when:
      def result = mockMvc.perform(get("/books/${isbn}"));

    then:
      result.andExpect(status().isOk())
      result.andExpect(
        content().string(containsString(title))
      );

    where:
      isbn                | title
      "978-1-78398-478-7"|"Orchestrating Docker"
      "978-1-78528-415-1"|"Spring Boot Recipes"
  }

  @Transactional
  def "Insert another book"() {
    setup:
      def existingBook =
        repository.findBookByIsbn("978-1-78528-415-1")
      def newBook = new Book("978-1-12345-678-9",
        "Some Future Book", existingBook.getAuthor(),
        existingBook.getPublisher()
      )

    expect:
      repository.count() == 3

    when:
      def savedBook = repository.save(newBook)

    then:
      repository.count() == 4
      savedBook.id > -1
  }
}
```

5. Execute the tests by running `./gradlew clean test` and the tests should get passed.

6. As Spock integrates with JUnit, we can see the execution report of the Spock tests together with the rest of our test suite. If we open `build/reports/tests/index.html` in the browser and click the **Classes** button, we will see our specification in the table, as shown in the following screenshot:

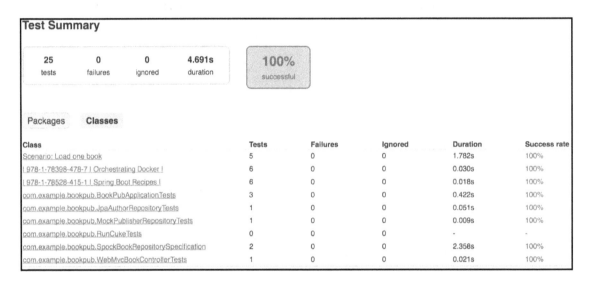

Class	Tests	Failures	Ignored	Duration	Success rate
Scenario: Load one book	5	0	0	1.782s	100%
978-1-78398-478-7	Orchestrating Docker		6	0	0	0.030s	100%
978-1-78528-415-1	Spring Boot Recipes		6	0	0	0.018s	100%
com.example.bookpub.BookPubApplicationTests	3	0	0	0.422s	100%
com.example.bookpub.JpaAuthorRepositoryTests	1	0	0	0.051s	100%
com.example.bookpub.MockPublisherRepositoryTests	1	0	0	0.009s	100%
com.example.bookpub.RunCukeTests	0	0	0	-	-
com.example.bookpub.SpockBookRepositorySpecification	2	0	0	2.358s	100%
com.example.bookpub.WebMvcBookControllerTests	1	0	0	0.021s	100%

7. Selecting the **com.example.bookpub.SpockBookRespositorySpecification** link will take us to the detailed report page, which is as follows:

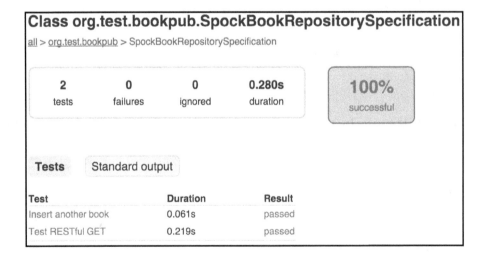

8. Next, we will take our tests a bit further and explore the mocking functionality of the database repositories. Let's use `PublisherRepository` as our candidate to mock, and wire it into the `BookController` class to provide a `getBooksByPublisher` functionality. Let's add the following content to the `BookController` class in the `src/main/java/com/example/bookpub/controllers` directory at the root of our project:

```
@Autowired
private PublisherRepository publisherRepository;

@RequestMapping(value = "/publisher/{id}", method =
RequestMethod.GET)
public List<Book> getBooksByPublisher(@PathVariable("id") Long id)
{
    Optional<Publisher> publisher =
        publisherRepository.findById(id);
    Assert.notNull(publisher);
    Assert.isTrue(publisher.isPresent());
    return publisher.get().getBooks();
}
```

9. Let's add the following to the `Publisher` class in the `src/main/java/com/example/bookpub/entity` directory at the root of our project:

```
@OneToMany(mappedBy = "publisher")
@JsonBackReference
private List<Book> books;
```

10. Lastly, let's add a getter and setter for the books to the `Publisher` entity class as well:

```
public List<Book> getBooks() {
    return books;
}

public void setBooks(List<Book> books) {
    this.books = books;
}
```

11. With all the code additions completed, we are ready to add another test to the `SpockBookRepositorySpecification.groovy` file in the `src/test/groovy/com/example/bookpub` directory at the root of our project with the following content:

```
...
class SpockBookRepositorySpecification extends Specification {
    ...
    @MockBean
    private PublisherRepository publisherRepository

    @Transactional
    def "Test RESTful GET books by publisher"() {
        setup:
          Publisher publisher =
                  new Publisher("Strange Books")
          publisher.setId(999)
          Book book = new Book("978-1-98765-432-1",
                  "Mystery Book",
                  new Author("John", "Doe"),
                  publisher)
          publisher.setBooks([book])
          Mockito.when(publisherRepository.count()).
                  thenReturn(1L)
          Mockito.when(publisherRepository.findById(1L)).
                  thenReturn(Optional.of(publisher))

        when:
          def result =
            mockMvc.perform(get("/books/publisher/1"))

        then:
          result.andExpect(status().isOk())
          result.andExpect(content().
                  string(containsString("Strange Books")))

        cleanup:
          Mockito.reset(publisherRepository)
    }
}
```

12. Execute the tests by running `./gradlew clean test` and the tests should continue to get passed.

How it works...

As you saw from this example, writing tests can be just as elaborate and sophisticated as the production code being tested itself. Let's examine the steps that we took in order to get the Spock tests integrated into our Spring Boot application.

The first thing that we did was to add a Groovy plugin in order to make our build Groovy-friendly, and we also added the required Spock library dependencies of `spock-core` and `spock-spring`, both of which are required to make Spock work with Spring's dependency injection and contexts.

The next step was to create the `SpockBookRepositorySpecification` Spock specification, which extends the Spock's specification abstract base class. Extending the `Specification` class is very important because this is how JUnit knows that our class is the test class that needs to be executed. If we look in the `Specification` source, we will see the `@RunWith(Sputnik.class)` annotation, just like the one that we used in the Cucumber recipe. In addition to the JUnit bootstrapping, the `Specification` class provides us with many helpful methods and mocking support as well.

 For more information about the detailed capabilities that are offered by Spock, you can refer to the Spock documentation that is available at `http://spockframework.github.io/spock/docs/current/index.html`.

It is also worth mentioning that we used the same annotations for the `SpockBookRepositorySpecification` class as we did for our Spring Boot-based tests, as shown in the following code:

```
@SpringBootTest
@AutoConfigureMockMvc
```

The reason that we had to add `@AutoConfigureMockMvc` in addition to `@SpringBootTest` is to add functionality to allow us to use the `@Autowire MockMvc` instance instead of having to create one ourselves. Regular `@SpringBootTest` does not automatically create and configure an instance of a `MockMvc` object, so we could have either created it manually, as we did in `BookPubApplicationTests`, or added the `@AutoConfigureMockMvc` annotation, which is what gets used inside `@WebMvcTest`, to let Spring handle it for us. The good news is that we can always use the same annotation compositions as used by Spring Boot, and annotate our classes directly, which is exactly what we did.

Unlike Cucumber, Spock combines all the aspects of the test in one `Specification` class, dividing it into multiple blocks, as follows:

- `setup`: This block is used to configure the specific test with variables, populating data, building mocks, and so on.
- `expect`: This block is one of the stimulus blocks, as Spock defines it, designed to contain simple expressions asserting a state or condition. Besides evaluating the conditions, we can only define variables in this block, and nothing else is allowed.
- `when`: This block is another stimulus type block, which always goes together with `then`. It can contain any arbitrary code and is designed to define the behavior that we are trying to test.
- `then`: This block is a response type block. It is similar to `expect` and can only contain conditions, exception checking, variable definition, and object interactions, such as how many times a particular method has been called and so forth.

 More information on interaction testing is available on Spock's website at `http://spockframework.github.io/spock/docs/current/interaction_based_testing.html`.

- `cleanup`: This block is used to clean the state of the environment and potentially undo whatever changes were done as part of the individual test execution. In our recipe, this is where we will reset our `PublisherRepository` mock object.

Spock provides us with the instance-based `setup()` and `cleanup()` methods as well, which can be used to define the setup and cleanup behavior that is common to all the tests in the specification.

If we look at our `setup()` method, this is where we can configure the database population with the test data. An interesting and important nuance is that the `setup()` method gets executed before every test method, not once per class. It is important to keep that in mind when doing things like populating a database to avoid re-insertion of the same data multiple times without proper rollback.

To help us with that is the @Transactional annotation of the test methods. Just like the @txn tag in the Cucumber feature files, this annotation instructs Spock to execute the annotated method and its corresponding setup() and cleanup() executions with a transaction scope, which get rolled back after the particular test method is finished. We rely on this behavior to get a clean database state for every test, so we don't end up inserting duplicate data during the execution of the setup() method every time each of our tests runs.

Most of you are probably wondering why we had to add the @JsonBackReference annotation to our Publisher entity class. The answer has to do with the Jackson JSON parser and how it handles circular dependency. In our model, we have a book belonging to a publisher and each publisher has multiple books. When we created our Publisher class with the Books mock and assigned a publisher instance to a book—which later got put in the publisher's book collection—we created a circular reference. During the execution of the BookController.getBooksByPublisher(...) method, the Jackson renderer would have thrown StackOverflowError while trying to write the object model to JSON. By adding this annotation to Publisher, we told Jackson how the objects reference each other, so instead of trying to write out the complete object tree, Jackson now handles it correctly, thus avoiding the circular reference loop situation.

The last thing that is important to keep in mind is how Spring Boot handles and processes the repository interfaces that are annotated with @RepositoryRestResource. Unlike the BookRepository interface, which we have annotated with a plain @Repository annotation and later explicitly declared as an autowire dependency of our BookController class, we did not create an explicit controller to handle RESTful requests for the rest of our repository interfaces such as PublisherRepository and others. These interfaces get scanned by Spring Boot and automatically wrapped with the mapped endpoints that trap the requests and delegate the calls to the backing SimpleJpaRepository proxy. Due to this setup, we can use only the mock object replacement approach for these objects that have been explicitly injected as bean dependencies such as with our example of BookRepository. The good news is that in these situations, where we don't explicitly expect beans to be wired and only use some annotations to stereotype the interfaces for Spring Boot to do its magic, we can rely on Spring Boot to do the job correctly. We know that it has tested all the functionalities behind it so that we don't have to test them. To test the actual repository and entity functionality, we can use the @DataJpaTest annotation to do a specific JPA slice test instead.

6

Application Packaging and Deployment

In this chapter, we will cover the following topics:

- Creating a Spring Boot executable JAR
- Creating Docker images
- Building self-executing binaries
- Spring Boot environment configuration, hierarchy, and precedence
- Adding custom PropertySource to the environment using EnvironmentPostProcessor
- Externalizing an environmental configuration using property files
- Externalizing an environmental configuration using environment variables
- Externalizing an environmental configuration using Java system properties
- Externalizing an environmental configuration using JSON
- Setting up Consul
- Externalizing an environmental configuration using Consul and envconsul

Introduction

What good is an application unless it is being used? In today's day and age—when DevOps has become the way of doing software development, when the cloud is the king, and when building microservices is considered the thing to do—a lot of attention is being focused on how applications get packaged, distributed, and deployed in their designated environments.

The Twelve-Factor App methodology has played an instrumental role in defining how a modern **Software as a Service (SaaS)** application is supposed to be built and deployed. One of the key principles is the separation of environmental configuration definitions from the application and storage of this in the environments. The Twelve-Factor App methodology also favors the isolation and bundling of the dependencies, development versus production parity, and ease of deployment and disposability of the applications, among other things.

 The Twelve-Factor App methodology can be found at
http://12factor.net/.

The DevOps model also encourages us to have complete ownership of our application, starting from writing and testing the code all the way to building and deploying it. If we are to assume this ownership, we need to ensure that the maintenance and overhead costs are not excessive and won't take away much time from our primary task of developing new features. This can be achieved by having clean, well-defined, and isolated deployable artifacts, which are self-contained, self-executed, and can be deployed in any environment without having to be rebuilt.

The following recipes will walk us through all the necessary steps to achieve the goal of low-effort deployment and maintenance while having clean and elegant code behind it.

Creating a Spring Boot executable JAR

The Spring Boot magic would not be complete without providing a nice way to package the entire application including all of its dependencies, resources, and so on in one composite, executable JAR file. After the JAR file is created, it can simply be launched by running a java -jar <name>.jar command.

We will continue with the application code that we built in the previous chapters and will add the necessary functionalities to package it. Let's go ahead and take a look at how to create the Spring Boot Uber JAR.

The Uber JAR is typically known as an application bundle encapsulated in a single composite JAR file that internally contains a /lib directory with all the dependent inner jars and optionally a /bin directory with the executables.

How to do it...

1. Let's go to our code directory from Chapter 5, *Application Testing*, and execute ./gradlew clean build

2. With the Uber JAR built, let's launch the application by executing java -jar build/libs/ch6-0.0.1-SNAPSHOT.jar

3. This will result in our application running in the JAR file with the following console output:

```
  .   ____          _            __ _ _
 /\\ / ___'_ __ _ _(_)_ __  __ _ \ \ \ \
( ( )\___ | '_ | '_| | '_ \/ _` | \ \ \ \
 \\/  ___)| |_)| | | | | || (_| |  ) ) ) )
  '  |____| .__|_| |_|_| |_\__, | / / / /
 =========|_|==============|___/=/_/_/_/
 :: Spring Boot ::  (v2.0.0.BUILD-SNAPSHOT)
...
(The rest is omitted for conciseness)
...
2017-12-17 INFO: Registering beans for JMX exposure on startup
2017-12-17 INFO: Tomcat started on port(s): 8080 (http) 8443
(https)
2017-12-17 INFO: Welcome to the Book Catalog System!
2017-12-17 INFO: BookRepository has 1 entries
2017-12-17 INFO: ReviewerRepository has 0 entries
2017-12-17 INFO: PublisherRepository has 1 entries
2017-12-17 INFO: AuthorRepository has 1 entries
2017-12-17 INFO: Started BookPubApplication in 12.156 seconds
(JVM
running for 12.877)
2017-12-17 INFO: Number of books: 1
```

How it works...

As you can see, getting the packaged executable JAR file is fairly straightforward. All the magic is already coded and provided to us as part of the Spring Boot Gradle plugin. The addition of the plugin adds a number of tasks, which allow us to package the Spring Boot application, run it and build the JAR, TAR, WAR files, and so on. For example, the `bootRun` task, which we have been using throughout this book, is provided by the Spring Boot Gradle plugin, among others. We can see a complete list of the available Gradle tasks by executing `./gradlew tasks`. When we run this command, we will get the following output:

```
------------------------------------------------------------
All tasks runnable from root project
------------------------------------------------------------
Application tasks
-----------------
bootRun - Run the project with support for auto-detecting main
class and reloading static resources
run - Runs this project as a JVM application
Build tasks
-----------
assemble - Assembles the outputs of this project.
bootJar - Assembles an executable jar archive containing the main
classes and their dependencies.
build - Assembles and tests this project.
buildDependents - Assembles and tests this project and all projects
that depend on it.
buildNeeded - Assembles and tests this project and all projects it
depends on.
classes - Assembles classes 'main'.
clean - Deletes the build directory.
jar - Assembles a jar archive containing the main classes.
testClasses - Assembles classes 'test'.
Build Setup tasks
-----------------
init - Initializes a new Gradle build. [incubating]
Distribution tasks
------------------
assembleBootDist - Assembles the boot distributions
assembleDist - Assembles the main distributions
bootDistTar - Bundles the project as a distribution.
bootDistZip - Bundles the project as a distribution.
distTar - Bundles the project as a distribution.
distZip - Bundles the project as a distribution.
installBootDist - Installs the project as a distribution as-is.
installDist - Installs the project as a distribution as-is.
```

The preceding output is not complete; I've excluded the non-relevant task groups such as IDE, documentation, and so on, but you will see them on your console. In the task list, we will see tasks such as `bootRun`, `bootJar`, and others. These tasks have been added by the Spring Boot Gradle plugin and executing them gets the required Spring Boot steps added to the build pipeline. You can see the actual task dependency if you execute `./gradlew tasks --all`, which will not only print the visible tasks, but also the depended, internal tasks, and the task dependencies. For example, when we were running the `build` task, all the following dependent tasks were executed as well:

```
build - Assembles and tests this project. [assemble, check]
assemble - Assembles the outputs of this project. [bootJar,
distTar, distZip, jar]
```

You can see that the `build` task will execute the `assemble` task, which in turn will call `bootJar`, where the creation of the Uber JAR is actually taking place.

The plugin also provides a number of very useful configuration options. While I am not going to go into detail about all of them, I'll mention the two that I find very useful:

```
bootJar {
   classifier = 'exec'
   baseName = 'bookpub'
}
```

This configuration allows us to specify the executable JAR file `classifier`, along with the JAR `baseName`, allowing for having the regular JAR contain just the application code and the executable JAR with the `classifier` in the name, `bookpub-0.0.1-SNAPSHOT-exec.jar`.

Another useful configuration option allows us to specify which dependency JARs require unpacking because, for some reason, they can't be included as nested inner JARs. This comes in very handy when you need something to be available in the system `Classloader` such as setting a custom `SecurityManager` via the startup system properties:

```
bootJar {
   requiresUnpack = '**/some-jar-name-*.jar'
}
```

In this example, the contents of the `some-jar-name-1.0.3.jar` dependency will be unpacked into a temporary folder on a filesystem when the application is launched.

Creating Docker images

Docker, Docker, Docker! I hear this phrase more and more in all the conferences and tech meetups that I have attended. The arrival of Docker has been welcomed by the community with open arms and it has instantly become a hit. The Docker ecosystem has been rapidly expanding with many other companies providing services, support, and complementing frameworks such as **Apache Mesos**, Amazon Elastic Beanstalk, ECS, and Kubernetes, just to name a few. Even Microsoft is providing Docker support in their Azure Cloud Service and is partnering with Docker to bring Docker to Windows operating system.

The reason for Docker's overwhelming popularity lies in its ability to package and deploy applications in a form of self-contained containers. The containers are more lightweight than the traditional full-blown virtual machines. Multiple numbers of them can be run on top of a single OS instance, thus increasing the number of applications that can be deployed on the same hardware compared to traditional VMs.

In this recipe, we will take a look at what it would take to package our Spring Boot application as a Docker image and how to deploy and run it.

Building a Docker image and just running it on your development machine is doable, but not as much fun as being able to share it with the world. You will need to publish it somewhere for it to be deployable, especially if you are thinking of using it with Amazon or some other cloud-like environment. Luckily, Docker provides us with not only the container solution, but also with a repository service, Docker Hub, located at `https://hub.docker.com`, where we can create repositories and publish our Docker images. So think of it like Maven Central for Docker.

How to do it...

1. The first step will be to create an account on Docker Hub so that we can publish our images. Go to `https://hub.docker.com` and create an account. You can also use your GitHub account and log in using it if you have one.
2. Once you have an account, we will need to create a repository named `springbootcookbook`.
3. With this account created, now is the time to build the image. For this, we will use one of the Gradle Docker plugins. We will start by changing `build.gradle` to modify the `buildscript` block with the following change:

```
buildscript {
  dependencies {
```

```
    classpath("org.springframework.boot:spring-boot-gradle-
        plugin:${springBootVersion}")
    classpath("se.transmode.gradle:gradle-docker:1.2")
  }
}
```

4. We will also need to apply this plugin by adding the `apply plugin: 'docker'` directive to the `build.gradle` file.

5. We also need to explicitly add the `application` plugin to `build.gradle` as well, since it is no longer automatically included by the Spring Boot Gradle plugin.

6. Add `apply plugin: 'application'` to the list of plugins in the `build.gradle` file.

7. Lastly, we will need to add the following Docker configuration to the `build.gradle` file as well:

```
task distDocker(type: Docker,
                overwrite: true,
                dependsOn: bootDistTar) {
  group = 'docker'
  description = "Packs the project's JVM application
  as a Docker image."

  inputs.files project.bootDistTar
  def installDir = "/" + project.bootDistTar.archiveName
                        - ".${project.bootDistTar.extension}"

  doFirst {
      tag "ch6"
      push false
      exposePort 8080
      exposePort 8443
      addFile file("${System.properties['user.home']}
      /.keystore"), "/root/"
      applicationName = project.applicationName
      addFile project.bootDistTar.outputs.files.singleFile

      entryPoint = ["$installDir/bin/${project.applicationName}"]
  }
}
```

8. Assuming that you already have Docker installed on your machine, we can proceed to creating the image by executing `./gradlew clean distDocker`.

9. For Docker installation instructions, please visit the tutorial that is located at `https://docs.docker.com/installation/#installation`. If everything has worked out correctly, you should see the following output:

```
> Task :distDocker
Sending build context to Docker daemon   68.22MB
  Step 1/6 : FROM aglover/java8-pier
   ---> 3f3822d3ece5
  Step 2/6 : EXPOSE 8080
   ---> Using cache
   ---> 73717aaca6f3
  Step 3/6 : EXPOSE 8443
   ---> Using cache
   ---> 6ef3c0fc3d2a
  Step 4/6 : ADD .keystore /root/
   ---> Using cache
   ---> 6efebb5a868b
  Step 5/6 : ADD ch6-boot-0.0.1-SNAPSHOT.tar /
   ---> Using cache
   ---> 0634eace4952
  Step 6/6 : ENTRYPOINT /ch6-boot-0.0.1-SNAPSHOT/bin/ch6
   ---> Using cache
   ---> 39a853b7ddbb
Successfully built 39a853b7ddbb
Successfully tagged ch6:0.0.1-SNAPSHOT
BUILD SUCCESSFUL
Total time: 1 mins 0.009 secs.
```

10. We can also execute the following Docker images command so as to see the newly created image:

```
$ docker images
REPOSITORY            TAG                 IMAGE ID
CREATED               VIRTUAL  SIZE
ch6                   0.0.1-SNAPSHOT      39a853b7ddbb       17
minutes ago       1.04 GB
aglover/java8-pier    latest              69f4574a230e       11
months ago        1.01 GB
```

11. With the image built successfully, we are now ready to start it in Docker by executing the following command:

```
docker run -d -P ch6:0.0.1-SNAPSHOT.
```

12. After the container has started, we can query the Docker registry for the port bindings so that we can access the HTTP endpoints for our service. This can be done via the `docker ps` command. If the container is running successfully, we should see the following result (names and ports will vary):

```
CONTAINER ID        IMAGE              COMMAND
CREATED             STATUS             PORTS
NAMES
37b37e411b9e        ch6:latest         "/ch6-boot-0.0.1-S..."
10 minutes ago      Up 10 minutes      0.0.0.0:32778->
8080/tcp,     0.0.0.0:32779->8443/tcp   drunk_carson
```

13. From this output, we can tell that the port mapping for the internal port 8080 has been set up to be 32778 (your port will vary for every run). Let's open http://localhost:32778/books in the browser to see our application in action, as shown in the following screenshot:

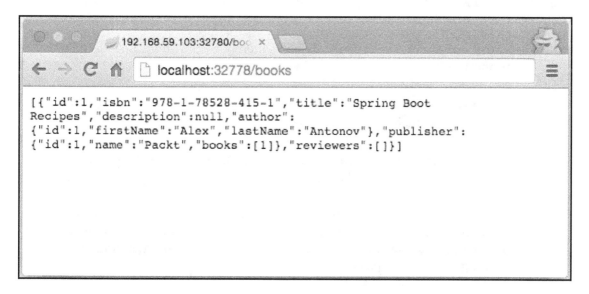

If you are using macOS X with `boot2docker`, then you won't be running the Docker container locally. In this scenario, you will be using the `boot2docker ip` instead of the local host to connect to the application. For more tips on how to make the `boot2docker` integration easier, please visit `http://viget.com/extend/how-to-use-docker-on-os-x-the-missing-gu ide`. One can also use a nice Docker façade, generously created by Ian Sinnott, which will automatically start boot2docker and handle the environment variables as well. To get the wrapper, go to `https://gist. github.com/iansinnott/0a0c212260386bdbfafb`.

How it works...

In the preceding example, we saw how easy it is to have our `build` package the application in a Docker container. The additional Gradle-Docker plugin does the bulk of the work of the `Dockerfile` creation, image building, and publishing; all we have to do is give it some instructions on what and how we want the image to be. Because the Spring Boot Gradle plugin uses a `boot` distribution, the Gradle-Docker plugin does not know that it needs to use a bootified TAR archive. To help with that, we override the `distDocker` task. Let's examine these instructions in detail:

- The `group` and `description` attributes merely help with displaying the task properly when the `./gradlew tasks` command is executed.
- The `inputs.files project.bootDistTar` directive is very important. This is what instructs the `distDocker` task to use the TAR archive created by the Spring Boot distribution, instead of the generic one.
- The `def installDir = "/" + project.bootDistTar.archiveName - ".${project.bootDistTar.extension}"` directive is creating a variable, containing the directory where the untarred artifacts will be placed inside the Docker container.
- The `exposePort` directive tells the plugin to add an `EXPOSE <port>` instruction to the Dockerfile so that when our container is started, it will expose these internal ports to the outside via port mapping. We saw this mapping while running the `docker ps` command.

- The `addFile` directive tells the plugin to add an `ADD <src> <dest>` instruction to the Dockerfile so that when the container is being built, we will copy the file from the source filesystem in the filesystem in the container image. In our case, we will need to copy the `.keystore` certificate file that we configured in one of our previous recipes for the HTTPS connector, which we instructed in `tomcat.https.properties` to be loaded from `${user.home}/.keystore`. Now, we need it to be in the `/root/ directory` directory as, in the container, our application will be executed under the root. (This can be changed with more configurations.)

The Gradle-Docker plugin uses the project name as a name for the image by default. The project name, in turn, is being inferred by Gradle from the project's directory name, unless an explicit property value is configured. As the code example is for `Chapter 6`, *Application Packaging and Deployment* the project directory is named `ch6`, thus the name of the image. The project name can be explicitly configured by adding `name='some_project_name'` in `gradle.properties`.

If you look at the resulting Dockerfile, which can be found in the `build/docker/` directory at the root of the project, you will see the following two instructions:

```
ADD ch6-boot-0.0.1-SNAPSHOT.tar /
ENTRYPOINT ["/ch6-boot-0.0.1-SNAPSHOT/bin/ch6"]
```

The `ADD` instruction adds the TAR application archive that was produced by the `bootDistTar` task and contains our application bundled up as a tarball. We can even see the contents of the produced tarball by executing `tar tvf build/distributions/ch6-boot-0.0.1-SNAPSHOT.tar`. During the building of the container, the contents of the TAR file will be extracted in the `/` directory in the container and later used to launch the application.

It is followed by the `ENTRYPOINT` instruction. This tells Docker to execute `/ch6-boot-0.0.1-SNAPSHOT/bin/ch6`, which we saw as part of the tarball content, once the container is started, thus automatically launching our application.

The first line in the Dockerfile, which is `FROM aglover/java8-pier`, is the instruction to use the `aglover/java8-pier` image, which contains the Ubuntu OS with Java 8 installed as a base image for our container, on which we will install our application. This image comes from the Docker Hub Repository and is automatically used by the plugin, but can be changed via the configuration settings, if so desired.

If you created an account on Docker Hub, we can also publish the created Docker image to the registry. As fair warning, the resulting image could be many hundreds of megabytes in size so uploading it could take some time. To publish this image, we will need to change the tag to `tag "<docker hub username>/<docker hub repository name>"` and add the `push true` setting to the `distDocker` task definition in `build.gradle`:

```
task distDocker(type: Docker,
                overwrite: true,
                dependsOn: bootDistTar) {
    ...
    doFirst {
        tag "<docker hub username>/<docker hub repository name>"
        push true
        ...
    }
}
```

The `tag` property sets up the created image tag and, by default, the plugin assumes that it is residing in the Docker Hub Repository. This is where it will be publishing it if the `push` configuration is set to `true`, as it is in our case.

For a complete list of all the Gradle-Docker plugin configuration options, take a look at the `https://github.com/Transmode/gradle-docker` GitHub project page.

When launching a Docker image, we use the `-d` and `-P` command-line arguments. Their uses are as follows:

- `-d`: This argument indicates the desire to run the container in a detached mode where the process starts in the background
- `-P`: This argument instructs Docker to publish all the internally exposed ports to the outside so that we can access them

For a detailed explanation of all the possible command-line options, refer to `https://docs.docker.com/reference/commandline/cli/`.

Building self-executing binaries

As of Spring Boot version 1.3, the Gradle and Maven plugins support the option of generating true executable binaries. These look like normal JAR files, but have the content of JAR fused together with the launch script that contains the command-building logic and is capable of self-starting itself without the need to execute the `java -jar file.jar` command explicitly. This capability comes in very handy as it allows for the easy configuration of Linux autostart services such as `init.d` or `systemd`, and `launchd` on macOS X.

Getting ready

For this recipe, we will use our existing application build. We will examine how the self-starting executable JAR files get created and how to modify the default launch script to add support for the custom JVM start up arguments, such as the `-D` start up system properties, JVM memory, Garbage Collection, and other settings.

For this recipe, make sure that `build.gradle` is using Spring Boot version 2.0.0 or above. If it is not, then change the following setting in the `buildscript` configuration block:

```
ext {
    springBootVersion = '2.0.0.BUILD-SNAPSHOT'
}
```

The same upgrade of the Spring Boot version should be done in the `db-counter-starter/build.gradle` file as well.

How to do it...

1. Building a default self-executing JAR file is very easy; actually, it is done automatically once we execute the `./gradlew clean bootJar` command.
2. We can proceed to launch the created application simply by invoking `./build/libs/bookpub-0.0.1-SNAPSHOT.jar`.

3. In an enterprise environment, it is rare that we are satisfied with the default JVM launch arguments as we often need to tweak the memory settings, GC configurations, and even pass the startup system properties in order to ensure that we are using the desired version of the XML parser or a proprietary implementation of class loader or security manager. To accomplish those needs, we will modify the default `launch.script` file to add support for the JVM options. Let's start by copying the default `launch.script` file from the `https://github.com/spring-projects/spring-boot/blob/master/spring-boot-project/spring-boot-tools/spring-boot-loader-tools/src/main/resources/org/springframework/boot/loader/tools/launch.script` Spring Boot GitHub repository in the root of our project.

The `launch.script` file is supported only on Linux and OS X environments. If you are looking to make self-executing JARs for Windows, you will need to provide your own `launch.script` file that is tailored for the Windows shell command execution. The good news is that it is the only special thing that is required; all the instructions and concepts in this recipe will work just fine on Windows as well, provided that the compliant `launch.script` template is being used.

4. We will modify the copied `launch.script` file and add the following content right above the *line 142* mark (this is showing only the relevant part of the script so as to condense the space):

```
...
# Find Java
if [[ -n "$JAVA_HOME" ]] &amp;&amp; [[ -x "$JAVA_HOME/bin/java" ]];
then
javaexe="$JAVA_HOME/bin/java"
elif type -p java 2>&amp;1> /dev/null; then
javaexe=java
elif [[ -x "/usr/bin/java" ]]; then
javaexe="/usr/bin/java"
else
echo "Unable to find Java"
exit 1
fi
# Configure JVM Options
jvmopts="{{jvm_options:}}"
arguments=(-Dsun.misc.URLClassPath.disableJarChecking=true $jvmopts
$JAVA_OPTS -jar $jarfile $RUN_ARGS "$@")
# Action functions
start() {
...
```

5. With the custom `launch.script` file in place, we will need to add the options setting to our `build.gradle` file with the following content:

```
applicationDefaultJvmArgs = [
    "-Xms128m",
    "-Xmx256m"
]

bootJar {
    classifier = 'exec'
    baseName = 'bookpub'
    launchScript {
        script = file('launch.script')
        properties 'jvm_options' : applicationDefaultJvmArgs.join('
')
    }
}
```

6. We are now ready to launch our application. First, let's use the `./gradlew clean bootRun` command, and if we look at the JConsole VM Summary tab, we will see that our arguments indeed have been passed to the JVM, as follows:

Current heap size:	69,370 kbytes
Maximum heap size:	233,472 kbytes
Garbage collector:	Name = 'PS MarkSweep', Collections = 2, Total time spent = 0.136 seconds
Garbage collector:	Name = 'PS Scavenge', Collections = 34, Total time spent = 0.144 seconds
Operating System:	Mac OS X 10.10.3
Architecture:	x86_64
Number of processors:	8
Committed virtual memory:	4,299,488 kbytes
VM arguments:	-Xms128m -Xmx256m -Dfile.encoding=UTF-8 -Duser.country=US -Duser.language=en -Duser.variant

7. We can also build the self-starting executable JAR by running the `./gradlew clean bootJar` command and then executing `./build/libs/bookpub-0.0.1-SNAPSHOT-exec.jar` in order to launch our application. We should expect to see a similar result in JConsole.

8. Alternatively, we can also use the `JAVA_OPTS` environment variable to override some of the JVM arguments. Say we want to change the minimum memory heap size to 128 megabytes. We can launch our application using the `JAVA_OPTS=-Xmx128m ./build/libs/bookpub-0.0.1-SNAPSHOT-exec.jar` command and this would show us the following effect in JConsole:

Current heap size: 49,311 kbytes	**Committed memory:** 125,952 kbytes	
Maximum heap size: 125,952 kbytes	**Pending finalization:** {0} objects	

Garbage collector: Name = 'PS MarkSweep', Collections = 2, Total time spent = 0.207 seconds
Garbage collector: Name = 'PS Scavenge', Collections = 81, Total time spent = 0.287 seconds

Operating System: Mac OS X 10.10.3	**Total physical memory:** 16,777,216 kbytes
Architecture: x86_64	**Free physical memory:** 410,752 kbytes
Number of processors: 8	**Total swap space:** 5,242,880 kbytes
Committed virtual memory: 4,161,596 kbytes	**Free swap space:** 1,152,000 kbytes

VM arguments: -Xms128m -Xmx256m -Xmx128m -Dsun.misc.URLClassPath.disableJarChecking=true

How it works...

With a small customization to `launch.script`, we were able to create a self-executing deployable application, packaged as a self-contained JAR file, which on top of everything else can also be configured in order to be launched using the various OS-specific autostarting frameworks.

The Spring Boot Gradle and Maven plugins provide us with lots of options for parameter customization and even an ability to embed mustache-like template placeholders in `launch.script`, which can later be replaced with values during build time. We have leveraged this capability to inject our JVM arguments into the file using the `launchScript{properties}` configuration setting.

In our custom version of `launch.script`, we added the `jvmopts="{{jvm_options:}}"` line, which will be replaced with the value of the `jvm_options` parameter during the build and packaging time. This parameter is declared in our `build.gradle` file as a value of the `launchScript.properties` argument : `launchScript{properties 'jvm_options' : applicationDefaultJvmArgs.join(' ')}`.

The JVM arguments can be hardcoded, but it is much better to maintain consistency between how our application starts using the bootRun task and how it starts when launched from the self-executing JAR. To achieve this, we will use the same applicationDefaultJvmArgs collection of arguments that we will define for the bootRun execution purpose, only with all the different arguments collapsed in a single line of text separated by white spaces. Using this approach, we have to define the JVM arguments only once and use them in both modes of execution.

 It is important to notice that this reuse also applies to the application distributions that are built using the distZip and distTar tasks defined by Gradle's application plugin, as well as Spring Boot Gradle's bootDistZip and bootDistTar.

We can modify the build to create the Docker image by launching our self-executing JAR instead of the contents of the TAR file produced by the distTar task by default. To do this, we will need to change our distDocker configuration block using the following code:

```
task distDocker(type: Docker, overwrite: true,
                dependsOn: bootJar) {
  ...
  inputs.files project.bootJar
  doFirst {
    ...
    addFile file("${System.properties['user.home']}/.keystore"),
      "/root/"
    applicationName = project.applicationName
    addFile project.bootJar.outputs.files.singleFile

    def executableName = "/" +
      project.bootJar.outputs.files.singleFile.name
    entryPoint = ["$executableName"]
  }
}
```

This will make our distDocker task put the executable jar inside a Docker image instead of a TAR archive.

Spring Boot environment configuration, hierarchy, and precedence

In the previous few recipes, we looked at how to package our application in a variety of ways and how it can be deployed. The next logical step is the need to configure the application in order to provide some behavioral control as well as some environment-specific configuration values, which could and most likely will vary from environment to environment.

A common example of such an environmental configuration difference is the database setup. We certainly don't want to connect to a production environment database with an application running on our development machine. There are also cases where we want an application to run in different modes or use a different set of profiles, as they are referred to by Spring. An example could be running an application in live or simulator mode.

For this recipe, we will pick up from the previous state of the code base and add the support for different configuration profiles as well as examine how to use the property values as placeholders in other properties.

How to do it...

1. We will start by adding an @Profile annotation to the @Bean creation of schedulerRunner by changing the definition of the schedulerRunner(...) method in BookPubApplication.java, located in the src/main/java/org/test/bookpub directory at the root of our project, to the following content:

```
@Bean
@Profile("logger")
public StartupRunner schedulerRunner() {
    return new StartupRunner();
}
```

2. Start the application by running ./gradlew clean bootRun.

3. Once the application is running, we should no longer see the previous log output from the StartupRunner class, which looked like this:

```
2017-12-17 --- org.test.bookpub.StartupRunner : Number of books: 1
```

4. Now, let's build the application by running `./gradlew clean bootJar` and start it by running `./build/libs/bookpub-0.0.1-SNAPSHOT-exec.jar --spring.profiles.active=logger`; we will see the log output line show up again.

5. Another functionality that is enabled by the profile selector is the ability to add profile-specific property files. Let's create an `application-inmemorydb.properties` file in the `src/main/resources` directory at the root of our project with the following content:

```
spring.datasource.url =
jdbc:h2:mem:testdb;DB_CLOSE_DELAY=-1;DB_CLOSE_ON_EXIT=FALSE
```

6. Let's build the application by running `./gradlew clean bootJar` and start it by running `./build/libs/bookpub-0.0.1-SNAPSHOT-exec.jar --spring.profiles.active=logger,inmemorydb`, which will use the `inmemorydb` profile configuration in order to use the in-memory database instead of the file-based one.

How it works...

In this recipe, we experimented with using profiles and applying additional configuration settings based on the active profiles. Profiles were first introduced in Spring Framework 3.2 and were used to conditionally configure the beans in context, depending on which profiles were active. In Spring Boot, this facility was extended even further to allow configuration separation as well.

By placing an `@Profile("logger")` annotation on our `StartupRunner@Bean` creation method, Spring will be instructed to create the bean only if the logger profile has been activated. Conventionally, this is done by passing the `--spring.profiles.active` option in the command line during the application startup. In the tests, another way that this can be done is using the `@ActiveProfiles("profile")` annotation on the `Test` class, but it is not supported for the execution of a normal application. It is also possible to negate profiles such as `@Profile("!production")`. When such an annotation is used (with ! marking the negation), the bean will be created only if no profile production is active.

During startup, Spring Boot treats all the options that get passed via the command line as application properties, and thus anything that gets passed during startup ends up as a property value that is capable of being used. This same mechanism not only works for new properties but can be used as a way of overriding the existing properties as well. Let's imagine a situation where we already have an active profile defined in our `application.properties` file that looks like this: `spring.profiles.active=basic`. By passing the `--spring.profiles.active=logger` option via the command line, we will replace the active profile from `basic` to `logger`. If we want to include some profiles regardless of the active configuration, Spring Boot gives us a `spring.profiles.include` option to configure. Any profiles that are set up this way will be added to the list of active profiles.

As these options are nothing more than regular Spring Boot application properties, they all follow the same hierarchy for override precedence. The options have been outlined as follows:

- **Command-line arguments**: These values supersede every other property source in the list, and you can always rest assured that anything passed via `--property.name=value` will take precedence over the other means.
- **JNDI attributes**: They are the next in precedence priority. If you are using an application container that provides data via a JNDI `java:comp/env` namespace, these values will override all the other settings from below.
- **Java system properties**: These values are another way to pass the properties to the application either via the `-Dproperty=name` command-line arguments or by calling `System.setProperty(...)` in the code. They provide another way to replace the existing properties. Anything coming from `System.getProperty(...)` will win over the others in the list.
- **OS environment variables**: Whether from Windows, Linux, OS X, or any other, they are a common way to specify a configuration, especially for locations and values. The most notable one is `JAVA_HOME`, which is a common way to indicate where the JVM location resides in the filesystem. If neither of the preceding settings are present, the `ENV` variables will be used for the property values instead of the ones mentioned as follows:

As the OS environment variables typically don't support dots (.) or dashes (-), Spring Boot provides an automatic remapping mechanism that replaces the underscores (_) with dots (.) during the property evaluation; it also handles the case conversion. Thus, `JAVA_HOME` becomes synonymous with `java.home`.

- `random.*`: This provides special support for the random values of primitive types that can be used as placeholders in configuration properties. For example, we can define a property named `some.number=${random.int}` where `${random.int}` will be replaced by some random integer value. The same goes for `${random.value}` for textual values and `${random.long}` for longs.
- `application-{profile}.properties`: They are the profile-specific files that get applied only if a corresponding profile gets activated.
- `application.properties`: They are the main property files that contain the base/default application configuration. Similar to the profile-specific ones, these values can be loaded from the following list of locations, with the top one taking priority over the lower entries:
  - `file:config/`: This is a `/config` directory located in the current directory:
  - `file:`: This is the current directory
  - `classpath:/config`: This is a `/config` package in the classpath
  - `classpath:`: This is a root of the classpath
- **@Configuration annotated classes annotated with @PropertySource**: These are any in-code property sources that have been configured using annotations. We have seen an example of such usage the *Adding custom connectors* recipe from `Chapter 3`, *Web Framework Behavior Tuning*. They are very low in the precedence chain and are only preceded by the default properties.
- **Default properties**: They are configured via the `SpringApplication.setDefaultProperties(...)` call and are seldom used, as it feels very much like hardcoding values in code instead of externalizing them in configuration files.

Adding a custom PropertySource to the environment using EnvironmentPostProcessor

In cases where the enterprise is already using a particular configuration system, custom written or off the shelf, Spring Boot provides us with a facility to integrate this into the application via the creation of a custom `PropertySource` implementation.

How to do it...

Let's imagine that we have an existing configuration setup that uses a popular Apache Commons Configuration framework and stores the configuration data in XML files:

1. To mimic our supposed pre-existing configuration system, add the following content to the dependencies section in the `build.gradle` file:

```
dependencies {
    ...
    compile project(':db-count-starter')
    compile("commons-configuration:commons-
        configuration:1.10")
    compile("commons-codec:commons-codec:1.6")
    compile("commons-jxpath:commons-jxpath:1.3")
    compile("commons-collections:commons-collections:3.2.1")
    runtime("com.h2database:h2")
    ...
}
```

2. Follow this up by creating a simple configuration file named `commons-config.xml` in the `src/main/resources` directory at the root of our project with the following content:

```
<?xml version="1.0" encoding="ISO-8859-1" ?>
<config>
  <book>
    <counter>
      <delay>1000</delay>
      <rate>${book.counter.delay}0</rate>
    </counter>
  </book>
</config>
```

3. Next, we will create the `PropertySource` implementation file named `ApacheCommonsConfigurationPropertySource.java` in the `src/main/java/org/test/bookpub` directory at the root of our project with the following content:

```
public class ApacheCommonsConfigurationPropertySource
    extends EnumerablePropertySource<XMLConfiguration> {
    private static final Log logger = LogFactory.getLog(
    ApacheCommonsConfigurationPropertySource.class);

    public static final String
```

```
    COMMONS_CONFIG_PROPERTY_SOURCE_NAME = "commonsConfig";

  public ApacheCommonsConfigurationPropertySource(
    String name, XMLConfiguration source) {
   super(name, source);
  }

  @Override
  public String[] getPropertyNames() {
   ArrayList<String> keys =
      Lists.newArrayList(this.source.getKeys());
   return keys.toArray(new String[keys.size()]);
  }

  @Override
  public Object getProperty(String name) {
   return this.source.getString(name);
  }

  public static void addToEnvironment(
    ConfigurableEnvironment environment, XMLConfiguration
      xmlConfiguration) {
   environment.getPropertySources().addAfter(
    StandardEnvironment.
      SYSTEM_ENVIRONMENT_PROPERTY_SOURCE_NAME, new
       ApacheCommonsConfigurationPropertySource(
        COMMONS_CONFIG_PROPERTY_SOURCE_NAME,
          xmlConfiguration));
   logger.trace("ApacheCommonsConfigurationPropertySource
    add to Environment");
  }
 }
```

4. We will now create the `EnvironmentPostProcessor` implementation class so as to bootstrap our `PropertySource` named `ApacheCommonsConfigurationEnvironmentPostProcessor.java` in the `src/main/java/org/test/bookpub` directory at the root of our project with the following content:

```
package com.example.bookpub;

import org.apache.commons.configuration.ConfigurationException;
import org.apache.commons.configuration.XMLConfiguration;
import org.springframework.boot.SpringApplication;
import org.springframework.boot.env.EnvironmentPostProcessor;
import org.springframework.core.env.ConfigurableEnvironment;
```

```
public class ApacheCommonsConfigurationEnvironmentPostProcessor
        implements EnvironmentPostProcessor {

    @Override
    public void postProcessEnvironment(
                    ConfigurableEnvironment environment,
                    SpringApplication application) {
        try {
            ApacheCommonsConfigurationPropertySource
                .addToEnvironment(environment,
                    new XMLConfiguration("commons-
                                        config.xml"));
        } catch (ConfigurationException e) {
            throw new RuntimeException("Unable to load commons-
config.xml", e);
        }
    }
}
```

5. Finally, we will need to create a new directory named META-INF in the src/main/resources directory at the root of our project and create a file named spring.factories in it with the following content:

```
# Environment Post Processors
org.springframework.boot.env.EnvironmentPostProcessor=\
com.example.bookpub.ApacheCommonsConfigurationEnvironmentPostProces
sor
```

6. With the setup done, we are now ready to use our new properties in our application. Let's change the configuration of the @Scheduled annotation for our StartupRunner class located in the src/main/java/org/test/bookpub directory at the root of our project, as follows:

```
@Scheduled(initialDelayString = "${book.counter.delay}",
    fixedRateString = "${book.counter.rate}")
```

7. Let's build the application by running ./gradlew clean bootJar and start it by running ./build/libs/bookpub-0.0.1-SNAPSHOT-exec.jar --spring.profiles.active=logger in order to ensure that our StartupRunner class is still logging the book count every ten seconds, as expected.

How it works...

In this recipe, we have explored how to add our own custom `PropertySource` that allowed us to bridge the existing system in the Spring Boot environment. Let's look into the inner workings of how the pieces fit together.

In the previous section, we learned how the different configuration definitions stacked up and what rules were used to overlay them on top of each other. This will help us to better understand how the bridging of an Apache Commons Configuration, using a custom `PropertySource` implementation, works. (This should not be confused with an `@PropertySource` annotation!)

In Chapter 4, *Writing Custom Spring Boot Starters*, we learned about the use of `spring.factories`, and so we already know that this file serves to define the classes that should automatically be incorporated by Spring Boot during application startup. The only difference this time is that instead of configuring the `EnableAutoConfiguration` settings, we will configure the `SpringApplicationRunListener` ones.

We created the following two classes to support our needs:

- `ApacheCommonsConfigurationPropertySource`: This is the extension of the `EnumerablePropertySource` base class that provides you with internal functionality in order to bridge XMLConfiguration from Apache Commons Configuration to the world of Spring Boot by providing transformation to get the specific property values by name via the `getProperty(String name)` implementation, and the list of all the supported property names via the `getPropertyNames()` implementation. In situations where you are dealing with the use case when the complete list of the available property names is not known or is very expensive to compute, you can just extend the `PropertySource` abstract class instead of using `EnumerablePropertySource`.

- `ApacheCommonsConfigurationEnvironmentPostProcessor`: This is the implementation of the `EnvironmentPostProcessor` interface that gets instantiated by Spring Boot during the application startup and receives notification callback after the initial environment initialization has been completed, but before the application context startup. This class is configured in `spring.factories` and is automatically created by Spring Boot.

In our post-processor, we implement the
`postProcessEnvironment(ConfigurableEnvironment environment,`
`SpringApplication application)` method, which gives us access to the
`ConfigurableEnvironment` instance. By the time this callback is invoked, we will get an
environment instance that has already been populated with all of the properties from the
preceding hierarchy. However, we will get the opportunity to inject our own
`PropertySource` implementation anywhere in the list, which we will successfully do in
the `ApacheCommonsConfigurationPropertySource.addToEnvironment(...)`
method.

In our case, we will choose to insert our source right below `systemEnvironment` in the
order of precedence, but if needs be, we can alter this order to whatever highest precedence
we desire. Just be careful not to place it so high that your properties become impossible to
override via the command-line arguments, system properties, or environment variables.

Externalizing an environmental configuration using property files

The previous recipe taught us about the application properties and how they are
provisioned. As was mentioned at the beginning of this chapter, during application
deployment, it is almost inevitable to have some property values that are environment
dependant. They can be database configurations, service topologies, or even simple feature
configurations where something might be enabled in development but not quite ready for
production just yet.

In this recipe, we will learn how to use an externally residing properties file for an
environment-specific configuration, which might reside in the local filesystem or out in the
wild on the internet.

In this recipe, we will use the same application with all the existing configurations as we
used in the previous recipe. We will use it to experiment with starting up using the external
configuration properties that are living in the local filesystem and from an internet URL,
such as GitHub or any other.

How to do it...

1. Let's start by adding a bit of code to log the value of our particular configuration property so that we can easily see the change in it as we do different things. Add an @Bean method to the BookPubApplication class located in the src/main/java/org/test/bookpub directory at the root of our project with the following content:

```
@Bean
public CommandLineRunner configValuePrinter(
   @Value("${my.config.value:}") String configValue) {
   return args -> LogFactory.getLog(getClass()).
      info("Value of my.config.value property is: " +
         configValue);
}
```

2. Let's build the application by running ./gradlew clean bootJar and start it by running ./build/libs/bookpub-0.0.1-SNAPSHOT-exec.jar --spring.profiles.active=logger so as to see the following log output:

```
2017-12-17 --- ication$$EnhancerBySpringCGLIB$$b123df6a : Value of
my.config.value property is:
```

3. The value is empty, as we expected. Next, we will create a file named external.properties in our home directly with the following content:

```
my.config.value=From Home Directory Config
```

4. Let's run our application by executing ./build/libs/bookpub-0.0.1-SNAPSHOT-exec.jar --spring.profiles.active=logger --spring.config.location=file:/home/<username>/external.properties in order to see the following output in the logs:

```
2017-12-17 --- ication$$EnhancerBySpringCGLIB$$b123df6a : Value of
my.config.value property is: From Home Directory Config
```

For macOS users, the home directories can be found in the /Users/<username> folder.

5. We can also load the file as an HTTP resource and not from the local filesystem. So, place a file named `external.properties` with the content of `my.config.value=From HTTP Config` somewhere on the web. It can even be checked in a GitHub or BitBucket repository, as long as it is accessible without any need for authentication.

6. Let's run our application by executing `./build/libs/bookpub-0.0.1-SNAPSHOT-exec.jar --spring.profiles.active=logger --spring.config.location=http://<your file location path>/external.properties` in order to see the following output in the logs:

```
2017-12-17 --- ication$$EnhancerBySpringCGLIB$$b123df6a : Value of
my.config.value property is: From HTTP Config
```

How it works...

Before delving into the details of an external configuration setup, let's quickly look at the code that was added in order to print the property value in the log. The element of focus is the `@Value` annotation that can be used on class fields or method arguments; it also instructs Spring to automatically inject the annotated variable with the value defined in the annotation. If the value is positioned in the wrapping curly braces prefixed with a dollar sign, (`${ }`), Spring will replace this with the value from the corresponding application property or with the default value, if it is provided, by adding the textual data after the colon (`:`).

In our case, we defined it as `@Value("${my.config.value:}") String configValue`, so unless an application property named `my.config.value` exists, the default value of an empty String will be assigned to the `configValue` method argument. This construct is quite handy and eliminates the need to explicitly wire in the instance of an environment object just to get a specific property value out of it, as well as simplifying the code during testing, with less objects to mock.

The support for being able to specify the location of the application properties configuration file is geared towards supporting a dynamic multitude of environmental topologies, especially in cloud environments. This is often the case when the compiled application gets bundled into different cloud images that are destined for different environments and are being specially assembled by deployment tools such as Packer, Vagrant, and others.

In this scenario, it is very common to drop a configuration file in the image filesystem while making the image, depending on what environment it is destined for. Spring Boot provides a very convenient ability to specify, via the command-line arguments, where the configuration properties file, which should be added to the application configuration bundle, resides.

Using the `--spring.config.location` startup option, we can specify a location of one or multiple files, which can then be separated by a comma (,) to be added to the default ones. The file designations can be either files from a local filesystem, a classpath, or a remote URL. The locations will be resolved either by the `DefaultResourceLoader` class or, if configured via a `SpringApplication` constructor or setter, by the implementation that is provided by the `SpringApplication` instance.

If the location contains directories, the names should end with a / so as to let Spring Boot know that it should look for the `application.properties` file in these directories.

If you want to change the default name of the file, Spring Boot provides you with this ability as well. Just set the `--spring.config.name` option to whatever filename that you want.

> It is important to remember that the default search paths for the configuration of `classpath:,classpath:/config,file:,file:config/` will always be used regardless of the presence of the `--spring.config.location` setting. This way, you can always retain your default configuration in `application.properties` and just override the ones that you need via the start up settings.

Externalizing an environmental configuration using environment variables

In the previous recipes, we have, a number of times, alluded to the fact that configuration values to a Spring Boot application can be passed and overridden by using OS environment variables. Operating systems rely on these variables to store information about various things. We probably have to set `JAVA_HOME` or `PATH` a few times, and these are examples of environment variables. OS environment variables is also a very important feature if one deploys their application using a PaaS system such as Heroku or Amazon AWS. In these environments, configuration values such as database access credentials and various API tokens are all provided over the environment variables.

Their power comes from the ability to completely externalize the configuration of simple key-value data pairs without the need to rely on placing a property or some other files in a particular location, and having this hardcoded in the application code base. These variables are also agnostic to the particular operating system and can be consumed in the Java program in the same way, `System.getenv()`, regardless of which OS the program is running on.

In this recipe, we will explore how this power can be leveraged to pass the configuration properties to our Spring Boot applications. We will continue to use the code base from the previous recipe and experiment with a few different ways of starting the application and using the OS environment variables in order to change the configuration values of some properties.

How to do it...

1. In the previous recipe, we added a configuration property named `my.config.value`. Let's build the application by running `./gradlew clean bootJar` and start it by running `MY_CONFIG_VALUE="From ENV Config" ./build/libs/bookpub-0.0.1-SNAPSHOT-exec.jar --spring.profiles.active=logger` so as to see the following output in the logs:

   ```
   2017-12-17 --- ication$$EnhancerBySpringCGLIB$$b123df6a : Value of
   my.config.value property is: From ENV Config
   ```

2. If we want to use the environment variables while running our application via the Gradle `bootRun` task, the command line will be `MY_CONFIG_VALUE="From ENV Config" ./gradlew clean bootRun` and should produce the same output as in the preceding step.

3. Conveniently enough, we can even mix and match how we set the configurations. We can use the environment variable to configure the `spring.config.location` property and use it to load other property values from the external properties file, as we did in the previous recipe. Let's try this by launching our application by executing `SPRING_CONFIG_LOCATION= file:/home/<username>/external.properties ./gradlew bootRun`. We should see the following in the logs:

```
2017-12-17 --- ication$$EnhancerBySpringCGLIB$$b123df6a : Value of
my.config.value property is: From Home Directory Config
```

While using environment variables is very convenient, it does have maintenance overhead if the number of these variables gets to be too many. To help deal with this issue, it is good practice to use a method of delegation by setting the `SPRING_CONFIG_LOCATION` variable to configure the location of the environment-specific properties file, typically by loading them from a URL location.

How it works...

As you learned from the section on environment configuration hierarchy, Spring Boot offers multiple ways of providing the configuration properties. Each of these is managed via an appropriate `PropertySource` implementation. We looked at how to create a custom implementation of `PropertySource` when we were implementing `ApacheCommonsConfigurationPropertySource`. Spring Boot already provides a `SystemEnvironmentPropertySource` implementation for us to use out of the box. This even gets automatically registered with the default implementation of the environment interface: the `SystemEnvironment`.

As the `SystemEnvironment` implementation provides a composite façade on top of a multitude of different `PropertySource` implementations, the overriding takes place seamlessly, simply because the `SystemEnvironmentPropertySource` class sits higher up in the list than the `application.properties` file one.

An important aspect that you should notice is the use of ALL_CAPS with underscores (_) in order to separate the words instead of the traditional conventional all.lower.cased format with dots (.) separating the words used in Spring Boot to name the configuration properties. This is due to the nature of some operating systems, namely Linux and OS X, which prevent the use of dots (.) in the names and instead encourages the use of the ALL_CAPS underscore-separated notation.

In situations where the usage of environment variables to specify or override the configuration properties is not desired, Spring provides us with the -Dspring.getenv.ignore system property, which can be set to true and prevents the usage of environment variables. You might want to change this setting to true if you see errors or exceptions in the log due to the running of your code on some application servers or a particular security policy configuration that might not allow access to environment variables.

Externalizing an environmental configuration using Java system properties

While environment variables can, on rare occasions, be hit or miss, the good old Java system properties can always be trusted to be there for you. In addition to using the environment variables and command-line arguments represented by the property names prefixed with a double dash (--), Spring Boot provides you with the ability to use the plain Java system properties to set or override the configuration properties.

This can be useful in a number of situations, particularly if your application is running in a container that sets certain values during startup via the system properties that you want to get access to, or if a property value is not set via a command-line -D argument, but rather in some library via code and by calling System.setProperty(...), especially if property value is being accessed from inside a static method of sorts. While arguably these cases are rare, it takes only one to make you bend over backwards in an effort to try and integrate this value into your application.

In this recipe, we will use the same application executable that was used for the previous one, with the only difference being that we are using Java system properties instead of command-line arguments or environment variables to set our configuration properties at runtime.

How to do it...

1. Let's continue our experiments by setting the `my.config.value` configuration property. Build the application by running `./gradlew clean bootJar` and start it by running `java -Dmy.config.value="From System Config" -jar ./build/libs/bookpub-0.0.1-SNAPSHOT-exec.jar` so as to see the following in the logs:

   ```
   2017-12-17 --- ication$$EnhancerBySpringCGLIB$$b123df6a : Value of
   my.config.value property is: From System Config
   ```

2. If we want to be able to set the Java system property while running our application using the Gradle's `bootRun` task, we will need to add this to the `applicationDefaultJvmArgs` configuration in the `build.gradle` file. Let's add `-Dmy.config.value=Gradle` to this list and start the application by running `./gradlew clean bootRun`. We should see the following in the logs:

   ```
   2017-12-17 --- ication$$EnhancerBySpringCGLIB$$b123df6a : Value of
   my.config.value property is: Gradle
   ```

3. As we made the `applicationDefaultJvmArgs` setting to be shared with `launch.script`, rebuilding the application by running `./gradlew clean bootJar` and starting it by running `./build/libs/bookpub-0.0.1-SNAPSHOT-exec.jar` should yield the same output in the logs as in the preceding step.

How it works...

You might have already guessed that Java system properties are consumed by a similar mechanism that is used for environment variables, and you would be correct. The only real difference is the implementation of `PropertySource`. This time, a more generic `MapPropertySource` implementation is used by `StandardEnvironment`.

What you have also probably noticed is the need to launch our application using the `java -Dmy.config.value="From System Config" -jar ./build/libs/bookpub-0.0.1-SNAPSHOT-exec.jar` command instead of just simply invoking the self-executing packaged JAR by itself. This is because, unlike the environment variables and command-line arguments, Java system properties have to be set on the Java executable ahead of everything else.

We did manage to work around this need by effectively hardcoding the values in our `build.gradle` file, which, combined with the enhancements that we made to `launch.script`, allowed us embed the `my.config.value` property in the command line in the self-executing jar, as well as use it with the Gradle's `bootRun` task.

The risk of using this approach with the configuration properties is that it will always override the values that we set in the higher layers of the configuration, such as `application.properties` and others. Unless you are explicitly constructing the Java executable command line and not using the self-launching capabilities of the packaged JAR, it is best not to use Java system properties and consider using the command-line arguments or environment variables instead.

Externalizing an environmental configuration using JSON

We have looked at a number of different ways to externally add or override the values of specific properties, either by using environment variables, system properties, or command-line arguments. All those options provide us with a great deal of flexibility, but with the exception of external property files, are all limited to setting one property at a time. When it comes to using property files, the syntax is not exactly the best at representing nested, hierarchical data structures, and can get a bit tricky. To avoid this situation, Spring Boot provides us with an ability to also pass, externally, JSON-encoded content containing an entire config hierarchy of settings.

In this recipe, we will use the same application executable that was used for the previous one, with the only difference being using external JSON content to set our configuration properties at runtime.

How to do it...

1. Let's continue our experiments by setting the `my.config.value` configuration property. Build the application by running `./gradlew clean bootJar` and start it by running `java -jar ./build/libs/bookpub-0.0.1-SNAPSHOT-exec.jar --spring.application.json={"my":{"config":{"value":"From external JSON"}}}` so as to see the following in the logs:

   ```
   2017-12-17 --- ication$$EnhancerBySpringCGLIB$$b123df6a : Value of
   my.config.value property is: From external JSON
   ```

2. If we want to be able to set the content using Java system properties, we can use `-Dspring.application.json` instead, assigning the same JSON content as the value.

3. Alternatively, we can also rely on the `SPRING_APPLICATION_JSON` environment variable to pass the same JSON content in the following way:

   ```
   SPRING_APPLICATION_JSON={"my":{"config":{"value":"From external
   JSON"}}} java -jar ./build/libs/bookpub-0.0.1-SNAPSHOT-exec.jar --
   spring.profiles.active=logger
   ```

How it works...

Just like every other configuration approach we have looked at, the JSON content is consumed by a dedicated `EnvironmentPostProcessor` implementation. The only difference is the flattening of the JSON tree into a flat property map, to match the dot-separated properties naming style. In our case, the `my->config->value` nested map gets converted into a flat map with only one key, `my.config.value`, with the value of `From external JSON`.

The setting of the JSON content can come from ANY property source, available from the environment at the time of loading, which contains a key named `spring.application.json` with a value of valid JSON content, and is not only limited to being set by an Environment Variable or using the `SPRING_APPLICATION_JSON` name or Java System Property.

This capability can be very useful to provide externally-defined, environment-specific configuration in bulk. The best way is to do so via setting the `SPRING_APPLICATION_JSON` environment variable on the machine instance using machine/image provisioning tools such as Chef, Puppet, Ansible, Packer, and so on. This enables you to store an entire configuration hierarchy in one JSON file externally, and then simply provision the correct content on the specific machine during provisioning time by just setting an Environment Variable. All applications running on that machine will automatically consume it upon startup.

Setting up Consul

So far, everything that we have been doing with the configuration was connected to the local set of data. In a real, large-scale enterprise environment, this is not always the case and quite frequently there is the desire to be able to make the configuration changes at large, across hundreds or even thousands of instances or machines.

There are a number of tools that exist to help you with this task, and in this recipe, we will take a look at one that, in my opinion, stands out from the group, giving you the ability to cleanly and elegantly configure the environment variables for a starting application using a distributed data store. The tool's name is **Consul**. It is an open source product from Hashicorp and is designed to discover and configure the services in a large, distributed infrastructure.

In this recipe, we will take a look at how to install and configure Consul and experiment with some key functionalities that it provides. This will give us the necessary familiarity for our next recipe, where we will be using Consul to provide the configuration values that are needed to start our application.

How to do it...

1. Go to `https://consul.io/downloads.html` and download the appropriate archive, depending on the operating system that you are using. Consul supports Windows, OS X, and Linux, so it should work for the majority of readers.

 If you are an OS X user, you can install Consul using Homebrew by running `brew install caskroom/cask/brew-cask` followed by `brew cask install consul`.

2. After the installation, we should be able to run `consul --version` and see the following output:

```
Consul v1.0.1
Protocol 2 spoken by default, understands 2 to 3 (agent will
automatically use protocol >2 when speaking to compatible agents)
```

3. With Consul successfully installed, we should be able to start it by running the `consul agent -server -bootstrap-expect 1 -data-dir /tmp/consul` command and our terminal window will display the following:

```
==> WARNING: BootstrapExpect Mode is specified as 1; this is the
same as Bootstrap mode.
==> WARNING: Bootstrap mode enabled! Do not enable unless necessary
==> WARNING: It is highly recommended to set GOMAXPROCS higher than
1
==> Starting Consul agent...
==> Starting Consul agent RPC...
==> Consul agent running!
          Node name: <your machine name>'
          Datacenter: 'dc1'
              Server: true (bootstrap: true)
         Client Addr: 127.0.0.1 (HTTP: 8500, HTTPS: -1, DNS: 8600,
RPC: 8400)
        Cluster Addr: 192.168.1.227 (LAN: 8301, WAN: 8302)
      Gossip encrypt: false, RPC-TLS: false, TLS-Incoming: false
               Atlas: <disabled>
==> Log data will now stream in as it occurs:
    2017/12/17 20:34:43 [INFO] serf: EventMemberJoin: <your machine
name> 192.168.1.227
    2017/12/17 20:34:43 [INFO] serf: EventMemberJoin: <your machine
name>.dc1 192.168.1.227
    2017/12/17 20:34:43 [INFO] raft: Node at 192.168.1.227:8300
[Follower] entering Follower state
    2017/12/17 20:34:43 [INFO] consul: adding server <your machine
name> (Addr: 192.168.1.227:8300) (DC: dc1)
    2017/12/17 20:34:43 [INFO] consul: adding server <your machine
name>.dc1 (Addr: 192.168.1.227:8300) (DC: dc1)
    2017/12/17 20:34:43 [ERR] agent: failed to sync remote state:
No cluster leader
    2017/12/17 20:34:45 [WARN] raft: Heartbeat timeout reached,
starting election
    2017/12/17 20:34:45 [INFO] raft: Node at 192.168.1.227:8300
[Candidate] entering Candidate state
    2017/12/17 20:34:45 [INFO] raft: Election won. Tally: 1
    2017/12/17 20:34:45 [INFO] raft: Node at 192.168.1.227:8300
[Leader] entering Leader state
```

```
2017/12/17 20:34:45 [INFO] consul: cluster leadership acquired
2017/12/17 20:34:45 [INFO] consul: New leader elected: <your
machine name>
2017/12/17 20:34:45 [INFO] raft: Disabling EnableSingleNode
(bootstrap)
2017/12/17 20:34:45 [INFO] consul: member '<your machine name>'
joined, marking health alive
2017/12/17 20:34:47 [INFO] agent: Synced service 'consul'
```

4. With the Consul service running, we can verify that it contains one member by running the `consul members` command, and should see the following result:

Node	Address	Status	Type	Build	Protocol
DC					
<your_machine_name>	192.168.1.227:8301	alive	server	0.5.2	2
dc1					

5. While Consul can also provide discovery for services, health checks, distributed locks, and more, we are going to focus on the key/value service as this is what will be used to provide the configuration in the next recipe. So, let's put the `From Consul Config` value in the key/value store by executing the `curl -X PUT -d 'From Consul Config'` `http://localhost:8500/v1/kv/bookpub/my/config/value` command.

 If you are using Windows, you can get curl from `http://curl.haxx.se/download.html`.

6. We can also retrieve the data by running the `curl` `http://localhost:8500/v1/kv/bookpub/my/config/value` command and should see the following output:

```
[{"CreateIndex":20,"ModifyIndex":20,"LockIndex":0,"Key":"bookpub/my
/config/value","Flags":0,"Value":"RnJvbSBDb25zdWwgQ29uZmln"}]
```

7. We can delete this value by running the `curl -X DELETE` `http://localhost:8500/v1/kv/bookpub/my/config/value` command.

8. In order to modify the existing value and change it for something else, execute the `curl -X PUT -d 'newval'` `http://localhost:8500/v1/kv/bookpub/my/config/value?cas=20` command.

How it works...

A detailed explanation about how Consul works and all the possible options for its key/value service would take a book of its own, so here we will look only at the basic pieces. It is strongly recommended that you read Consul's documentation at
`https://consul.io/intro/getting-started/services.html`.

In *step 3*, we started the Consul agent in server mode. It acts as a main master node and, in real deployment, the local agents running on the individual instances will be using the server node to connect to and retrieve data from. For our test purposes, we will just use this server node as if it were a local agent.

The information displayed upon startup shows us that our node has started as a server node, establishing an HTTP service on port `8500` as well as the DNS and RPC services, if that's how one chooses to connect to it. We can also see that there is only one node in the cluster, ours, and we are the elected leader running in a healthy state.

As we will be using the convenient RESTful HTTP API via cURL, all of our requests will be using localhost on port `8500`. Being a RESTful API, it fully adheres to CRUD verb terminology, and to insert the data, we will use a `PUT` method on a `/v1/kv` endpoint in order to set the `bookpub/my/config/value` key.

Retrieving the data is even more straightforward: we just make a `GET` request to the same `/v1/kv` service using the desired key. The same goes for `DELETE`, with the only difference being the method name.

The update operation requires a bit more information in the URL, namely the `cas` parameter. The value of this parameter should be the `ModifyIndex` of the desired key, which can be obtained from the `GET` request. In our case, it has a value of 20.

Externalizing an environmental configuration using Consul and envconsul

In the previous recipe, we had our Consul service installed and experimented with its key/value capabilities to learn how we could manipulate the data in it in order to integrate Consul with our application and make the data extraction process seamless and non-invasive from an application standpoint.

As we don't want our application to know anything about Consul and have to explicitly connect to it, even though such a possibility exists, we will employ another utility, also created as open source by Hashicorp, called **envconsul**. It will connect to the Consul service for us, extract the specified configuration key/value tree, and expose it as the environment variables to be used while also launching our application. Pretty cool, right?

Getting ready

Before we get started with launching our application, which was created in the previous recipes, we need to install the envconsul utility.

Download the binary for your respective operating system from `https://github.com/hashicorp/envconsul/releases` and extract the executable to any directory of your choice, though it is better to put it somewhere that is in the PATH.

Once envconsul is extracted from the downloaded archive, we are ready to start using it so as to configure our application.

How to do it...

1. If you have not already added the value for the `my/config/value` key to Consul, let's add it by running `curl -X PUT -d 'From Consul Config' http://localhost:8500/v1/kv/bookpub/my/config/value`.

2. The first step is to make sure envconsul can connect to the Consul server and that it extracts the correct data based on our configuration key. Let's execute a simple test by running the `envconsul --once --sanitize --upcase --prefix bookpub env` command. We should see the following in the output:

```
. . .
TERM=xterm-256color
SHELL=/bin/bash
LANG=en_US.UTF-8
HOME=/Users/<your_user_name>
. . .
MY_CONFIG_VALUE=From Consul Config
```

3. After we have verified that envconsul is returning the correct data to us, we will use it to launch our `BookPub` application by running `envconsul --once --sanitize --upcase --prefix bookpub ./gradlew clean bootRun`. Once the application has started, we should see the following output in the logs:

```
2017-12-17 --- ication$$EnhancerBySpringCGLIB$$b123df6a : Value of
my.config.value property is: From Consul Config
```

4. We can do the same thing by building the self-starting executable JAR by running `./gradlew clean bootJar`, and start it by running `envconsul --once --sanitize --upcase --prefix bookpub ./build/libs/bookpub-0.0.1-SNAPSHOT-exec.jar` to make sure we see the same output in the logs as in the preceding step. If you see `Gradle` instead of `From Consul Config`, make sure the `applicationDefaultJvmArgs` configuration in `build.gradle` does not have `-Dmy.config.value=Gradle` in it.

5. Another marvelous ability of envconsul is not only to export the configuration key values as environment variables, but also to monitor for any changes and restart the application if the values in Consul change. Let's launch our application by running `envconsul --sanitize --upcase --prefix bookpub ./build/libs/bookpub-0.0.1-SNAPSHOT-exec.jar`, and we should see the following value in the log:

```
2017-12-17 --- ication$$EnhancerBySpringCGLIB$$b123df6a : Value of
my.config.value property is: From Consul Config
```

6. We will now use the consul command to get the current `ModifyIndex` of our key and update its value to `From UpdatedConsul Config` by opening another terminal window and executing `curl http://localhost:8500/v1/kv/bookpub/my/config/value`, grabbing the `ModifyIndex` value, and using it to execute `curl -X PUT -d 'From UpdatedConsul Config' http://localhost:8500/v1/kv/bookpub/my/config/value?cas=<Modify Index Value>`. We should see our running application magically restart itself and our newly updated value displayed in the log at the end:

```
2017-12-17 --- ication$$EnhancerBySpringCGLIB$$b123df6a : Value of
my.config.value property is: From UpdatedConsul Config
```

How it works...

What we just did was pretty sweet, right? Let's examine the magic going on behind the scenes in more detail. We will start by dissecting the command line and explaining what each argument control option does.

Our first execution command line was `envconsul --once --sanitize --upcase -- prefix bookpub ./gradlew clean bootRun`, so let's take a look at exactly what we did, as follows:

- First, one might notice that there is no indication about which Consul node we should be connecting to. This is because there is an implicit understanding or an assumption that you already have a Consul agent running locally on `localhost:8500`. If this is not the case for whatever reason, you can always explicitly specify the Consul instance to connect via the `--consul localhost:8500` argument added to the command line.

- The `--prefix` option specifies the starting configuration key segment in which to look for the different values. When we were adding keys to Consul, we used the following key: `bookpub/my/config/value`. By specifying the `--prefix bookpub` option, we tell envconsul to strip the `bookpub` part of the key and use all the internal tree elements in `bookpub` to construct the environment variables. Thus, `my/config/value` becomes the environment variable.

- The `--sanitize` option tells envconsul to replace all the invalid characters with underscores (_). So, if we were to only use `--sanitize`, we would end up with `my_config_value` as an environment variable.

- The `--upcase` option, as you might already have guessed, changes the environment variable key to all upper case characters, so when combined with the `--sanitize` option, `my/config/value` key gets transformed into the `MY_CONFIG_VALUE` environment variable.

- The `--once` option indicates that we only want to externalize the keys as environment variables once and do not want to continuously monitor for changes in the Consul cluster. If a key in our prefix tree has changed its value, we re-externalize the keys as environment variables and restart the application.

This last option, --once, provides a very useful choice of functionalities. If you are interested only in the initial bootstrapping of your application via the use of a Consul-shared configuration, then the keys will be set as environment variables, the application will be launched, and envconsul will consider its job done. However, if you would like to monitor the Consul cluster for changes to keys/values and, after the change has taken place, restart your application reflecting the new change, then remove the --once option and envconsul will restart the application once the change has occurred.

Such behavior can be very useful and handy for things such as a near-instantaneous changes to the database connection configuration. Imagine that you need to do a quick failover from one database to another and your JDBC URL is configured via Consul. All you need to do is push a new JDBC URL value and envconsul will almost immediately detect this change and restart the application, telling it to connect to a new database node.

Currently, this functionality is implemented by sending a traditional SIGTERM signal to an application running process, telling it to terminate and, once the process is exited, restart the application. This might not always be the desired behavior, especially if it takes some time for an application to start up and be capable of taking traffic. You don't want your entire cluster of web applications to be shut down, even if it will only be for a few minutes.

To provide a better handling of this scenario, envconsul was enhanced to be able to send a number of standard signals that can be configured via a newly added --kill-signal option. Using this option, we can specify any of the SIGHUP, SIGTERM, SIGINT, SIGQUIT, SIGUSR1, or SIGUSR2 signals to be used instead of the default SIGTERM, to be sent to a running application process once the key/value changes have been detected.

The process signal handling in Java is not as clear and straightforward due to most of the behavior being very specific to a particular operating system and the JVM that is run atop it. Some of the signals in the list will terminate the application anyway or, in the case of SIGQUIT, the JVM will print Core Dump into the standard output. However, there are ways to configure the JVM, depending on the operating system, to let us use SIGUSR1 and SIGUSR2 instead of acting on those signals itself, but unfortunately that topic falls outside the scope of this book.

Here is a sample example of how to deal with **Signal Handlers**: https://github.com/spotify/daemon-java, or see the Oracle Java documentation at https://docs.oracle.com/javase/8/docs/technotes/guides/troubleshoot/signals.html for a detailed explanation.

7
Health Monitoring and Data Visualization

In this chapter, we will cover the following recipes:

- Writing custom health indicators
- Configuring management context
- Emitting metrics
- Monitoring Spring Boot via JMX
- Managing Spring Boot via SSHd Shell and writing custom remote Shell commands
- Integrating Micrometer metrics with Graphite
- Integrating Micrometer metrics with Dashing

Introduction

In the previous chapter, you learned a few techniques to efficiently package and get the application ready for deployment and we looked at a number of techniques to provide an environmental configuration without changing the code. With the deployment and configuration woes behind us, the last (but not least) important step remains—ensuring that we have complete visibility, monitoring, and management control of our application, as it is running in the production environment and is exposed to the harsh environment of customers' (ab)use.

Just as airline pilots don't like to fly blind, developers don't get excited if they can't see how their beloved application, that they worked hard on, performs in production. We want to know, at any given time, what the CPU utilization is like, how much memory we are consuming, whether our connection to the database is up and available, the number of customers who use the system in any given time interval, and so on. Not only do we want to know all these things, but we also want to be able to see it in pretty charts, graphs, and visual dashboards. These come in very handy to put on the big Plasma displays for monitoring as well as impressing your boss, so as to show that you are on the top of things and have it all under control.

This chapter will help you learn the necessary techniques to enhance our application in order to expose custom metrics, health statuses, and so on, as well as how to get the monitoring data out of our application and either store it in Graphite for historical reference or use this data to create real-time monitoring dashboards using the Dashing and Grafana frameworks. We will also take a look at the capability to connect to running instances and perform various management tasks using the powerful CRaSH framework integration.

Writing custom health indicators

Knowing the state of the application that is running in production, especially in a large-scale distributed system, is just as (if not more) important as having things such as automated testing and deployment. In today's fast-paced IT world, we can't really afford much downtime, so we need to have the information about the health of the application at our fingertips, ready to go at a minute's notice. If the all-so-important database connections go down, we want to see it right away and be able to quickly remedy the situation; the customers are not going to be waiting around for long before they go to another site.

We will resume working on our `BookPub` application in the state in which we left it in the previous chapter. In this recipe, we will add the necessary Spring Boot starters to enable the monitoring and instrumentation of our application and will even write our own health indicator.

How to do it...

1. The first thing that we need to do is add a dependency to the Spring Boot
   Actuator starter in our `build.gradle` file with the following content:

```
dependencies {
    ...
    compile("org.springframework.boot:spring-boot-starter-
    data-rest")
    // compile("org.springframework.boot:spring-boot-starter-
    jetty") //
    Need to use Jetty instead of Tomcat
    compile("org.springframework.boot:spring-boot-starter-
    actuator")
    compile project(':db-count-starter')
    ...
}
```

2. Adding this dependency alone already gives us the ability to access the Spring
   management `/actuator/*` endpoints, such as `/env`, `/info`, `/metrics`,
   and `/health`, (though they are disabled by default, unless
   a `management.endpoints.web.exposure.include=*` property is configured
   in the `application.properties` file). So, let's start our application by
   executing the `./gradlew clean bootRun` command line and then we can
   access the newly available `/health` endpoint by opening our browser and going
   to `http://localhost:8080/actuator/health` so as to see the new endpoint
   in action, as shown in the following screenshot:

3. To get more details about the health state of our application, let's configure it to show the detailed health output by adding the `management.endpoint.health.show-details=always` property to the `application.properties` file and then restarting our application. Now, when we go to `http://localhost:8080/actuator/health` in the browser, we should see something similar to the following screenshot:

4. With the `actuator` dependency added, and detailed `/health` endpoint configured, we can now add and perform all kinds of monitoring functions on our application. Let's go ahead and populate the `/info` endpoint with some data by adding a directive to the `build.gradle` file located at the root of our project with the following content:

```
springBoot {
    buildInfo {
        properties {
            additional = [
                'description' : project.description
            ]
        }
    }
}
```

5. Next, we will create a new properties file named `gradle.properties` in the root directory of our project with the following content:

```
version=0.0.1-SNAPSHOT
description=BookPub Catalog Application
```

6. We will also add `rootProject.name='BookPub-ch7'` to the `settings.gradle` file located in the root directory of our project.

7. Now, let's start our application by executing `./gradlew clean bootRun` and then we can access the newly available `/info` endpoint by opening our browser and going to `http://localhost:8080/actuator/info` to see the new endpoint in action, as follows:

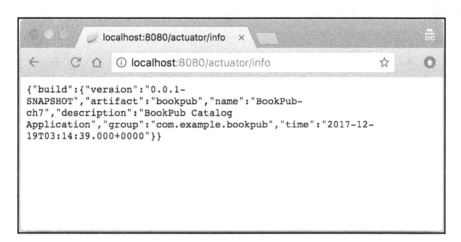

8. As we have got the hang of how things work, let's go ahead and make our custom health indicator, which will be accessible via the `/health` endpoint in order to report the count status of the entries for each of our repositories. If they are greater than or equal to zero, we are UP, otherwise we are not really sure what's going on. Obviously, if an exception has occurred, we would be reporting DOWN. Let's start by relaxing the `getRepositoryName(...)` method visibility from `private` to `protected` in the `DbCountRunner.java` file located in the `db-count-starter/src/main/java/com/example/bookpubstarter/dbcount` directory at the root of our project.

9. Next, we will add the same dependency to the `compile("org.springframework.boot:spring-boot-starter-actuator")` library in the `build.gradle` file in the `db-count-starter` directory at the root of our project.

10. Now, we will create a new file named `DbCountHealthIndicator.java` in the `db-count-starter/src/main/java/com/example/bookpubstarter/dbcount` directory at the root of our project with the following content:

```java
public class DbCountHealthIndicator implements HealthIndicator {
    private CrudRepository repository;

    public DbCountHealthIndicator(CrudRepository repository) {
        this.repository = repository;
    }

    @Override
    public Health health() {
        try {
            long count = repository.count();
            if (count >= 0) {
                return Health.up().withDetail("count",
                count).build();
            } else {
                return Health.unknown().withDetail("count",
                count).build();
            }
        } catch (Exception e) {
            return Health.down(e).build();
        }
    }
}
```

11. Next, we will modify the `@Import` annotation in the `EnableDbCounting.java` file located in the `db-count starter/src/main/java/com/example/bookpubstarter/dbcount` directory at the root of our project with the following content:

```java
@Import({DbCountAutoConfiguration.class,
        HealthIndicatorAutoConfiguration.class})
```

12. Finally, for the automatic registration of our `HealthIndicator` class, we will enhance the `DbCountAutoConfiguration.java` file located in the `db-count-starter/src/main/java/com/example/bookpubstarter/dbcount` directory at the root of our project with the following content:

```
@Autowired
private HealthAggregator healthAggregator;
@Bean
public HealthIndicator
dbCountHealthIndicator(Collection<CrudRepository> repositories) {
    CompositeHealthIndicator compositeHealthIndicator = new
      CompositeHealthIndicator(healthAggregator);
    for (CrudRepository repository : repositories) {
        String name = DbCountRunner.getRepositoryName
          (repository.getClass());
        compositeHealthIndicator.addHealthIndicator(name, new
          DbCountHealthIndicator(repository));
    }
    return compositeHealthIndicator;
}
```

13. So, let's start our application by executing the `./gradlew clean bootRun` command line, and then we can access the `/health` endpoint by opening our browser and going to `http://localhost:8080/actuator/health` to see our new `HealthIndicator` class in action, as follows:

How it works...

The Spring Boot Actuator starter adds a number of important features that give insight into the runtime state of the application. The library contains a number of autoconfigurations that add and configure the various endpoints to access the runtime monitoring data and health of the application. Those endpoints all share a common context path: `/actuator`. To expose any other endpoints besides `/info` and `/health`, we need to explicitly expose them by setting the `management.endpoints.web.exposure.include=*` property. When the value is set to `*`, it will expose all of the endpoints. The following endpoints are available to aid us in getting an insight into the application runtime state and configuration:

- `/env`: This endpoint enables us to query the application about all of the environment variables that the application has access to via the environment implementation, which we have seen earlier. It is very useful when you need to debug a particular issue and want to know a value of any given configuration property. If we access the endpoint by going to `http://localhost:8080/actuator/env`, we will see a number of different configuration sections, for example, the class path resource `[tomcat.https.properties]`, `applicationConfig`: `[classpath:/application.properties]`, `commonsConfig`, `systemEnvironment`, `systemProperties`, and others. They all represent an instance of an individual `PropertySource` implementation that is available in the environment and depending on their place in the hierarchy, may or may not be used to provide the value resolution at the runtime. To find out exactly which entry is used to resolve a particular value, for example, for the `book.count.rate` property, we can query it by going to the `http://localhost:8080/actuator/env/book.counter.rate` URL. By default, we should get 10,000 as a result unless, of course, a different value was set via the system environment or command-line arguments as an override. If you really want to dig deep into the code, the `EnvironmentEndpoint` class is responsible for handling the logic behind this capability.

- `/configprops`: This endpoint provides you with an insight into the settings of the various configuration property objects, such as our `WebConfiguration.TomcatSslConnectorProperties` starter. It is slightly different from the `/env` endpoint as it provides insight into the configuration object bindings. If we open the browser to go to `http://localhost:8080/actuator/configprops` and search for `custom.tomcat.https`, we will see the entry for our configuration property object that we will use to configure `TomcatSslConnector`, which was automatically populated and bound for us by Spring Boot.

- `/conditions`: This endpoint serves as a web-based analog to the AutoConfiguration Report, which we saw in `Chapter 4`, *Writing Custom Spring Boot Starters*. This way, we can get the report using the browser at any time without having to start the application with the specific flags to get it printed.
- `/beans`: This endpoint is designed to list all the beans that have been created by Spring Boot and are available in application context.
- `/mappings`: This endpoint exposes a list of all the URL mappings that are supported by the application as well as a reference to the `HandlerMapping` bean implementation. This is very useful for answering the question of where would a specific URL get routed to. Try going to `http://localhost:8080/actuator/mappings` to see the list of all the routes that our application can handle.
- `/threaddump`: This endpoint allows extraction of the Thread Dump information from the running application. It is rather useful when trying to diagnose a potential thread deadlock.
- `/heapdump`: This endpoint is similar to `/dump` with the exception that it produces Heap Dump information instead.
- `/info`: This endpoint shows the basic description and application information that we added and we've seen this in action, so it should be familiar to us as of now. The nice support in the build tools gives us the ability to configure additional or replace existing values inside our `build.gradle` configuration, which would then be propagated to be consumed by the `/info` endpoint. Additionally, any properties defined in the `application.properties` file, that start with `info.` will be displayed while accessing the `/info` endpoint, so you are definitely not limited to only the `build.gradle` configuration. Configuring this specific endpoint in order to return the relevant information can be very helpful when building various automated discovery and monitoring tools as it is a great way to expose application-specific information in the form of a nice JSON RESTful API.
- `/actuator`: This endpoint gives a nice JSON-formatted list of links in a **Hypertext Application Language** (**HAL**) style for all the available actuator endpoints.
- `/health`: This endpoint provides information about the general application health status as well as a detailed breakdown and health status of the individual components.

- `/metrics`: This endpoint gives an overview of all the various data points that are emitted by the metrics subsystem. You can experiment with it by accessing it via the `http://localhost:8080/actuator/metrics` URL in the browser. We will cover this in more detail in the next recipe.

Now that we know in general what is being provided for us by Spring Boot Actuator, we can move on to take a look at the details of what we did to get our custom `HealthIndicator` class working and how the whole health monitoring subsystem in Spring Boot functions.

As you saw, getting the basic `HealthIndicator` interface to work is very easy; all we have to do is create an implementing class that will return a `Health` object upon a call to the `health()` method. All you have to do is expose the instance of the `HealthIndicator` class as `@Bean` for Spring Boot to pick it up and add it to the `/health` endpoint.

In our case, we went a step further because we had to deal with the need to create `HealthIndicator` for each `CrudRepository` instance. To accomplish this, we created an instance of `CompositeHealthIndicator` to which we added all the instances of `DbHealthIndicator` for each `CrudRepository`. We then returned this as `@Bean` and this is what was used by Spring Boot to represent the health status. Being a composite, it preserved the inner hierarchy as is evident from the returned JSON data representing the health status. We also added some extra data element to provide the indication of the entry count as well as the name of each particular repository so that we can tell them apart.

Looking at the code, you are probably wondering: what is this `HealthAggregator` instance that we've wired in? The reason that we needed a `HealthAggregator` instance is because `CompositeHealthIndicator` needs to know how to decide if the inner composition of all the nested `HeathIndicators` represents good or bad health as a whole. Imagine that all the repositories, but one, return UP but one is DOWN. What does this mean? Is the composite indicator healthy as a whole or should it also report DOWN because one inner repository has issues?

By default, Spring Boot already creates and uses an instance of `HealthAggregator`, so we just autowired it and used it in our use case as well. We did have to explicitly add the import of the `HealthIndicatorAutoConfiguration` and `MetricsDropwizardAutoConfiguration` classes in order to satisfy the bean dependency during slice tests for `DataJpaTest` and `WebMvcTest`, since those only partially instantiate the context, and the actuator autoconfigurations are missing.

Even though the default implementation is an instance of `OrderedHealthAggregator`, which just collects all the inner status responses and chooses the lowest on the priority level out of `DOWN`, `OUT_OF_SERVICE`, `UP`, and `UNKNOWN`, it doesn't always have to be that way. For example, if the composite indicator consists of the indicators for redundant service connections, your combined result could be `UP` as long as at least one of the connections is healthy. Creating a custom `HealthAggregator` interface is very easy; all you have to do is either extend `AbstractHealthAggregator` or implement a `HealthAggregator` interface itself.

Configuring management context

Spring Boot Actuator out of the box creates a set of management endpoints and the supporting beans in the main application context and those endpoints are available on the `server.port` configured HTTP port. There are, however, cases where for security or isolation reasons we would want to separate the main application context from the management one or expose the management endpoints on a different port than the main application.

Spring Boot provides us with an ability to configure a separate child application context for the management beans, which would inherit everything from the main application context, but allow for defining beans that are only available for the management functions as well. The same goes for exposing the endpoints on a different port or even using different connector security in such a way that the main application could be using SSL, but the management endpoints are accessible using plain HTTP.

How to do it...

Let's imagine that, for whatever reason, we want to change our JSON converter to output field names using `SNAKE_CASE` (all lowercase letters separating words with an underscore).

1. First, let's create a class holding our configuration for the management context named `ManagementConfiguration.java` located in the `src/main/java/com/example/bookpub` directory at the root of our project with the following content:

```
@ManagementContextConfiguration
public class ManagementConfiguration
        implements WebMvcConfigurer {
    @Override
```

```
public void configureMessageConverters(
        List<HttpMessageConverter<?>> converters) {
    HttpMessageConverter c = new
     MappingJackson2HttpMessageConverter(
        Jackson2ObjectMapperBuilder.json().
        propertyNamingStrategy(PropertyNamingStrategy.SNAKE_CAS).
        build()
        );
    converters.add(c);
  }
}
```

2. We also need to add this class to `spring.factories` located in the `src/main/resources/META-INF` directory at the root of our project with the following content:

```
org.springframework.boot.actuate.autoconfigure.web.ManagementContex
tConfiguration=com.example.bookpub.ManagementConfiguration
```

3. To avoid our configuration being detected by the component scan for the main application context, we need to exclude it by adding the following to `BookPubApplication.java` located in the `src/main/java/com/example/bookpub` directory at the root of our project:

```
@ComponentScan(excludeFilters =
    @ComponentScan.Filter(
        type = FilterType.ANNOTATION,
        classes = ManagementContextConfiguration.class
    )
)
```

4. To have a separate management context, we need to launch it using a different port, so let's amend `application.properties` located in the `src/main/resources` directory at the root of our project with the following content:

```
management.server.port=8081
management.endpoints.web.exposure.include=*
```

5. Finally, let's start our application by executing `./gradlew clean bootRun` and then we can access the `/threaddump` endpoint by opening our browser and going to `http://localhost:8081/actuator/threaddump` to see our new configuration take place. The field names of the returned JSON should all be in lowercase and words should be separated using an underscore, or in `SNAKE_CASE`, as it is called. Alternatively, by going to the `http://localhost:8080/books/978-1-78528-415-1` endpoint, we should continue seeing JSON field names in the `LOWER_CAMEL_CASE` format.

How it works...

Spring Boot recognizes that there are many reasons and it needs to be able to provide separate configuration for the way management endpoints and other actuator components work, which is different from the main application. The first level of such configurations can be achieved by setting the myriad of available properties that intuitively start with `management.*`. We have used one such property, `management.server.port`, to set the port for the management interface to be `8081`. We could also set things like the SSL configuration, security settings, or network IP interface address to bind the listener to. We also have the capability to configure each individual `actuator` endpoint by setting their corresponding properties, which start with `management.endpoint.<name>.*` and have a variety of settings, depending on the specific endpoint goals.

For security reasons, the data that is exposed by the various management endpoints, especially the ones from sensitive ones such as `/health`, `/env`, and others can be very lucrative for malicious people on the outside. To prevent this from happening, Spring Boot provides us with the ability to configure if we want the endpoints to be available via `management.endpoint.<name>.enabled=false`. We can specify which individual endpoints we want to disable by setting an appropriate `management.endpoint<name>.enabled=false` property as well, or using `management.endpoints.web.exposure.exclude=<name>` to tell Spring Boot if this endpoint should be enabled, but not exposed via the WEB HTTP API method of access.

Alternatively, we can set `management.server.port=-1` to disable the HTTP exposure of these endpoints or use a different port number in order to have the management endpoints and live services on different ports. If we want to enable access only via a localhost, we can achieve this by configuring `management.server.address=127.0.0.1` to prevent external access. Even the context URL path can be configured to something else, say `/admin`, via `management.server.context-path=/admin`. This way, to get access to a `/health` endpoint, we would go to `http://127.0.0.1/admin/health` instead of the default `/actuator` context path. This can be useful if you want to control and restrict access via the firewall rules, so you can just add a filter to block external access to anything, `/admin/*`, for all the applications from the outside. With the addition of Spring Security, an authentication can also be configured to require a user login to get access to the endpoints.

In situations when controlling behavior using properties is not enough, Spring Boot provides a mechanism to provide alternative application context configuration via the use of `spring.factories` and the accompanying `ManagementContextConfiguration` annotation. This enables us to tell Spring Boot which configurations should be automatically loaded when management context is being created. The intended use of this annotation is to have the configuration live in a separate, sharable dependency library, outside of the main application's code.

In our example, because we put it in the same codebase (for simplicity), we had to do an extra step and define the exclusion filter in the `BookPubApplication.java` file to exclude the `ManagementContextConfiguration` classes from component scan when setting up the main application. The reason we had to do that is simple—if we look inside the `ManagementContextConfiguration` annotation definition, we will see that it is a meta-annotation with the `@Configuration` annotation inside it. What this means is that when our main application is being configured, the component scan will automatically detect all the classes in the classpath tree of the application code that are annotated with `@Configuration`, and as such, it will put all the configurations marked with `ManagementContextConfiguration` in the main context as well. We have avoided that using the exclusion filter. Alternatively, a better way is to have those configurations in a separate library using a different package hierarchy, which would prevent the component scan picking them up, but the autoconfiguration will still works because of the `spring.factories` entry for `org.springframework.boot.actuate.autoconfigure.web.ManagementContextConfiguration` telling Spring Boot to automatically add those configurations to the management context.

In order to have the management context separate from the main application, it is necessary to configure it to run on a separate port using the `management.server.port` property. Without this setting, all of the objects will be using shared application context.

Emitting metrics

The previous recipe gave an overview of the capabilities provided by Spring Boot Actuators. We played with different management endpoints such as /info and /health and even created our own health metrics to add to the default set. However, besides the health status, there are a number of things that we, as developers and operations folks, want to be able to see and monitor on an ongoing basis, and just knowing that the uplink is functional is not good enough. We would also like to see the number of open sessions, concurrent requests to the application, latency, and so on. In this recipe, you will learn about the metric reporting facilities in Spring Boot as well as how to add our own metrics and some quick and simple ways of visualizing them.

Getting ready

To help us visualize the metrics better, we will use a great open source project, spring-boot-admin, located at https://github.com/codecentric/spring-boot-admin. It provides a simple web UI on top of the Spring Boot Actuators to give a nicer view of the various data.

We will create a simple admin application in Gradle using the instructions from https://github.com/codecentric/spring-boot-admin#server-application by performing the following simple steps:

1. Go to start.spring.io and create a new application template with the following fields:

   - **Generate a: Gradle Project**
   - **With: Java**
   - **Spring Boot: 2.0.0 (SNAPSHOT)**
   - **Group:** org.sample.admin
   - **Artifact:** spring-boot-admin-web
   - **Name:** Spring Boot Admin Web
   - **Description:** Spring Boot Admin Web Application
   - **Package Name:** org.sample.admin
   - **Packaging: Jar**
   - **Java Version: 8**

2. Select the **Actuator** option under **Search for dependencies**
3. Click on **Generate Project alt +** to download the application template archive
4. Extract the contents from the directory of your choice
5. In the extracted directory, execute the `gradle wrapper` command line to generate a gradlew script
6. In the `build.gradle` file, add the following dependencies to the `dependencies` block:

```
compile("de.codecentric:spring-boot-admin-server:2.0.0-SNAPSHOT")
compile("de.codecentric:spring-boot-admin-server-ui:2.0.0-SNAPSHOT")
```

7. We also need to update the `repositories` block with a reference to use the `snapshots` repository (as the time of writing, the SBA is not yet released):

```
maven { url
"https://oss.sonatype.org/content/repositories/snapshots/" }
```

8. Open the `SpringBootAdminWebApplication.java` file located in the `src/main/java/spring-boot-admin-web` directory and add the following annotations to the `SpringBootAdminWebApplication` class:

```
@SpringBootApplication
@EnableAdminServer
public class SpringBootAdminWebApplication {

  public static void main(String[] args) {
    SpringApplication.run(
                    SpringBootAdminWebApplication.class,
                    args);
  }
}
```

9. Open the `application.properties` file located in the `src/main/resources` directory and add the following settings:

```
server.port: 8090
spring.application.name: Spring Boot Admin Web
spring.cloud.config.enabled: false
spring.jackson.serialization.indent_output: true
```

10. We are now ready to start our Admin Web Console by running `./gradlew bootRun` and open the browser to `http://localhost:8090` to see the following output:

How to do it...

1. With the **Admin Web** up and running, we are now ready to start adding various metrics to our `BookPub` application. Let's expose the same information about our data repositories as we did in `HealthIndicators`, but this time, we will expose the counts data as a metric. We will continue to add code to our `db-count-starter` subproject. So, let's create a new file named `DbCountMetrics.java` in the `db-count-starter/src/main/java/com/example/bookpubstarter/dbcount` directory at the root of our project with the following content:

```
public class DbCountMetrics implements MeterBinder {
    private Collection<CrudRepository> repositories;

    public DbCountMetrics(Collection<CrudRepository> repositories)
    {
        this.repositories = repositories;
    }

    @Override
    public void bindTo(MeterRegistry registry) {
```

```
                    for (CrudRepository repository : repositories) {
                        String name = DbCountRunner.getRepositoryName
                            (repository.getClass());
                        String metricName = "counter.datasource."
                                            + name;
                        Gauge.builder(metricName, repository,
                                        CrudRepository::count)
                            .tags("name", name)
                            .description("The number of entries in "
                                        + name + "repository")
                            .register(registry);
                    }
                }
            }
```

2. Next, for the automatic registration of `DbCountMetrics`, we will enhance `DbCountAutoConfiguration.java` located in the `db-count-starter/src/main/java/com/example/bookpubstarter/dbcount` directory at the root of our project with the following content:

```
@Bean
public DbCountMetrics
    dbCountMetrics(Collection<CrudRepository> repositories) {
        return new DbCountMetrics(repositories);
}
```

3. In order for the Thread Dump to properly display in the Spring Boot Admin UI, we need to change our JSON converter from `SNAKE_CASE` to `LOWER_CAMEL_CASE` by changing `ManagementConfiguration.java` located in the `src/main/java/com/example/bookpub` directory at the root of our project with the following content:

```
propertyNamingStrategy(
        PropertyNamingStrategy.LOWER_CAMEL_CASE
)
```

4. So, let's start our application by executing `./gradlew clean bootRun` and then we can access the `/metrics` endpoint by opening our browser and going to `http://localhost:8081/actuator/metrics` to see our new `DbCountMetrics` class added to the existing metrics list, as follows:

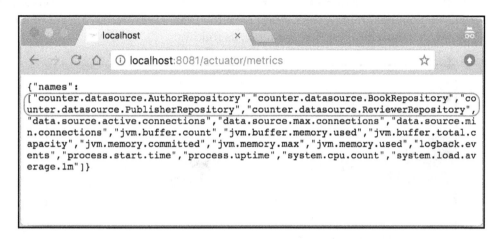

5. Our next step would be to get our application to appear in the Spring Boot Admin Web, which we created earlier. To make this happen, we will need to add a dependency on the `compile("de.codecentric:spring-boot-admin-starter-client:2.0.0-SNAPSHOT")` library to `build.gradle` in the directory at the root of our project.

6. Additionally, `application.properties` located in the `src/main/resources` directory in the root of our project needs to be enhanced with the following entries:

```
spring.application.name=BookPub Catalog Application
server.port=8080
spring.boot.admin.client.url=http://localhost:8090
```

7. Once again, let's start our application by executing `./gradlew clean bootRun`, and if we now go to Spring Boot Admin Web by directing our browser to `http://localhost:8090`, we should see a new entry for our application named `BookPub Catalog Application` appear in the list. If we click on the **Details** button on the right-hand side and scroll down to the **Health** section, we will see our custom health indicators along with the others reported in a form of nicer looking hierarchical entries in a table, as follows:

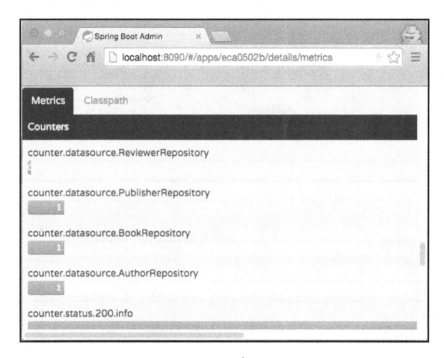

How it works...

A few words about Spring Boot Admin Web before we delve into the details of creating and emitting metrics. It is a simple web GUI that, in the backend, uses the same endpoints exposed by Spring Boot Actuator, which we learned about in the previous recipe. The data is extracted from the application as we click on the various links in Admin Web and displayed in a nice graphical way—no magic!

We only had to configure a few properties in addition to adding the client library dependency in order to get our application to connect and register with Admin Web:

- `spring.application.name=BookPub Catalog Application`: This configures the name of the application that we have chosen to use. It is also possible to take the value from the description property defined in `gradle.properties` using the resource processing task in Gradle. Admin Web uses this value when displaying the application list.

- `spring.boot.admin.client.url=http://localhost:8090`: This configures the location of the Admin Web application so that our application knows where to go in order to register itself. As we are running on port `8080`, we chose to configure Admin Web to listen on port `8090`, but any port can be chosen as desired. You can see more configuration options by visiting `https://codecentric.github.io/spring-boot-admin/current/`.

If we also want to enable the logging level control through the UI, we will need to add a Jolokia JMX library to our `compile("org.jolokia:jolokia-core:+")` build dependency as well as a `logback.xml` file in the `src/main/resources` directory in the root of the project with the following content:

```
<configuration>
  <include
      resource="org/springframework/boot/logging/logback/base.xml"/>
  <jmxConfigurator/>
</configuration>
```

The metrics facility in Spring Boot is very powerful and extendable, offering a number of different approaches for emitting and consuming metrics. Starting with Spring Boot 2.0, the `Micrometer.io` library is being used under the hood to provide a very comprehensive monitoring solution. Out of the box, Spring Boot already configures a number of data metrics that monitor the system resources, such as heap memory, thread counts, system uptime, and many others as well as the database usage and HTTP session counts. The MVC endpoints are also instrumented to gauge the request latency, which is measured in milliseconds, as well as a counter for each endpoint request status.

Various metrics, such as gauges, counters, timers, and so on, are emitted via the `MeterRegistry` implementation that is provided by Spring Boot at runtime. The registry can be easily autowired into any Spring-managed object and be used to emit metrics.

For example, we can easily count the number of times a particular method gets invoked. All we need to do is to autowire an instance of `MeterRegistry` into our object during creation, and place the following line at the beginning of the method:

```
meterRegistry.counter("objectName.methodName.invoked").increment();
```

Each time the method gets called, the particular metric count will be incremented.

This approach will give us the counts that we can increment, but if we want to measure latency or any other arbitrary value, we will need to use `Gauge` to submit our metrics. To measure how long it will take for our method to execute, we can use `MeterRegistry` and at the beginning of the method, record the time:

```
long start = System.currentTimeMillis();
```

We will then place our code and before the return, capture the time again:

```
long end = System.currentTimeMillis();.
```

Then, we will emit the metric `meterRegistry.gauge("objectName.methodName.latency", end - start);`, which will update the last. The use of `gauge` for timing purposes is very rudimentary and `MeterRegistry` actually provides a specialized type of meter—Timer. The Timer meter, for example, provides the ability to wrap runnable or callable lambdas and automatically time the execution. Another benefit of using a Timer instead of `Gauge` is that a Timer meter keeps both the event counts as well as the latency it took to execute each occurrence.

The `MeterRegistry` implementation covers most of the simple use cases and is very handy when we operate in our own code and have the flexibility to add them where we need to. However, it is not always the case, and in these cases, we will need to resort to wrapping whatever it is we want to monitor by creating a custom implementation of `MeterBinder`. In our case, we will use it to expose the counts for each of the repositories in the database as we can't insert any monitoring code into the `CrudRepository` proxy implementations.

Whenever the `MeterRegistry` implementation does not provide enough flexibility, for example, when there is a need to wrap an object in a meter like `Gauge`, most meter implementations provide fluid builders to gain more flexibility. In our example, to wrap the repository metrics, we used a `Gauge` fluid builder to construct `Gauge`:

```
Gauge.builder(metricName, repository, CrudRepository::count)
```

The main builder method takes the following three arguments:

- `metricName`: This specifies the name to use to uniquely identify this metric
- `repository`: This provides an object on which we invoke the method that should return a numeric value that `gauge` will report
- `CrudRepository::count`: This is the method that should be called on the `repository` object to get the current count of entries

This enables us to build flexible wrappers because all we have to do is provide an object that would expose the necessary numeric value and a function reference to a function that should be called on the instance to get that value during the `gauge` evaluation.

The `MeterBinder` interface, used to export the Meter, has only one method defined, `void bindTo(MeterRegistry);`, which the implementer needs to code with the definition of what exactly is being monitored. The implementation class needs to be exposed as `@Bean`, and it will automatically be picked up and processed during the application initialization. Assuming that one actually registered the created `Meter` instance with the provided `MeterRegistry` implementation, typically by terminating the fluid builder's chain by calling `.builder(...).register(registry)`, the metrics will be exposed via `MetricsEndpoint`, which will expose all the meters registered with the registry every time the `/metrics` actuator is called.

It is important to mention that we have created the `MeterBinder` and `HealthIndicator` beans inside the main application context and not in the management one. The reason being that even though the data is being exposed via the management endpoints, the endpoint beans, such as `MetricsEndpoint`, get defined in the main application context, and thus expect all the other autowired dependencies to be defined there as well.

This approach is safe because in order to get access to the information, one needs to go through the `WebMvcEndpointHandlerMapping` implementation facade, which is created in the management context and use the delegate endpoint from the main application context. Take a look at the `MetricsEndpoint` class and the corresponding `@Endpoint` annotation to see the details.

Monitoring Spring Boot via JMX

In today's day and age, the RESTful HTTP JSON services are a de facto way of accessing data, but this is not the only way to do so. Another fairly popular and common way of managing systems in real time is via JMX. The good news is that Spring Boot already comes with the same level of support to expose the management endpoints over JMX as it does over HTTP. Actually, these are exactly the same endpoints; they are just wrapped around the MBean container.

In this recipe, we will take a look at how to retrieve the same information via JMX as we did via HTTP as well as how to expose some MBeans, which are provided by third-party libraries through HTTP using the Jolokia JMX library.

Getting ready

If you haven't done so already for the previous recipe, then add the Jolokia JMX library to our `compile("org.jolokia:jolokia-core:+")` build dependency and add the `management.jolokia.enabled=true` property to `application.properties`, as we will need them to expose MBeans via HTTP.

How to do it...

1. After we add the Jolokia JMX dependency, all we need to do is build and start our application by executing `./gradlew clean bootRun` and now we can simply launch jConsole to see the the various endpoints exposed under the `org.springframework.boot` domain:

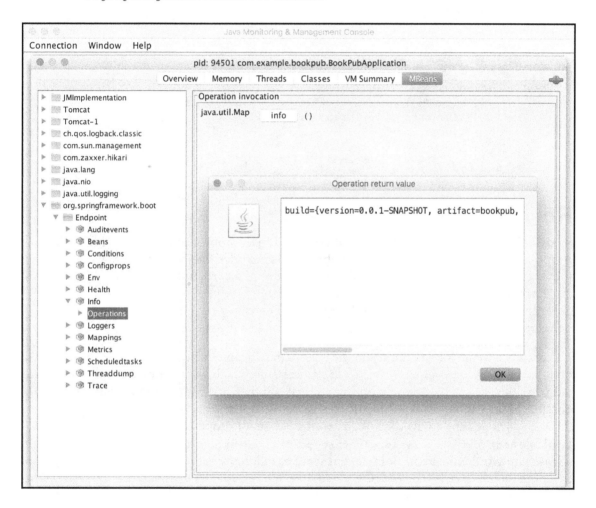

2. Having the Jolokia JMX library added to the classpath, Spring Boot also enables the accessing of all the registered MBeans via HTTP API using the `/jolokia` endpoint. To find out the `maxThreads` setting for our Tomcat HTTP port `8080` connector, we can either look it up using jConsole by selecting the `maxThreads` attribute on the `Tomcat:type=ThreadPool,name="http-nio-8080"` MBean to get the value of `200` or we can use Jolokia JMX HTTP by opening our browser and going to `http://localhost:8081/actuator/jolokia/read/Tomcat:type=ThreadPool,name=%22http-nio-8080%22/maxThreads` and we should see the following JSON response:

```
{"request":
  {"mbean":"Tomcat:name="http-nio-8080",type=ThreadPool",
   "attribute":"maxThreads",
   "type":"read"
  },
 "value":200,"timestamp":1436740537,"status":200}
```

How it works...

By default, the Spring Boot Actuator, when added to the application, comes with all the endpoints and management services enabled. This includes the JMX access as well. If, for some reason, one would like to disable the exposure of a particular endpoint via JMX, this can easily be configured by adding `management.endpoints.jmx.exclude=<id>` or in order to disable the exporting of all the Spring MBeans, we can configure the `spring.jmx.enabled=false` setting in `application.properties`.

The presence of the Jolokia library in the classpath triggers Spring Boot `JolokiaManagementContextConfiguration`, which would automatically configure `ServletRegistrationBean` accepting requests on the `/jolokia` actuator path. It is also possible to set various Jolokia-specific configuration options via the `management.endpoint.jolokia.config.*` set of properties. A complete list is available at `https://jolokia.org/reference/html/agents.html#agent-war-init-params`. In case you would like to use Jolokia, but want to manually set it up, we can tell Spring Boot to ignore its presence by configuring a `management.endpoint.jolokia.enabled=false` property setting in `application.properties`.

Managing Spring Boot via SSHd Shell and writing custom remote Shell commands

Some of you are probably reminiscing about the good old days where all the administration was done via SSH directly on the machine, where one has complete flexibility and control, or even using SSH to connect to a management port and apply whatever changes were needed directly to a running application. Even though Spring Boot has removed native integration with the CRaSH Java Shell in version 2.0, there is an open source project, sshd-shell-spring-boot, which brings back that ability.

For this recipe, we will use the health indicator and management endpoint, which we created earlier in this chapter. We will expose the same capabilities via the SSH console access.

How to do it...

1. The first step to getting SSHd Shell to work is to add the necessary dependency starters to our build.gradle file, as follows:

```
dependencies {
    ...
    compile("org.springframework.boot:spring-boot-starter-
actuator")
    compile("io.github.anand1st:sshd-shell-spring-boot-
starter:3.2.1")
    compile("de.codecentric:spring-boot-admin-starter-client:2.0.0-
SNAPSHOT")
    compile("org.jolokia:jolokia-core:+")
    ...
}
```

2. We also need to explicitly enable it by setting the following property in application.properties, located in the src/main/resources directory in the root of our project it needs to be enhanced with the following entries:

```
sshd.shell.enabled=true
management.endpoint.shutdown.enabled=true
```

3. Now, let's start our application by executing `./gradlew clean bootRun` and then connect to it via SSH by executing `ssh -p 8022 admin@localhost`.

4. We will be prompted for a password so let's find the autogenerated hash key in the application startup log, which would look as follows:

```
********** User password not set. Use following password to login:
8f20cf10-7d67-42ac-99e4-3a4a77ca6c5f **********
```

5. If the password is entered correctly, we will be greeted by the following welcome prompt:

```
Enter 'help' for a list of supported commands
app>
```

6. Next, we will invoke our existing `/health` endpoint by typing health and we should get the following result:

```
{
  "status" : "UP",
  "details" : {
    "dbCount" : {
      "status" : "UP",
      "details" : {
        "ReviewerRepository" : {
          . . .
        },
        "PublisherRepository" : {
          . . .
        },
        "AuthorRepository" : {
          . . .
        },
        "BookRepository" : {
          . . .
        }
      }
    },
    "diskSpace" : {
      "status" : "UP",
      "details" : {
        "total" : 249795969024,
        "free" : 14219882496,
        "threshold" : 10485760
      }
    },
    "db" : {
```

```
        "status" : "UP",
        "details" : { "database" : "H2", "hello" : 1 }
    }
  }
}
```

7. Typing `help` will show the list of all the existing commands so you can play with some of them to see what they do and then we will proceed with adding our own SSHd Shell command, which will enable us to add new publishers to the system via the command line.

8. Make a new directory named commands in `src/main/java/com/example/bookpub/command` at the root of our project.

9. Add a file named `Publishers.java` in the `src/main/java/com/example/bookpub/command` directory at the root of our project with the following content:

```java
package com.example.bookpub.command;

import com.example.bookpub.entity.Publisher;
import com.example.bookpub.repository.PublisherRepository;
import org.springframework.beans.factory.annotation.Autowired;
import org.springframework.stereotype.Component;
import sshd.shell.springboot.autoconfiguration.SshdShellCommand;
import sshd.shell.springboot.console.ConsoleIO;

import java.util.HashMap;
import java.util.Map;

@Component
@SshdShellCommand(value = "publishers", description = "Publisher
management. Type 'publishers' for supported subcommands")
public class PublishersCommand {
    @Autowired
    private PublisherRepository repository;

    @SshdShellCommand(value = "list", description = "List of
publishers")
    public String list(String _arg_) {
        List list = new ArrayList();

        repository.findAll().forEach(publisher ->
            list.add(publisher);
        );

        return ConsoleIO.asJson(list);
```

```
        }

        @SshdShellCommand(value = "add", description = "Add a new
    publisher. Usage: publishers add <name>")
        public String add(String name) {
            Publisher publisher = new Publisher(name);
            try {
                publisher = repository.save(publisher);
                return ConsoleIO.asJson(publisher);
            } catch (Exception e) {
                return String.format("Unable to add new publisher named
    %s%n%s", name, e.getMessage());
            }
        }

        @SshdShellCommand(value = "remove", description = "Remove
    existing publisher. Usage: publishers remove <id>")
        public String remove(String id) {
            try {
                repository.deleteById(Long.parseLong(id));
                return ConsoleIO.asJson(String.format("Removed
    publisher %s", id));
            } catch (Exception e) {
                return String.format("Unable to remove publisher with
    id %s%n%s", id, e.getMessage());
            }
        }
    }
```

10. With the commands built up, now let's start our application by executing `./gradlew clean bootRun` and then connect to it via SSH by executing `ssh -p 8022 admin@localhost` and log in using the generated password hash.

11. When we type publishers, we will see the list of all the possible commands, as follows:

```
app> publishers
Supported subcommand for publishers
add       Add a new publisher. Usage: publishers add <name>
list      List of publishers
remove    Remove existing publisher. Usage: publishers remove <id>
```

12. Let's add a publisher by typing `publishers add Fictitious Books` and we should see the following message:

```
{
    "id" : 2,
    "name" : "Fictitious Books"
}
```

13. If we will now type publishers list, we will get a list of all the books:

```
[ {
    "id" : 1,
    "name" : "Packt"
}, {
    "id" : 2,
    "name" : "Fictitious Books"
} ]
```

14. Removing a publisher is a simple command `publishers remove 2` that should respond with the `"Removed publisher 2"` message.

15. Just to confirm that the publisher is really gone, execute publishers list and we should see the following output:

```
[ {
    "id" : 1,
    "name" : "Packt"
} ]
```

How it works...

The SSHd Shell integration with Spring Boot provides you with many commands out of the box. We can invoke the same management end points that were available to us over HTTP and JMX. We can get access to the JVM information, make changes to the logging configuration, and even interact with the JMX server and all the registered MBeans. The list of all the possibilities is really impressive and very rich in functionalities, so I would definitely advise you to read the reference documentation on SSHd Shell by going to `https://github.com/anand1st/sshd-shell-spring-boot`.

In Spring Boot, the expectation is that any class annotated with `@SshdShellCommand` will be automatically picked up and registered as an SSHd Shell command. The value of the annotation attribute translates into the main command name. In our case, we set the class annotation attribute value field to `publishers` and this became the top-level command name in the SSH Shell console.

If the command contains sub-commands, as in our publishers command example, then, the methods of the class that are also annotated with `@SshdShellCommand` get registered as sub-commands to the main command. If a class has only one method, it will automatically become the only command for a given class that would be executed when the command name is typed. If we want multiple sub-commands to reside in the class command, as we did with publishers, each method that translates into a command needs to be annotated with `@SshdShellCommand`.

Currently, SSHd Shell framework has a limitation of being able to pass only one attribute argument to the command, but there is work going on to expand on that capability. In the mean time, it is recommended that JSON payload is used to communicate with the commands as inputs or outputs.

The following attributes are available on the annotations:

- `value`: This attribute defines the command or sub-command name. Even though the name of the method does not need to match the name of the command, it is a good convention for keeping the two in sync to make the code more readable.
- `description`: This attribute defines the text that gets displayed when the `help` command is invoked. It is a good place to communicate with the users how the command is expected to be used, what inputs it takes, and so on. It is a good idea to provide as much description and documentation as possible as in the Shell, one would like to clearly educate the users of what needs to happen and how to call the command. The man pages are great so keep the documentation top notch.
- `roles`: This attribute enables us to define a security constraint on who is allowed to execute the given command. If Spring Security is also used, SSHd Shell provides the ability to configure a custom or specific `AuthenticationProvider` to be used for handling user authentication and role binding. For example, it would be easy to connect your application to the company's LDAP server and allow developers to use their regular credentials and also configure different role access controls, based on the needs of the particular organization.

Each command can be queried for its usage by using help, or in the case of a command containing sub-commands, by typing the name of the top-level command.

While SSHd Shell comes with many built-in commands, one can easily add custom commands, taking advantage of standard Spring / Spring Boot programming style, using the `@Autowired` and `@Component` annotations to get the necessary dependencies to be wired in and automatically configured during the application start life cycle.

SSHd Shell also provides a nice functionality enabling the use of post-processors, invoked by a pipe (|) symbol. The current support allows for output highlighting | h packt, which will highlight the word packt in the output, or emailing response output | m my@email.com, which will email the response of a command to the specified email address, given that **Spring Mail** is also configured and available.

It would be great if we could chain different commands together, like in Linux proper, so as to help process the output and filter out the necessary data when the amount of information tends to get overwhelming. Imagine that our publishers list command returns not 2, but 2000 publishers. From this list, we want to find the ones that start with Pa.

Even though SSHd Shell does not provide this type of functionality out of the box, it does offer us an ability to implement our own post-processors by defining beans that extend the BaseUserInputProcessor class. Let's create one that would provide support for filtering JSON responses, something similar to how the jq command-line utility works.

To achieve this, let's create another class named JsonPathUserInputProcessor.java in the src/main/java/com/example/bookpub/command directory at the root of our project with the following content:

```
@Component
@Order(3)
public class JsonPathUserInputProcessor
            extends BaseUserInputProcessor {

    private final Pattern pattern = Pattern.compile("[\w\W]+\s?\|\s?jq
(.+)");

    @Override
    public Optional<UsageInfo> getUsageInfo() {
        return Optional.of(new UsageInfo(Arrays.<UsageInfo.Row>asList(
                new UsageInfo.Row("jq <arg>", "JSON Path Query <arg> in
response output of command execution"),
                new UsageInfo.Row("", "Example usage: help | jq
$.<name>"))));
    }

    @Override
    public Pattern getPattern() {
        return pattern;
    }

    @Override
    public void processUserInput(String userInput) throws
      InterruptedException, ShellException{
```

```
    String[] part = splitAndValidateCommand(userInput, "\|", 2);
    Matcher matcher = pattern.matcher(userInput);
    Assert.isTrue(matcher.find(), "Unexpected error");
    String jsonQuery = matcher.group(1).trim();
    try {
        String output = processCommands(part[0]);
        Object response = JsonPath.read(output, jsonQuery);
        ConsoleIO.writeJsonOutput(response);
    } catch (Exception e) {
        ConsoleIO.writeOutput(String.format("Unable to process
        query %s%n%s", jsonQuery, e.getMessage()));
    }
  }
}
```

Using the pipe functionality, we can easily chain the `publishers list` command with the `jq` command in the following way:

```
publishers list | jq $..[?(@.name =~ /Pa.*/i)]
```

In our example, this should return us only one record, as follows:

```
[ {
    "id" : 1,
    "name" : "Packt"
} ]
```

While it is not a full-fledged pipe functionality, the use of input processors allows for adding functionalities such as sorting, filtering, and displaying rendering, which give more flexibility to modularize and reuse common behaviors.

The SSHd Shell Spring Boot integration comes with a number of configuration options allowing us to disable the component, configure authentication settings, and specify usernames, passwords, and even key certificates. For example, if we want to use a specific username and password, we can do so by configuring the following properties:

```
sshd.shell.username=remote
sshd.shell.password=shell
```

In a real-world enterprise environment, it is more common to use the shared keys for restricted access and these can be configured using the `sshd.shell.publicKeyFile=<key path>` or `sshd.shell.hostKeyFile=<key path>` properties. Alternatively, and probably a better approach, as was already mentioned earlier, using a custom `AuthenticationProvider` implementation together with Spring Security allows the integrate of authentication mechanisms into the company's authentication system.

Integrating Micrometer metrics with Graphite

Earlier in this chapter, you learned about the monitoring capabilities that are provided by Spring Boot. We saw examples of writing custom `HealthIndicators`, creating metrics, and using `MeterRegistry` to emit data. The simple Spring Boot Admin Web framework gave us some nice graphical UI to visualize the data, but all of these metrics were in-the-moment, with no long-term retention and historical access. Not being able to observe the trends, detect the deviations from the baseline, and compare today with last week is not a very good strategy, especially for an enterprise-complex system. We all want to be able to have access to the time series data going weeks, if not months, back and set up alarms and thresholds, if something goes unplanned.

This recipe will introduce us to an amazing time series graphical tool: Graphite. Graphite is a two-part system. It provides storage for numeric time series data as well as a service to render this data in a form of on-demand graphs or expose the graph data as a JSON stream. You will learn how to integrate and configure Spring's Micrometer monitoring framework with Graphite in order to send the monitoring data from a Spring Boot application to Graphite and play a bit with Graphite to visualize the different statistics that we've gathered.

Getting ready

Graphite is an application that is written in Python and is, thus, capable of running on virtually any system supporting Python and its libraries. There are multiple ways of installing Graphite on any given system, ranging from compilation from a source, using `pip` all the way, to prebuilt RPMs for various Linux distributions.

For all the different installation strategies, take a look at the Graphite documentation at `http://graphite.readthedocs.org/en/latest/install.html`. OS X users can read a very good step-by-step guide located at `https://gist.github.com/relaxdiego/7539911`.

For the purposes of this recipe, we will use a premade Docker container containing Graphite as well as its counterpart Grafana. While there is an abundance of various prebuilt variants of Docker images containing combinations of Graphite and Grafana, we will use the one from `https://registry.hub.docker.com/u/alexmercer/graphite-grafana/` as it contains all the right configurations that will make it easy for us to get started quickly:

1. The first step will be to download the desired Docker container image. We will do this by executing `docker pull alexmercer/graphite-grafana`. The container size is about 500 MB; so the download might take a few minutes depending on your connection speed.

2. Both Graphite and Grafana store their data in the database files. We will need to create external directories, which will reside outside the container, and we will connect them to a running instance via Docker data volumes.
   - Make a directory for the Graphite data anywhere in your system, for example, in `<user_home>/data/graphite`.
   - Make a directory for the Grafana data, for example, in `<user_home>/data/grafana`.

3. In this container, the Graphite data will go to `/var/lib/graphite/storage/whisper`, while Grafana stores its data in `/usr/share/grafana/data`. So, we will use these paths as internal volume mount destinations when starting the container.

4. Run the container by executing `docker run -v <user_home>/data/graphite:/var/lib/graphite/storage/whisper -v <user_home>/data/grafana:/usr/share/grafana/data -p 2003:2003 -p 3000:3000 -p 8888:80 -d alexmercer/graphite-grafana`.
   - In Docker, the `-v` option configures a volume mount binding. In our example, we configured the external `<user_home>/data/graphite` directory to be the same as the `/var/lib/graphite/storage/whisper` directory reference in the container. The same goes for the `<user_home>/data/grafana` mapping. We can even look in the `<user_home>/data/graphite` or `data/grafana` directories to see them contain the subdirectories and files.

- The -p option configures the port mappings similar to the directory volumes. In our example, we mapped the following three different ports to be accessible from outside the container to the internal ports to which the various services are bound:

  2003:2003: This port mapping externalizes the Graphite data stream listener known as **Carbon-Cache Line Receiver**, to which we will connect in order to send the metrics data.

  3000:3000: This port mapping externalizes the Grafana Web Dashboard UI, which we will use to create visual dashboards on top of the Graphite data.

  8888:80: This port mapping externalizes the Graphite Web UI. Though it is running on port 80 in the container, it is unlikely that on our development machine, port 80 is open; so it is better to map it to some other higher number port such as 8080 or 8888 in our case, as 8080 is already taken by our BookPub application.

5. If everything has gone according to the plan, Graphite and Grafana should be up and running and thus, we can access Graphite by pointing our browser to http://localhost:8888 and we should see the following output:

6. To see Grafana, point the browser to `http://localhost:3000` so as to see the following output:

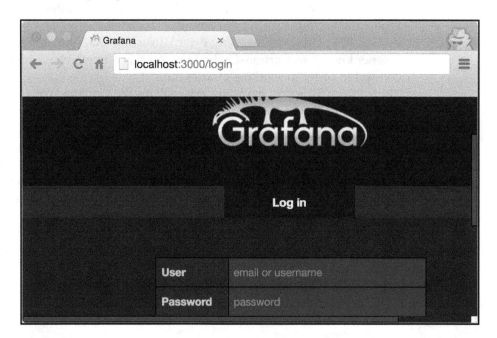

7. The default login and password for Grafana are `admin/admin` and can be changed via the Web UI Admin.

   For the OS X users who use boot2docker, the IP would not be of the `localhost`, but rather a result of the boot2docker IP call.

8. Once we are in Grafana, we will need to add our Graphite instance as `DataSource`, so click on the icon, go to **Data Sources**, and add a new source of the `Type Graphite, Url http://localhost:80, Access` proxy:

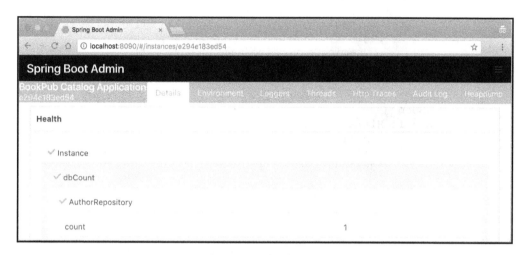

How to do it...

With Graphite and Grafana up and running, we are now ready to start configuring our application in order to send the metrics to the Graphite listener on port `2003`. To do this, we will use the Codahale/Dropwizard metrics library, which is fully supported by Spring Boot and thus requires a minimum amount of configuration:

1. The first thing on our list is to add the necessary library dependencies. Extend the dependencies block in the `build.gradle` file with the following content:

   ```
   compile("io.micrometer:micrometer-registry-
   graphite:latest.release")
   ```

2. Create a file named `MonitoringConfiguration.java` in the `src/main/java/com/example/bookpub` directory at the root of our project with the following content:

   ```
   @Configuration
   @ConditionalOnClass(GraphiteMeterRegistry.class)
   public class MonitoringConfiguration {

       private static final Pattern blacklistedChars =
   ```

```
                             Pattern.compile("[{}(),=\[\]/]");

@Bean
public MeterRegistryCustomizer<GraphiteMeterRegistry>
                            meterRegistryCustomizer() {
    return registry -> {
       registry.config()
         .namingConvention(namingConvention());
    };
}

@Bean
public HierarchicalNameMapper hierarchicalNameMapper(){
    return (id, convention) -> {
        String prefix = "bookpub.app.";
        String tags = "";

        if (id.getTags().iterator().hasNext()) {
            tags = "."
                    + id.getConventionTags(convention)
                    .stream()
                    .map(t -> t.getKey() + "."
                                        + t.getValue()
                    )
                    .map(nameSegment ->
                        nameSegment.replace(" ", "_")
                    )
                    .collect(Collectors.joining("."));
        }

        return prefix
                + id.getConventionName(convention)
                + tags;
    };
}

@Bean
public NamingConvention namingConvention() {
    return new NamingConvention() {
        @Override
        public String name(String name,
                           Meter.Type type,
                           String baseUnit) {
            return format(name);
        }

        @Override
        public String tagKey(String key) {
```

```
            return format(key);
        }

        @Override
        public String tagValue(String value) {
            return format(value);
        }

        private String format(String name) {
            String sanitized =
                Normalizer.normalize(name,
                                Normalizer.Form.NFKD);
            // Changes to the original
            // GraphiteNamingConvention to use "dot"
            // instead of "camelCase"
            sanitized =
                NamingConvention.dot.tagKey(sanitized);

            return blacklistedChars
                    .matcher(sanitized)
                    .replaceAll("_");
        }
    };
    }
}
```

3. We will also need to add the configuration property settings for our Graphite instance to the `application.properties` file in the `src/main/resources` directory at the root of our project:

```
management.metrics.export.graphite.enabled=true
management.metrics.export.graphite.host=localhost
management.metrics.export.graphite.port=2003
management.metrics.export.graphite.protocol=plaintext
management.metrics.export.graphite.rate-units=seconds
management.metrics.export.graphite.duration-units=milliseconds
management.metrics.export.graphite.step=1m
```

4. Now, let's build and run our application by executing `./gradlew clean bootRun` and if we have configured everything correctly, it should start without any issues.

5. With the application up and running, we should start seeing some data that is in the Graphite and `bookpub` data nodes getting added to the tree under metrics. To add some more realism, let's open our browser and load a book URL, `http://localhost:8080/books/978-1-78528-415-1/`, a few dozen times to generate some metrics.

6. Let's go ahead and look at some of the metrics in Graphite and set the data time range to 15 minutes in order to get some close-look graphs, which will look similar to the following screenshot:

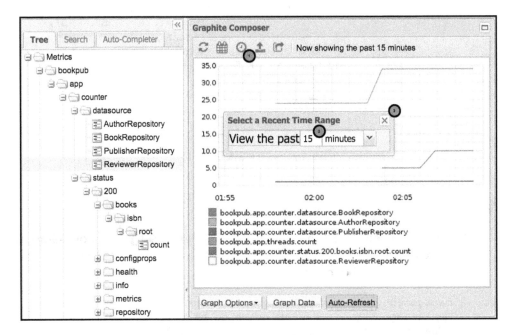

7. We can also create some fancy looking dashboards using this data in Grafana by creating a new dashboard and adding a **Graph** panel, as shown in the following screenshot:

8. The newly created **Graph** panel will look like this:

9. Click on the **no title (click here)** label, choose **edit**, and enter the metric name `bookpub.app.http.server.requests.exception.None.method.GET.status.200.uri._books__isbn_.count` in the text field as shown in the following screenshot:

10. Clicking on **Dashboard** will take you out of the edit mode.

For a more detailed tutorial, visit `http://docs.grafana.org/guides/gettingstarted/`.

How it works...

To enable exporting metrics via Graphite, we added an extra dependency on the `io.micrometer:micrometer-registry-graphite` library. Under the hood, however, it depends on the Dropwizard metrics library to provide Graphite integration, so it will add the following new dependencies to our `build` file:

- `io.dropwizard.metrics:metrics-core`: This dependency adds the basic Dropwizard functionality, `MetricsRegistry`, common API interfaces, and base classes. This is the bare minimum that is required to get Dropwizard working and integrated into Spring Boot to handle the metrics.

- `io.dropwizard.metrics:metrics-graphite`: This adds support for `GraphiteReporter` and is needed in order to configure Dropwizard to send the monitoring data that it collects to our Graphite instance.

In order to keep things clean and nicely separated, we created a separate configuration class with all the monitoring-related beans and settings: `MonitoringConfiguration`. In this class, we configured three `@Bean` instances: a custom `MeterRegistryCustomizer` implementation to customize the `GraphiteMeterRegistry` instance, `HigherarchicalNameMapper`, and `NamingConvention` to go along with it.

The reason why we had to create our own customization is twofold. We wanted to comply with the classic Graphite metric naming scheme, which uses the dot (`.`) notation to separate metric names in a hierarchy. Unfortunately, for whatever reason, Micrometer Graphite implementation has opted for using the `camelCase` collapsing notation instead, which made metric names like `counter.datasource.BookRepository` translate into the `counterDatasourceBookRepository` name to be displayed inside Graphite. Having such a long name, without hierarchical tree makes for a very difficult search and discovery inside Graphite UI, when many metrics are present. Also, all the metrics get placed under a root (`/`) tree, without creating a dedicated application folder, which also leads to poor readability and usage. We have added code to our `HigherarchicalNameMapper` instance to prepend the application prefix to all the metrics being exported to Graphite so that they all get put into `subtree: /bookpub/app/*.`:

```
String prefix = "bookpub.app.";
...
return prefix + id.getConventionName(convention) + tags;
```

The `NamingConvention` provides precise configuration about how to convert particular Meter names, keys, values, and tags into proper Graphite variants. Inside the `format(String name)` method, we declare that we want to use a dot (`.`) separation between elements via the `NamingConvention.dot` implementation.

The `management.metrics.export.graphite` group of properties define how to send the data to the Graphite instance. We configured it to do so every 1 minute, translate all the time duration intervals, such as the latency measurements, into milliseconds and all the variable rates, such as the number of requests per some time frame, into seconds. Most of these values have their default configuration settings for Graphite provided, but can be changed, if desired.

Notice that we've used the `@ConditionalOnClass` annotation to indicate that we only want to apply this `@Configuration` if the Micrometer Graphite provided class `GraphiteMeterRegistry.class` is present in the classpath. This is needed to not try to instantiate Graphite beans during tests, as there might not be a Graphite instance running and available in the testing environment.

As you can see from the available metrics from Graphite UI, there are many metrics that are provided out of the box. Some notable ones are about JVM and OS metrics, which expose the memory and thread metrics to Graphite in the memory and threads data nodes among other data. They can be found in `Metrics/bookpub/app/jvm`, `Metrics/bookpub/app/process`, or `Metrics/bookpub/app/system` in the Graphite tree.

Micrometer core library provides a number of meter binders for additional system metrics. If there is a need to export things like thread or executor information, or get a view into the file descriptors, one can export additional beans by simply declaring a method returning `new JvmThreadMetrics()` or `new FileDescriptorMetrics()` for example.

The running application will gather all the metrics registered with `MeterRegistry` and every configured exporter (in our case, `GraphiteMeterRegistry`) reports all these metrics at a timed interval to its destination. The proper exporter implementations run in a separate `ThreadPool`, thus outside of the main application threads and not interfering with them. However, this should be kept in mind in case the Meter implementations use some `ThreadLocal` data internally, which would not be available to exporters.

Integrating Micrometer metrics with Dashing

The previous recipe has given us a glimpse of how we can collect the various metrics from our application during its runtime. We've also seen how powerful the ability to visualize this data as a set of graphs of historical trends can be.

While Grafana and Graphite offer us the very powerful capability of manipulating the data in the form of graphs and building elaborate dashboards that are full of thresholds, applied data functions, and much more, sometimes we want something simpler, more readable, and something widgety. This is exactly the kind of dashboard experience that is provided by Dashing.

Dashing is a popular dashboard framework developed by Shopify and written in Ruby/Sinatra. It provides you with an ability to create an assortment of dashboards that are comprised of different types of widgets. We can have things such as graphs, meters, lists, numeric values, or just plain text to display the information.

In this recipe, we will install the Dashing framework, learn how to create dashboards, send and consume the data to report from an application directly as well as fetch it from Graphite, and use the Dashing API to push the data to the Dashing instance.

Getting ready

In order to get Dashing to run, we will need to have an environment that has a Ruby 1.9+ installed with RubyGems.

Typically, Ruby should be available on any common distribution of Linux and OS X. If you are running Windows, I would suggest using `http://rubyinstaller.org` in order to get the installation bundle.

Once you have such an environment available, we will install Dashing and create a new dashboard application for our use, as follows:

1. Installing Dashing is very easy; simply execute the gem install dashing command to install Dashing RubyGems on your system.
2. With the RubyGem successfully installed, we will create the new dashboard named `bookpub_dashboard` by executing the dashing new `bookpub_dashboard` command in the directory where you want the dashboard application to be created.
3. Once the dashboard application has been generated, go to the `bookpub_dashboard` directory and execute the `bundle` command to install the required dependency gems.
4. After the gems bundle has been installed, we can start the dashboard application by executing the `dashing start` command and then pointing our browser to `http://localhost:3030` to see the following result:

How to do it...

If you look carefully at the URL of our shiny new dashboard, you will see that it actually says `http://localhost:3030/sample` and displays a sample dashboard that was automatically generated. We will use this sample dashboard to make some changes in order to display some metrics from our application directly as well as get some raw metrics from the Graphite data API endpoint.

To demonstrate how to connect the data from the application `/actuator/metrics` endpoint so as to display it in the Dashing dashboard, we will change the `Buzzwords` widget to display the counts of our data repositories, as follows:

1. Before we start, we will need to add the `'httparty'`, `'>= 0.13.3'` gem to the `Gemfile` file located in the `bookpub_dashboard` directory, which will enable us to use an HTTP client in order to extract the monitoring metrics from the HTTP endpoints.

2. After adding the gem, run the `bundle` command one more time to install the newly added gem.

3. Next, we will need to modify the `sample.erb` dashboard definition located in the `bookpub_dashboard/dashboards` directory, replacing `<div data-id="buzzwords" data-view="List" data-unordered="true" data-title="Buzzwords" data-moreinfo="# of times said around the office"></div>` with `<div data-id="repositories" data-view="List" data-unordered="true" data-title="Repositories Count" data-moreinfo="# of entries in data repositories"></div>`.

4. With the widget replaced, we will create a new data provisioning job file named `repo_counters.rb` in the `bookpub_dashboard/jobs` directory with the following content:

```
require 'httparty'

repos = ['AuthorRepository', 'ReviewerRepository',
'BookRepository', 'PublisherRepository']

SCHEDULER.every '10s' do
  data =
JSON.parse(HTTParty.get("http://localhost:8081/metrics").body)
  repo_counts = []

  repos.each do |repo|
    current_count = data["counter.datasource.#{repo}"]
    repo_counts << { label: repo, value: current_count }
```

```
    end

    send_event('repositories', { items: repo_counts })
  end
```

5. With all the code changes in place, let's start our dashboard by executing the `dashing start` command. Go to `http://localhost:3030/sample` in the browser to see our new widget displaying the data as shown in the following icon:

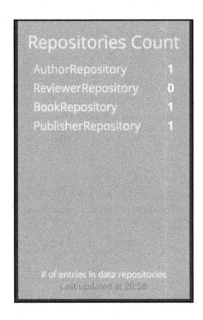

6. If we use the remote Shell to log in to the application, as we did earlier in this chapter, and add a publisher, we would see the counter on the dashboard increase.

7. Another way to push the data to the dashboard is to use their RESTful API. Let's update the text in the top left text widget by executing `curl -d '{ "auth_token": "YOUR_AUTH_TOKEN", "text": "My RESTful dashboard update!" }' http://localhost:3030/widgets/welcome`.

8. If everything has worked correctly, we should see the text updated to our new value, My RESTful dashboard update!, under the **Hello** title.

9. In an environment where multiple instances of the same application kind are running, it is probably not a good idea to directly pull the data from each node, especially if they are very dynamic and can come and go as they please. It is advised that you consume the data from a more static and well-known location, such as a Graphite instance. To get a demonstration of volatile data metrics, we will consume the memory pool data for the Eden, Survivor, and OldGen spaces and display them instead of the **Convergence**, **Synergy**, and **Valuation** graph dashboards. We will start by replacing the content of the sample.rb job file located in the bookpub_dashboard/jobs directory with the following content:

```ruby
require 'httparty'
require 'date'

eden_key = "bookpub.app.jvm.memory.used.area.heap.id.PS_Eden_Space"
survivor_key =
"bookpub.app.jvm.memory.used.area.heap.id.PS_Survivor_Space"
oldgen_key = "bookpub.app.jvm.memory.used.area.heap.id.PS_Old_Gen"

SCHEDULER.every '60s' do
  data =
JSON.parse(HTTParty.get("http://localhost:8888/render/?from=-11minu
tes&target=#{eden_key}&target=#{survivor_key}&target=#{oldgen_key}&
format=json&maxDataPoints=11").body)

  data.each do |metric|
    target = metric["target"]
    # Remove the last data point, which typically has empty value
    data_points = metric["datapoints"][0...-1]
    if target == eden_key
      points = []
      data_points.each_with_index do |entry, idx|
        value = entry[0] rescue 0
        points << { x: entry[1], y: value.round(0) }
      end
      send_event('heap_eden', points: points)
    elsif target == survivor_key
      current_survivor = data_points.last[0] rescue 0
      current_survivor = current_survivor / 1048576
      send_event("heap_survivor", { value:
                current_survivor.round(2) })
    elsif target == oldgen_key
      current_oldgen = data_points.last[0] rescue 0
```

```
                    last_oldgen = data_points[-2][0] rescue 0
                    send_event("heap_oldgen", {
                                current: current_oldgen.round(2),
                                last: last_oldgen.round(2)
                            })
            end
        end
    end
```

10. In the `sample.erb` template located in the `bookpub_dashboard/dashboards` directory, we will replace the **Synergy**, **Valuation**, and **Convergence** graphs with the following alternatives:

    - `<div data-id="synergy" data-view="Meter" data-title="Synergy" data-min="0" data-max="100"></div>` gets replaced with `<div data-id="heap_survivor" data-view="Meter" data-title="Heap: Survivor" data-min="0" data-max="100" data-moreinfo="In megabytes"></div>`

    - `<div data-id="valuation" data-view="Number" data-title="Current Valuation" data-moreinfo="In billions" data-prefix="$"></div>` gets replaced with `<div data-id="heap_oldgen" data-view="Number" data-title="Heap: OldGen" data-moreinfo="In bytes" ></div>`

    - `<div data-id="convergence" data-view="Graph" data-title="Convergence" style="background-color:#ff9618"></div>` gets replaced with `<div data-id="heap_eden" data-view="Graph" data-title="Heap: Eden" style="background-color:#ff9618" data-moreinfo="In bytes"></div>`

11. After all the changes are made, we can restart the dashboard application and reload our browser to `http://localhost:3030` to see the following result:

How it works...

In this recipe, we have seen how to extract the data directly from our application and via Graphite, and render it using the Dashing dashboard as well as pushing information directly to Dashing using their RESTful API. It is no secret that it is better to see something once than hear about it seven times. This is true when it comes to trying to get a holistic picture of the key metrics that represent how the systems behave at runtime and to be able to act on the data quickly.

Without going in to great detail about the internals of Dashing, it is still important to mention a few things about how data gets in to Dashing. This can happen in the following two ways:

- **Scheduled jobs**: This is used to pull data from the external sources
- **RESTful API**: This is used to push data to Dashing from outside

The scheduled jobs are defined in the jobs directory in the generated dashboard application. Each file has a piece of ruby code wrapped in the SCHEDULER.every block, which computes the data points and sends an event to an appropriate widget with the new data for an update.

In our recipe, we created a new job named `repo_counters.rb` where we used the `httparty` library in order to make a direct call to our application instance's `/actuator/metrics/#{name}` endpoint and extracted the counters for each of the predefined repositories. Looping over the metrics, we created a `repo_counts` collection with data for each repository containing a label display and a value count. The resulting collection was sent to the repositories widget for an update in the form of `event:` `send_event('repositories', { items: repo_counts })`.

We configured this job to get executed every 10 seconds, but if the rate of data change is not very frequent, the number can be changed to a few minutes or even hours. Every time the scheduler runs our job, the repositories widget is updated via the client-side websockets communication with the new data. Looking in dashboards/`sample.erb`, we can find the widget's definition using `data-id="repositories"`.

Besides adding our own new job, we also changed the existing `sample.rb` job to pull data from Graphite using Graphite's RESTful API to populate the different types of widgets in order to display the memory heap data. As we were not pulling data directly from the application instance, it was a good idea not to put the code in the same job because the jobs could—and in our case, do—have different time intervals. As we send data to Graphite only once every minute, it does not make sense to pull it any less frequently than this.

To get the data out of Graphite, we used the following API call:

```
/render/?from=-11minutes&target=
bookpub.app.jvm.memory.used.area.heap.id.PS_Eden_Space &target=
bookpub.app.jvm.memory.used.area.heap.id.PS_Survivor_Space &target=
bookpub.app.jvm.memory.used.area.heap.id.PS_Old_Gen
&format=json&maxDataPoints=11
```

Take a look at the following parameters mentioned in the preceding code snippet:

- `target`: This parameter is a repeated value that defines a list of all the different metrics that we want to retrieve.
- `from`: This parameter specifies the time range; in our case, we asked for data going back 11 minutes to.
- `format`: This parameter configures the desired output format. We chose JSON but many others are available. Refer to `http://graphite.readthedocs.org/en/latest/render_api.html#format`.
- `maxDataPoints`: This parameter indicates how many entries we want to get.

The reason we asked for 11 entries and not 10 is due to a frequent occurrence where the last entry of short-ranged requests, which consist of only a few minutes, sometimes get returned as empty. We just use the first 10 entries and ignore the most recent ones to avoid weird data visualization.

Iterating over the target data, we will populate the appropriate widgets such as `heap_eden`, `heap_survivor`, and `heap_oldgen`, with their designated data, as follows:

- `heap_eden`: This is a `Graph` widget, as defined in the `sample.erb` template in the form of a `data-view="Graph"` attribute, so it wants a data input in the form of the points collection containing a value for x and y. The x value represents a timestamp, which conveniently gets returned to us by Graphite and is automatically converted to the minutes display value by the Graph widget. The y value represents the memory pool utilization in bytes. As the value from Graphite is in the form of a decimal number, we will need to convert it to a whole number so as to make it look better.

- `heap_survivor`: This is a `Meter` widget, as defined in the `sample.erb` template in the form of a `data-view="Meter"` attribute, so it wants a data input as a simple value number between a template configured range. In our case, the range is set as the `data-min="0" data-max="100"` attribute. Even though we chose to round the number to two decimal positions, it could probably just be an integer as it is precise enough for the purpose of a dashboard display. You will also notice that inside `sample.rb`, we convert the raw value, which is in bytes, into megabytes, for better readability— `current_survivor = current_survivor / 1048576`.

- `heap_oldgen`: This is a `Number` widget, as defined in the `sample.erb` template in the form of a `data-view="Number"` attribute, so it wants a data input as a current value and optionally a last value; in this case, a percentage change with the change direction will be displayed as well. As we get the last 10 entries, we have no issues in retrieving both the current and last values so we can easily satisfy this requirement.

In this recipe, we also experimented with Dashing's RESTful API by trying to use a `curl` command to update the value of the welcome widget. This was a push operation and can be used in situations where there is no data API exposed, but you have the capability of creating some sort of a script or piece of code that could send the data to Dashing instead. To achieve this, we used the following command: `curl -d '{ "auth_token": "YOUR_AUTH_TOKEN", "text": "My RESTful dashboard update!" }' http://localhost:3030/widgets/welcome`.

The Dashing API accepts data in a JSON format, sent via a POST request that contains the following parameters needed for the widgets as well as the widget ID, which is a part of the URL path itself:

- `auth_token`: This allows for a secure data update and can be configured in the dashboard root directory in the `config.ru` file.
- `text`: This is a `widget` property that is being changed. As we are updating a Text widget, as defined in the `sample.erb` template in the form of a `data-view="Text"` attribute, we need to send it to text to update.
- `/widgets/<widget id>`: This URL path identifies the particular widget where the update is destined to. The `id` corresponds to a declaration in the `sample.erb` template. In our case, it looks like `data-id="welcome"`.

The definition of the various widgets can also be manipulated and a very rich collection of the various widgets has been created by the community, which is available at `https://github.com/Shopify/dashing/wiki/Additional-Widgets`. The widgets get installed in the widgets directory in the dashboard and can be installed by simply running `dashing install <GIST>`, where `GIST` is the hash of the GitHub Gist entry.

The dashboard template files, similar to our `sample.erb` template, can be modified in order to create the desired layout for each particular dashboard as well as multiple dashboard templates, which can be rotated or directly loaded manually.

Each dashboard represents a grid in which the various widgets get placed. Each widget is defined by a `<div>` entry with the appropriate configuration attributes and it should be nested in the `<li>` grid element. We can use the data element attributes to control the positioning of each widget in the grid, which is as follows:

- `data-row`: This represents the row number where the widget should be positioned
- `data-col`: This represents the column number where the widget should be positioned
- `data-sizex`: This defines the number of columns the widget will span horizontally
- `data-sizey`: This defines the number of rows the widget will span vertically

The existing widgets can be modified to change their look and feel as well as extend their functionality; so the sky is the limit for what kind of information display we can have. You should definitely check out `http://dashing.io` for more details.

8

Spring Boot DevTools

In this chapter, we will learn about the following topics:

- Adding Spring Boot DevTools to a project
- Configuring LiveReload
- Configuring dynamic application restart triggers
- Using Remote Update

Introduction

In a world of DevOps, agile software development practices, the introduction of microservices, and with more and more teams doing continuous development and deployment, it becomes even more important to be able to quickly see the code changes to an application without going through the whole process of re-compiling the entire project, rebuilding, and restarting the application.

The arrival of containerization services such as Docker has also presented a challenge in terms of access to the actual application running environment. It has changed the notion of a machine by abstracting and encapsulating the runtime environment, removing the ability to use any port to get access.

Spring Boot DevTools provides the ability to do selective class reloading and debugging applications running inside Docker containers using HTTP remote debug tunnel, in order to give developers a quick feedback loop to see their changes reflected in the running application without long rebuild and restart cycles.

Adding Spring Boot DevTools to a project

Starting with Spring Boot 1.3, we have the ability to take advantage of DevTools components in our projects to enable things like automatic application restarts upon code change, reloading the browser windows for the UI, or remotely reloading applications.

The DevTools module is available for both Maven and Gradle, and works nicely with either Eclipse or IntelliJ IDEA editors.

 In this chapter, we will cover integration with Gradle and IntelliJ IDEA, but for detailed information about using Spring Boot DevTools, take a look at the documentation at `http://docs.spring.io/spring-boot/docs/current/reference/html/using-boot-devtools.html`.

How to do it...

Continuing with our `BookPub` project, we will be adding a DevTools module to the main build configuration by performing the following steps:

1. Add the following content to the `build.gradle` file located at the root of the project:

```
dependencies {
    ...
    compile("io.dropwizard.metrics:metrics-graphite:3.1.0")
    compile("org.springframework.boot:spring-boot-devtools")
    runtime("com.h2database:h2")
    ...
}
```

2. Start the application by running `./gradlew clean bootRun`.

3. After application startup, you might notice in the console log an output warning about the inability to register with Spring Boot admin (unless you have one running) that looks like this: **Failed to register application as Application....** Let's make a live change to the `application.properties` file located in the `build/resources/main` directory from the root of our project and add a property entry with the following content:

```
spring.boot.admin.auto-registration=false
```

4. Without doing anything else, upon saving the file, we should see the console log showing us that the application context is being restarted.

How it works...

As you have probably learned by now, when we add a `spring-boot-devtools` module as a dependency there is some autoconfiguration magic that takes place to add a number of components. A number of listeners and autoconfigurations extend the application context to handle the code changes and do appropriate restarts and reloads, both local and remote.

In our recipe, we did a quick test to make sure the restart functionality worked and everything had been configured by making a property change in the `application.properties` file. You have probably noticed that instead of making the change in `src/main/resources/application.properties`, we made the change to the compiled version located under the `build/resources/main` directory. The reason for this was because of the property placeholder replacements for the `info.` block that we used during the Gradle build phase. If we were to only make a change in the original file and use the IntelliJ compile option, it would not perform the required replacements and thus result in a restart failure.

When the DevTools are enabled, the application after being started, begins to monitor the classpath for changes to the classes that are on that classpath. When any class or a resource changes, it will serve as a trigger for DevTools to reload the application by refreshing the classloader containing the project's codebase (which is not the same classloader that holds the classes from the static dependency artifacts).

 See the detailed explanation of the inner workings at the following link:
`http://docs.spring.io/spring-boot/docs/current/reference/html/`
`using-boot-devtools.html#using-boot-devtools-restart`

After the reloadable classloader has completed the refresh, the application context gets restarted automatically, thus effectively causing the application restart.

Configuring LiveReload

Those who work on frontend web applications will probably agree that being able to automatically reload the page once the backend code or resource change has taken place will save a few clicks and prevent situations where a forgotten reload leads to wasteful debugging efforts and chasing an error that does not exist. Thankfully, DevTools comes to the rescue by providing a LiveReload server implementation, which can be used together with a LiveReload browser extention to automatically reload the page when the backend change occurs.

How to do it...

If the DevTools module is added to the build dependencies, the LiveReload server has been automatically started. We do, however, need to install and enable the browser extensions by performing the following steps:

1. Unless the browser already has the LiveReload extension installed, go to `http://livereload.com/extensions/` and install the appropriate extension for your browser of choice (Firefox, Safari, and Chrome are supported).

 For Internet Explorer users, there is a third-party extension available that can be found at `https://github.com/dvdotsenko/livereload_ie_extension/downloads`.

2. After the extension is installed, it typically needs to be enabled on the page by clicking a button in the toolbar. This is what it would look like in the Chrome browser:

3. After enabling the extension, we can go ahead and make another change as we did in the previous recipe (or any other code or resource change), or simply execute the `touch build/resources/main/application.properties` command. We should see the application reload taking place on the backend as well as the browser page reloading after.

How it works...

With the addition of the LiveReload browser extension, and a running LiveReload server embedded into our `BookPub` application, the browser is now capable of connecting to the backend server using a web socket to monitor changes. When the Spring Boot DevTools detects a change that should trigger a reload, it will trigger the reload as well as send a notification to the browser to reload the page as well.

If there is ever a need to disable the LiveReload part of the DevTools functionality, it can easily be achieved by adding the `spring.devtools.livereload.enabled=false` property via any of the supported configuration options, be that a property file, environment variable, or a system property.

Configuring dynamic application restart triggers

In the previous recipes, we have looked into the basic capabilities of DevTools when it comes to restarting the application upon code or resource change and communicating to the browser to reload the page. This section will address the various configuration options that we can leverage to indicate to Spring Boot DevTools exactly what we want those events to be triggered by, and when.

How to do it...

By default, adding a DevTools module to a project will make it monitor all the classes or resources, which could become undesired behavior, especially when it comes to multi-module repositories. This becomes true when building and launching projects from within an IDE like IntelliJ or Eclipse. We need to tell DevTools to exclude the `db-count-starter` sub-module in our project from the watch list by adjusting the configuration settings:

1. Let's create a file named `spring-devtools.properties` under the `db-count-starter/src/main/resources/META-INF` directory from the root of our project with the following content:

   ```
   restart.exclude.db-count-starter=/db-count-
   starter/build/(classes|resources)/main
   ```

2. Next we need to launch our application from within an IDE by opening the `BookPubApplication` class located under the `src/main/java/com/example/bookpub` directory from the root of our project and starting the `main(String[] args)` method either in **run** or **debug** mode

3. With the `db-count-starter` module excluded, we can safely make a change to a file, for example a `spring.factories` resource located under the `db-count-starter/build/resources/main/META-INF` directory from the root of our project, only to see the application not being restarted

4. If we want to completely disable the restart capability, we can do so by adding the following property to `application.properties` located under the `src/main/resources` directory from the root of our project:

```
spring.devtools.restart.enabled=false
```

5. After relaunching our application, even the changes to the `build/resources/main/application.properties` file, which is what's being loaded from the classpath, will not trigger the application restart

How it works...

In this recipe, we have looked at a number of different reload trigger configurations, so let's look at each of them individually to understand where best to use them:

- `spring.devtools.restart.enabled`: This property offers the simplest of controls, fully enabling or disabling the restart functionality of DevTools. With the value of `false`, no restart of the application will take place, regardless of the class or resource changes on the classpath.

- `spring.devtools.restart.exclude`: This property provides an ability to stop specific classpaths from being reloaded. This property accepts values in a comma-separated form using the Ant Path matching pattern style. The default exclude value is `"META-INF/maven/**,META-INF/resources/**,resources/**,static/**,public/**,templates/**,**/*Test.class,**/*Tests.class,git.properties,META-INF/build-info.properties"`.

- `spring.devtools.restart.additional-exclude`: This property provides the convenience of being able to add to the default excludes list without having to copy/paste the default values, but rather simply adding to them while retaining the original defaults. It takes the same comma-separated Ant Path matching pattern style of input.

- `spring.devtools.restart.additional-paths`: This property provides the ability to watch for resources that are outside of the classpath. For example, this could be a `config` directory that gets loaded at application startup, and you want to restart the application if the config entry changes. It takes a comma-separated list of absolute file paths.
- `spring.devtools.restart.poll-interval`: This property specifies how long to pause, in milliseconds, between checking for classpath changes. The default value is `1000` milliseconds, but if there is a need to save some CPU cycles, this will do the trick.
- `spring.devtools.restart.quiet-period`: This property controls how much time should pass, in milliseconds, without any changes to the classpath before the restart will take place. This is needed to ensure the restarts don't get overwhelming if there are continuous changes taking place. The default value is `400` milliseconds, but it can be changed if needed.
- `spring.devtools.restart.trigger-file`: This property provides explicit control over when a restart happens by watching a `trigger` file for change. This is useful for situations where the classpath gets continuously changed, and you don't want to get caught in a restart loop.

All the preceding property settings listed are usually shared between all the application projects that developers work on, so DevTools provides the ability to have global properties defined in this, making it convenient to share the development configurations across many projects without having to copy/paste the same values in all the different codebases.

> Internally, this capability is implemented as `PropertySource`, which gets added to the top of the configuration precedence hierarchy. This means that not only the `spring.devtools` configuration family, but any property added to the global file will be applied to all applications using DevTools.

Another way to control reload triggers is with the use of `META-INF/spring-devtools.properties` with the `restart.exclude.<name>` and `restart.include.<name>` configurations inside them. By default, the restart of the application only gets triggered by changes to the actual classes or resources that are directly on the classpath and not bundled into JARs. This allows you to keep the majority of the classes in the non-reloadable base classloader, greatly limiting the number of entries that need to be monitored for changes.

In situations where developers work with multiple projects that are dependent on each other, or work in a multi-module repository, like the `BookPub` one, it might be desirable to add some JARs into a reloadable classloader and watch them for change. This would typically be applied to dependencies that point to the `build/libs` or `target` directories, where the JARs inside them are a direct result of a build task execution and typically get rebuilt frequently.

Another use case, which we explored in this recipe, is the inclusion or exclusion of `build/classes` or `target/classes` from the watch list. If a multi-module project is loaded in an IDE, it is common for the classpath to contain direct reference to the build directories of the sub-modules instead of the compiled JAR artifact, and depending on the use case, we might or might not choose to include or exclude those from triggering the reload.

The `<name>` part of the keys is not important as long as it is unique, because all the `META-INF/spring-devtools.properties` files will be loaded as composites, regardless whether if they live inside the JARs or right in the project. The suggested approach is to use a sub-module/artifact name, as it will typically ensure uniqueness. If more than one pattern applies, the name can be appended with a sequence number, for example `restart.exclude.db-count-starter-1` and `restart.exclude.db-count-starter-2`. The value of each key should contain a valid regex pattern that can be evaluated against every entry in the classpath to determine whether that particular classpath URL should go into the reloadable or base classloader.

Using Remote Update

With the growing popularity of Docker, more and more applications are being built and deployed as Docker containers. One of the great features of Docker is the isolation of the runtime environment from the host OS, but that same isolation makes it difficult to make continuous changes and test your application in a true environment. Each time there is a change to a property file or a Java class, one needs to rebuild everything, create a new Docker image, restart the container, and so on. That's a lot of work to be doing for every change.

Even though, unfortunately, as of version 2.0, Spring Boot has removed the capability of doing a remote debug, there is still the very helpful ability to remotely reload the code changes from within your IDE as you work on the code, without the need to at least rebuild the application JAR and Docker image.

The **Remote Restart** capability provides a solution for better continuous development and makes it possible to do dynamic application restarts remotely, as if it were on a local machine.

How to do it...

As you have probably guessed, Remote Restart involves an agent running locally and sending instructions to the remote client. DevTools provides an implementation of such an agent—RemoteSpringApplication:

1. In order to enable Remote Restart, we need to add a property to application.properties located under the src/main/resources directory from the root of our project with the following content:

   ```
   spring.devtools.remote.secret=our-secret
   ```

2. The next step would be to create a Java application launch configuration for the RemoteSpringApplication class in the IDE.

It is important to make sure the program arguments field has the base URL of the application you are trying to debug together with the port. Ensure that the working directory points to the main project, and the classpath of the module is pointing to the main project module as well.

The figure on the next page shows what such a configuration would look like in IntelliJ IDEA. The Eclipse IDE would have a similar form as well.

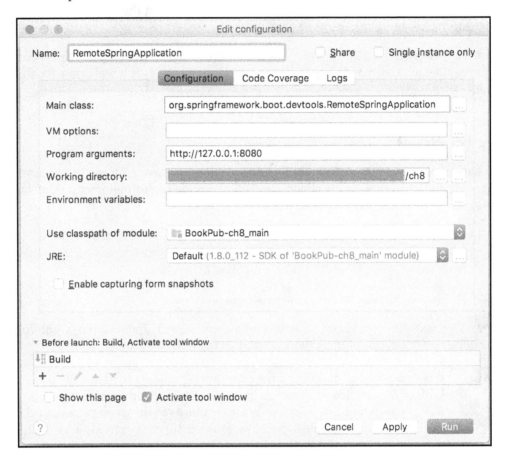

3. After filling out all the fields, we need to start `RemoteSpringApplication` from within our IDE by clicking **Run**. If all has been configured correctly, we should see a similar output in the log:

```
  .   ____          _            __ _ _
 /\\ / ___'_ __ _ _(_)_ __  __ _ \ \ \ \
( ( )\___ | '_ | '_| | '_ \/ _` | \ \ \ \
 \\/  ___)| |_)| | | | | || (_| []::::::[]   / -_) ' / _ _/ -_) ) ) ) )
  '  |____| .__|_| |_|_| |_\__, | / / / /
 =========|_|==============|___/=================================/_/_/_/
 :: Spring Boot Remote ::   (v2.0.0.BUILD-SNAPSHOT)
    2017-12-26 21:33:28.520  INFO o.s.b.devtools.RemoteSpringApplication
 : Starting RemoteSpringApplication v2.0.0.BUILD-SNAPSHOT ...
    2017-12-26 21:33:28.524  INFO o.s.b.devtools.RemoteSpringApplication
 : No active profile set, falling back to default profiles: default
    2017-12-26 21:33:28.781  INFO s.c.a.AnnotationConfigApplicationContext
 : Refreshing
 org.springframework.context.annotation.AnnotationConfigApplicationContext@6
 babf3bf: startup date [Tue Dec 26 21:33:28 CST 2017]; root of context
 hierarchy
    2017-12-26 21:33:29.295  WARN o.s.b.d.r.c.RemoteClientConfiguration
 : The connection to http://127.0.0.1:8080 is insecure. You should use a URL
 starting with 'https://'.
    2017-12-26 21:33:29.368 DEBUG o.s.b.devtools.restart.ChangeableUrls
 : Matching URLs for reloading : [file:/.../ch8/build/classes/main/,
 file:/.../ch8/build/resources/main/]
    2017-12-26 21:33:29.401  INFO o.s.b.d.a.OptionalLiveReloadServer
 : LiveReload server is running on port 35729
    2017-12-26 21:33:29.443  INFO o.s.b.devtools.RemoteSpringApplication
 : Started RemoteSpringApplication in 1.497 seconds (JVM running for 2.248)
```

4. To simulate remoteness, we will launch the application in a separate command shell, executing the `./gradlew clean bootJar` command followed by executing `./build/libs/bookpub-0.0.1-SNAPSHOT-exec.jar`.

5. Once the application has started, take a look at one of the last lines in the log that should look something like the following:

```
INFO 50926 --- [           main]
ication$$EnhancerBySpringCGLIB$$11c0ff63 : Value of my.config.value
property is:
```

6. The property value of `my.config.value` is not being set, because we don't have one defined in our `application.properties` file, and we didn't use any environment variables or startup system property settings to set it.

7. Let's pretend we need to do a live change and modify our `application.properties` file located under the `build/resources/main` directory from the root of our project with the following content:

```
my.config.value=Remote Change
```

8. Now we should see in the console that our application has automatically restarted and, after all is done, we should see something similar to the following:

```
INFO 50926 --- [  restartedMain]
ication$$EnhancerBySpringCGLIB$$11c0ff63 : Value of my.config.value
property is: Remote Change
```

How it works...

It might look like voodoo magic, but the science behind the Remote Restart functionality is pretty straightforward. Under the hood, when a DevTools module is included, the HTTP endpoint handler for `/.~~spring-boot!~/restart` automatically gets added. This allows the `RemoteSpringApplication` process to send the code change payload via an HTTP tunnel to the remote application and back.

To make sure that no malicious outside debug connection gets to connect to our remote application, the value of the `spring.devtools.remote.secret` property gets sent across and verified to establish the authenticity of the request.

In *step 2* of the recipe, we launched the `RemoteSpringApplication` process with a program arguments value of `http://127.0.0.1:8080`, which is how `RemoteSpringApplication` knows how to communicate with our remote application. The `RemoteSpringApplication` class itself scans for the local file changes from an IDE by monitoring the classpath.

In *step 6* of the recipe, when we added the property to our config in the code, it is very important to note that we made the change to the `application.properties` file located in the running classpath of the `RemoteSpringApplication` class not under `src/main/resources`, but under the `build/resources/main` directory, where Gradle has placed all the compiled files—hopefully that's the same directory your IDE is using as a classpath to run `RemoteSpringApplication`. If that's not the path your IDE is using, you should make the change in the appropriate folder, where the IDE has compiled the classes—for IntelliJ IDEA that would be the `out/production/resources` directory by default.

If DevTools needs to be enabled inside an application running as a Docker container, we need to explicitly configure the `build` script to do so by adding the following to the `build.gradle` file in the main project:

```
bootJar {
    ...
    excludeDevtools = false
}
```

The reason we need to do this is because, by default, when a Spring Boot application gets re-packaged for production deployment, which is the case when building a Docker container image, the DevTools module is excluded from the classpath during build time. To prevent this from happening, we need to tell the build system to not exclude the module in order to take advantage of its capabilities, namely the Remote Restart.

9
Spring Cloud

In this chapter, we will learn about the following topics:

- Getting started with Spring Cloud
- Service discovery using Spring Cloud Consul
- Using Spring Cloud Netflix—Feign
- Service discovery using Spring Cloud Netflix—Eureka
- Using Spring Cloud Netflix—Hystrix

Introduction

Throughout this book, we have learned how to create an application, configure RESTful services, do testing, integrate metrics and other management components, and handle packaging and deployment, among other things. Now, the time has come to look at the world outside the application—the ubiquitous cloud environment.

In this chapter, we will look at how to make applications cloud-friendly, how to deal with the dynamic nature of the distributed applications running in the cloud, how to make our applications visible to the world, how to discover other service endpoints, how to call them, and how to handle various error conditions.

Getting started with Spring Cloud

The Spring Cloud family of projects provides integration extensions for Spring Boot of various frameworks, which offer functionality for distributed service discovery, configuration, routing, service invocation, and more. Through the use of uniform API, we can add these concepts to our applications and later have the flexibility to change the specific implementation if such a need arises without making deep-cutting changes to our codebase.

How to do it...

We will start by enhancing our `BookPub` project with base Spring Cloud modules by adding them to the main build configuration:

1. Add the following content to the `build.gradle` file located at the root of the project:

```
...
apply plugin: 'docker'

dependencyManagement {
    imports {
        mavenBom 'org.springframework.cloud:spring-cloud-
dependencies:Finchley.BUILD-SNAPSHOT'
    }
}

jar {
    baseName = 'bookpub'
    version = '0.0.1-SNAPSHOT'
}

...

dependencies {
    ...
    compile("org.springframework.boot:spring-boot-devtools")
    compile("org.springframework.cloud:spring-cloud-context")
    compile("org.springframework.cloud:spring-cloud-commons")
    runtime("com.h2database:h2")
    ...
}
```

2. Start the application by running `./gradlew clean bootRun`

3. After the application has been started, even though it seems like nothing new has happened, if we open our browser at `http://localhost:8081/actuator/env` (the management endpoint for environment), we will see new property sources appear:

```
{
    "name": "springCloudClientHostInfo",
    "properties": {
      "spring.cloud.client.hostname": {
        "value": "127.0.0.1"
      },
      "spring.cloud.client.ip-address": {
        "value": "127.0.0.1"
      }
    }
}
```

4. Create a `bootstrap.properties` file under the `src/main/resources` directory from the root of our project with the following content (the same properties should be commented out inside `application.properties` at this point):

```
spring.application.name=BookPub-ch9
```

5. Start the application by running `./gradlew clean bootRun`

6. After the application has been started, open our browser at `http://localhost:8081/env` and we will see new property sources appear:

```
{
    "name": "applicationConfig: [classpath:/bootstrap.properties]",
    "properties": {
      "spring.application.name": {
        "value": "BookPub-ch9",
        "origin": "class path resource [bootstrap.properties]:1:25"
      }
    }
}
```

How it works...

Before we dive under the hood of how things work, let's review the changes that we have made to our project. The first step was to enhance the `build.gradle` build configuration by importing a **Bill of Material** (**BOM**) declaration for a Spring Cloud release train—mavenBom `'org.springframework.cloud:spring-cloud-dependencies:Finchley.BUILD-SNAPSHOT'`. While we could have selectively imported explicitly-defined versions of the `spring-cloud-context` and `spring-cloud-commons` libraries, by relying on a packaged BOM, we are sure that we will be using the correct versions of different artifacts that have been tested for compatibility with each other.

 Specific versions of each Spring Cloud modules that are included in a particular Release Train can be seen at `http://cloud.spring.io/`.

We start by adding dependencies on the `spring-cloud-context` and `spring-cloud-commons` libraries, to illustrate the basic common facilities Spring Cloud provides, before diving into a specific starter integration such as `spring-cloud-netflix` or `spring-cloud-consul`. Those basic libraries provide a foundation of interfaces and common functionality that is being used to build upon in all the different cloud-specific integrations. Here is what their purpose is:

- `spring-cloud-commons`: This provides a collection of shared common interfaces and base classes that define the notions of service discovery, service routing, load balancing, circuit breaking, feature capabilities, and some basic configuration. For example, this is the library that autoconfigures the environment with the `springCloudClientHostInfo` property source.
- `spring-cloud-context`: This is the base foundation that is responsible for bootstrapping and configuring the various integrations, such as a specific implementation of service discovery like Consul, or a specific implementation of circuit breaker like **Hystrix**. This is achieved by creating an isolated Bootstrap application context, which is responsible for loading and configuring all the components before the main application is started.

Bootstrap application context gets created early on in the application start cycle and it is configured by a separate file—bootstrap.properties (a YAML variant is also supported). Since it is very typical for an application running in the cloud to rely on many external sources of configuration, service lookup, and so on, the purpose of the Bootstrap context is to configure those functions and obtain all of the necessary configuration from outside.

To clearly separate application configuration from Bootstrap, we put things that describe the application, or configure external configs, or other environmental variants like where to call for service discovery, into bootstrap.properties instead of application.properties. In our example, we have placed spring.application.name config into bootstrap.properties, because that information will be needed during the Bootstrap phase; it could be used to look up configuration from a remote config store.

Since Bootstrap application context is indeed a real Spring application context, there exists a parent-child relationship between the two, where Bootstrap application context becomes the parent of the Spring Boot application context. This means that all the beans and the property sources defined in the Bootstrap context become available for consumption from within the application context as well.

When Spring Cloud is added to the application, it automatically provides the integration framework for specific Spring Cloud modules, like Spring Cloud Consul, to be plugged in via the use of the by now well-known spring.factories configuration declarations. The annotations provided inside spring-cloud-commons, namely @SpringCloudApplication, @EnableDiscoveryClient, @EnableCircuitBreaker, and the @BootstrapConfiguraion and PropertySourceLocator interfaces provided by the spring-cloud-context library, are designed to define the integration points to be used to self-configure specific components such as discovery clients like Consul, circuit breakers like Hystrix, or remote configuration sources like **ZooKeeper**.

Let's examine those in detail:

- @SpringCloudApplication: This annotation is like @SpringBootApplication, meta-annotation in nature, except it also wraps the @EnableDiscoveryClient and @EnableCircuitBreaker annotations in addition to also being meta-annotated with @SpringBootApplication. It is a good idea to use this annotation when you want to enable both the discovery client and the circuit breaker functionality in your application.

- `@EnableDiscoveryClient`: This annotation is used to indicate that Spring Cloud should initialize the provided discovery client for service registry, depending on the included integration library, such as Consul, Eureka, ZooKeeper, and so on.
- `@EnableCircuitBreaker`: This annotation is used to indicate that Spring Cloud should initialize the circuit breaker capabilities, based on the specific dependency of the integration library, such as Hystrix.
- `PropertySourceLocator`: This is used by the integration libraries to implement specific functionality of how to extract remote configuration from the provided datastore. Each integration module, providing ability to load remote configuration, would register an implementing bean of this type that exposes an implementation of `PropertySource` that is backed by the integration.
- `@BootstrapConfiguration`: This annotation is like the `@ManagementContextConfiguration` annotation, and is (mostly) a marker annotation geared to identify the key inside the `spring.factories` descriptor to indicate which configuration classes should be loaded during the Spring Cloud Bootstrap process and be part of the Bootstrap application context. Those configurations are read by `BootstrapApplicationListener` during startup and initialize the specified configurations. Typically, this is where the configuration classes, which define and expose `PropertySourceLocator`—implementing beans, are configured.

Service discovery using Spring Cloud Consul

In a world of distributed computing, it is very common for services to become a disposable commodity. The typical life cycle of a service could be measured in days, if not in hours, and it is not unheard of for an instance to just crash for whatever reason, only to have a new one come up automatically seconds later. When the state of applications is so ephemeral, it becomes really hard to maintain a statically-connected architecture, with services knowing where exactly their dependent services are located, as the topology is always changing.

To help with this problem, the service discovery layer comes into play, maintaining a centralized and distributed state of service registrations, ready to reply on demand with the most current information. Applications register themselves upon startup, providing information about their location and possibly about their capabilities, level of service, health check status, and even more.

Earlier in the book, in Chapter 6, *Application Packaging and Deployment*, we were introduced to Consul, and used it for external application configuration consumption. In this recipe, we will continue to look further into the capabilities of Consul and will learn about how to use the spring-cloud-consul modules to automatically register our application with Consul.

How to do it...

Take a look at the following steps to set up service discovery:

1. Replace the spring-cloud-commons and spring-cloud-context modules with spring-cloud-starter-consul-all by modifying the build.gradle file located in the root of our project with the following content:

```
...

dependencies {
    ...
    compile("io.dropwizard.metrics:metrics-graphite:3.1.0")
    compile("org.springframework.boot:spring-boot-devtools")
    //compile("org.springframework.cloud:spring-cloud-context")
    //compile("org.springframework.cloud:spring-cloud-commons")
    compile("org.springframework.cloud:spring-cloud-starter-consul-
all")
    runtime("com.h2database:h2")
    ...
}
...
```

2. With Consul dependencies added, we will proceed with enabling our application to automatically register with the local agent upon startup by modifying the BookPubApplication.java file located under the src/main/java/com/example/bookpub directory from the root of our project with the following content:

```
...
@EnableScheduling
@EnableDbCounting
@EnableDiscoveryClient
public class BookPubApplication {
    ...
}
```

3. Given that Consul was successfully installed using the steps described in the *Setting up Consul* recipe in `Chapter 6`, *Application Packaging and Deployment,* we should be able to start it by running `consul agent -server -bootstrap-expect 1 -data-dir /tmp/consul` and our Terminal window should display the following output:

```
==> Starting Consul agent...
==> Starting Consul agent RPC...
==> Consul agent running!
          Version: 'v1.0.2'
...
```

4. After the Consul agent is up and running successfully, we will proceed by starting our application by running `./gradlew clean bootRun`

5. As we watch the startup logs scroll by, there are a couple of interesting entries that indicate the application is interacting with the agent, so watch for the following content in the logs:

```
...
2017-12-26 --- b.c.PropertySourceBootstrapConfiguration : Located
property source: CompositePropertySource [name='consul',
propertySources=[ConsulPropertySource [name='config/BookPub-ch9/'],
ConsulPropertySource [name='config/application/']]]
...
2017-12-26 --- o.s.c.consul.discovery.ConsulLifecycle    :
Registering service with consul: NewService{id='BookPub-ch9-8080',
name='BookPub-ch9', tags=[], address='<your_machine_name>',
port=8080, check=Check{script='null', interval=10s, ttl=null,
http=http://<your_machine_name>:8081/health, tcp=null,
timeout=null}}
2017-12-26 --- o.s.c.consul.discovery.ConsulLifecycle    :
Registering service with consul: NewService{id='BookPub-ch9-8080-
management', name='BookPub-ch9-management', tags=[management],
address='://<your_machine_name>', port=8081,
check=Check{script='null', interval=10s, ttl=null,
http=http://chic02qv045g8wn:8081/health, tcp=null, timeout=null}}
...
```

6. Just to verify that our application has registered and is in communication with the local Consul agent, let's open `http://localhost:8081/actuator/consul` in the browser to see the Consul agent information, as shown in the following screenshot:

```
{"catalogServices":{"BookPub-Catalog-Application":
[{"node":"127.0.0.1","address":"127.0.0.1","serviceId":"BookPub-Catalog-Application-
8080","serviceName":"BookPub-Catalog-Application","serviceTags":
[]},"serviceAddress":"192.168.1.194","servicePort":8080}],"BookPub-Catalog-Application-
management":[{"node":"127.0.0.1","address":"127.0.0.1","serviceId":"BookPub-Catalog-
Application-8080-management","serviceName":"BookPub-Catalog-Application-
management","serviceTags":
["management"],"serviceAddress":"192.168.1.194","servicePort":8081}],"consul":
[{"node":"127.0.0.1","address":"127.0.0.1","serviceId":"consul","serviceName":"consul"
,"serviceTags":[],"serviceAddress":"","servicePort":8300}]},"agentServices":{"BookPub-
Catalog-Application-8080":{"id":"BookPub-Catalog-Application-8080","service":"BookPub-
Catalog-Application","tags":[],"address":"192.168.1.194","port":8080},"BookPub-
Catalog-Application-8080-management":{"id":"BookPub-Catalog-Application-8080-
management","service":"BookPub-Catalog-Application-management","tags":
["management"],"address":"192.168.1.194","port":8081}},"catalogNodes":
[{"node":"127.0.0.1","address":"127.0.0.1"}]}
```

How it works...

When we added `spring-cloud-starter-consul-all` as a build dependency, it automatically pulled all the necessary components to enable Consul functionality for our application. We automatically got the `spring-cloud-consul-binder`, `spring-cloud-consul-core`, `spring-cloud-consul-config`, and `spring-cloud-consul-discovery` artifacts added to our classpath. Let's take a look at the them:

- `spring-cloud-consul-core`: This artifact provides base autoconfiguration to expose generic `ConsulProperties`, as well as the `ConsulClient` initialization and setting of the `/consul` management endpoint, if the Spring Boot Actuator functionality is enabled.

- `spring-cloud-consul-config`: This provides the `ConsulPropertySourceLocator` implementation, used during Bootstrap, to configure the `ConsulPropertySource` bean, which allows remote configuration consumption from the Consul key/value store. It also sets up a `ConfigWatch` change observer, which fires `RefreshEvent` to the application context, if a configuration key value changes in Consul key/value store while the application is running. This allows for a possible configuration properties reload without having to redeploy and restart the application.
- `spring-cloud-consul-discovery`: This provides all the functionality and implementations needed for service discovery, service registration, and service invocation.
- `spring-cloud-consul-binder`: This provides integration of Consul event functionality with Spring Cloud Stream Framework, enabling it to send and receive events from Consul and respond to them within the application. While outside of the scope of this chapter, more information can be obtained from `http://cloud.spring.io/spring-cloud-stream/`.

While addition of `spring-cloud-consul-config` to the classpath will automatically register `ConsulPropertySource`, it is not so for the `spring-cloud-consul-discovery` module. The service discovery functionality is more intrusive and thus requires an additional step of acknowledgement from the developers to indicate that it is indeed wanted. This is accomplished by adding the `@EnableDiscoveryClient` annotation to the main application class; in our case it is `BookPubApplication`.

Once the `@EnableDiscoveryClient` annotation is added, Spring Cloud (`EnableDiscoveryClientImportSelector` class from the `spring-cloud-commons` module, to be more precise) scans all `spring.factories` files for the presence of the `org.springframework.cloud.client.discovery.EnableDiscoveryClient` key, and loads all the associated configurations into the main application context. If we look inside the `spring.factories` file located in the `spring-cloud-consul-discovery` JAR under the `META-INF/` directory, we will see the following entry:

```
# Discovery Client Configuration
org.springframework.cloud.client.discovery.EnableDiscoveryClient=\
org.springframework.cloud.consul.discovery.ConsulDiscoveryClientConfigurati
on
```

This tells us that when the discovery client is enabled, `ConsulDiscoveryClientConfiguration` will be consumed and all of its defining beans will be added to the application context.

A similar approach can be used if a custom service discovery mechanism is being used. One will need to create a custom configuration class, exposing a custom implementation of the `DiscoveryClient` interface, and configure it in the `spring.factories` file bundled within the archive. Once that JAR gets loaded, the configuration will be automatically consumed if discovery client functionality is enabled.

 Spring Cloud Consul libraries provide very fine-grained ability to configure and pick and choose the selected functions, if not all apply for a particular use-case. For detailed information about various configuration and usage options see `http://cloud.spring.io/spring-cloud-consul/`.

Using Spring Cloud Netflix – Feign

In the previous recipe, we looked at how to enable service discovery capability for our application in order to be able to register our service with the world as well as to know what other services exist and where they are located. This recipe will help us better interact with that information and consume those services without having to explicitly code any logic to handle service discovery and all of the related concerns that come with it.

To achieve this goal, we will look at another Spring Cloud integration, provided by the Spring Cloud Netflix module family—Netflix Feign. Feign, which makes writing Java HTTP clients easier. Its purpose is to simplify the process of binding service API calls to their corresponding HTTP API counterparts. It provides automatic service mapping and discovery, ability to translate Java types to HTTP request URL paths, parameters and response payloads, as well as error handling.

For the sake of simplicity, in this recipe, we will be creating a `Client` controller, which will act as an external client of our `BookPub` application service, calling our APIs via Feign-annotated Java service interfaces, relying on Consul to provide service discovery functionality.

How to do it...

1. We will start by adding Netflix Feign module dependencies to our project. Let's modify our `build.gradle` file located in the root of our project with the following content:

```
dependencies {
    ...
    compile("org.springframework.cloud:spring-
    cloud-starter-consul-all")
    compile("org.springframework.cloud:spring-
    cloud-starter-openfeign")
    runtime("com.h2database:h2")
    ...
}
```

2. With the dependency added, our next step is to create a Java API interface describing how we want to define our interaction with the `BookPub` service. Let's create an `api` package under the `src/main/java/com/example/bookpub` directory from the root of our project.

3. Inside the newly-created `api` package, let's create our API class file named `BookPubClient.java` with the following content:

```
package com.example.bookpub.api;

import com.example.bookpub.entity.Book;
import org.springframework.cloud.netflix.feign.FeignClient;
import org.springframework.web.bind.annotation.PathVariable;
import org.springframework.web.bind.annotation.RequestMapping;
import org.springframework.web.bind.annotation.RequestMethod;

@FeignClient("http://BookPub-ch9")
public interface BookPubClient {
    @RequestMapping(value = "/books/{isbn}",
                    method = RequestMethod.GET)
    public Book findBookByIsbn(@PathVariable("isbn") String isbn);
}
```

4. After we have defined the API, it is time to tell our application that we want to enable Feign support. We will do that by making a change to the `BookPubApplication.java` file located under the `src/main/java/com/example/bookpub directory` from the root of our project with the following content:

```
...
@EnableDiscoveryClient
@EnableFeignClients
public class BookPubApplication {...}
```

5. Finally, let's create a client controller to invoke `BookPubClient` by making a new file named `ClientController.java` under the `src/main/java/com/example/bookpub/controllers` directory from the root of our project with the following content:

```
...
@RestController
@RequestMapping("/client")
public class ClientController {

    @Autowired
    private BookPubClient client;

    @RequestMapping(value = "/book/{isbn}",
                    method = RequestMethod.GET)
    public Book getBook(@PathVariable String isbn) {
        return client.findBookByIsbn(isbn);
    }
}
```

6. With everything set and done, let's start the application by executing the `./gradlew clean bootRun` command.

Make sure that the Consul agent is also running in the background, otherwise service registration will fail.

7. Once the application is up and running, let's
   open `http://localhost:8080/client/book/978-1-78528-415-1` in the
   browser to see the Consul agent information, as shown in the following
   screenshot:

8. If we look at the application console logs, we will also see entries indicating that
   our Feign client is initialized and functioning. You should see something similar
   to this:

```
2017-12-26 --- c.n.u.concurrent.ShutdownEnabledTimer : Shutdown
hook installed for: NFLoadBalancer-PingTimer-BookPub-ch9
2017-12-26 --- c.netflix.loadbalancer.BaseLoadBalancer :
Client:BookPub-ch9 instantiated a
LoadBalancer:DynamicServerListLoadBalancer:{NFLoadBalancer:name=Boo
kPub-ch9,current list of Servers=[],Load balancer stats=Zone stats:
{},Server stats: []}ServerList:null
2017-12-26 --- c.n.l.DynamicServerListLoadBalancer : Using
serverListUpdater PollingServerListUpdater
 2017-12-26 --- c.netflix.config.ChainedDynamicProperty : Flipping
property: BookPub-ch9.ribbon.ActiveConnectionsLimit to use NEXT
property:
niws.loadbalancer.availabilityFilteringRule.activeConnectionsLimit
= 2147483647
 2017-12-26 --- c.n.l.DynamicServerListLoadBalancer :
DynamicServerListLoadBalancer for client BookPub-ch9 initialized:
DynamicServerListLoadBalancer:{NFLoadBalancer:name=BookPub-
ch9,current list of Servers=[192.168.1.194:8080],Load balancer
stats=Zone stats: {unknown=[Zone:unknown; Instance count:1; Active
connections count: 0; Circuit breaker tripped count: 0; Active
connections per server: 0.0;]
```

```
        },Server stats: [[Server:192.168.1.194:8080; Zone:UNKNOWN; Total
        Requests:0; Successive connection failure:0; Total blackout
        seconds:0; Last connection made:Wed Dec 31 18:00:00 CST 1969; First
        connection made: Wed Dec 31 18:00:00 CST 1969; Active
        Connections:0; total failure count in last (1000) msecs:0; average
        resp time:0.0; 90 percentile resp time:0.0; 95 percentile resp
        time:0.0; min resp time:0.0; max resp time:0.0; stddev resp
        time:0.0]
        ]}ServerList:ConsulServerList{serviceId='BookPub-ch9', tag=null}
```

9. One last thing that we should do is to get our tests to work with all the newly added frameworks. Because Spring Cloud does not add itself to the test life cycle, we should explicitly disable any reliance on beans created by Spring Cloud libraries during tests. To do so let's add to our `application.properties` file located under the `src/test/resources` directory from the root of the project of the following properties:

```
spring.cloud.bus.enabled=false
spring.cloud.consul.enabled=false
spring.cloud.consul.discovery.enabled=false
eureka.client.enabled=false
autoconfigure.exclude=com.example.bookpub.
MonitoringConfiguration.class
```

10. We also need to add a Mock dependency on `BookPubClient` into the `JpaAuthorRepositoryTests.java` and `WebMvcBookControllerTests.java` files located under the `src/test/java/com/example/bookpub` directory from the root of the project with the following content:

```
@MockBean
private BookPubClient client;
```

How it works...

Similar to what we saw in the previous recipe, the use of the `@EnableFeignClients` annotation on the main application class, `BookPubApplication`, explicitly tells Spring Cloud that it should scan for all the interfaces annotated with `@FeignClient` and create service client implementations based on their definitions. The `@EnableFeignClients` annotation is similar in nature to the `@ComponentScan` one, providing attributes to control which packages to scan for the `@FeignClient` annotated classes or explicitly list the API classes that should be used.

Out of the box, all Feign client implementations are configured using components defined in the `FeignClientsConfiguration` class, but one can provide alternative configuration classes using the `defaultConfiguration` attribute of the `@EnableFeignClients` annotation.

In a nutshell, every interface definition, annotated with `@FeignClient`, gets a service implementation consisting of a Java dynamic proxy object, which handles all the interface method calls (usually using `FeignInvocationHandler` to handle all the requests). The invocation handler is responsible for doing a few things.

Once any method is invoked, first the service instances are located using the provided discovery client (in our case it is `ConsulDiscoveryClient`) based on the `name` attribute of the `@FeignClient` annotation. In our example, we have declared the value of `name` attribute to be `http://BookPub-ch9`, so all the service instances from the registry which have their name set to `BookPub-ch9` will be returned as possible candidates. This name can be just a service name itself, or, as we did in our example, an optional protocol can be specified. This is a useful feature, as not all service discovery providers support ability to specify exactly how the service should be called, so if we want to make a secure call using HTTPS, we can explicitly specify the protocol to help Feign make the right call.

There are a number of other configuration attributes available on the annotation, for example, to tell Feign to make a direct call to a specified URL instead of doing a service lookup, there is a `url` attribute that can be configured.

 To see a complete list of possible attributes and their use-cases, go to `https://cloud.spring.io/spring-cloud-netflix/single/spring-cloud-netflix.html#spring-cloud-feign`.

The list of instances for a given service gets wrapped with an internal load balancer, provided by another Netflix library—Ribbon. It uses a specified algorithm to rotate between the instances of a service as well as to take the bad instances out of circulation if the discovery client says they are unhealthy.

 To see a complete list of possible configuration options for things like load balancing rules, and other settings, go to `https://cloud.spring.io/spring-cloud-netflix/single/spring-cloud-netflix.html#spring-cloud-ribbon`.

When a specific instance has been determined, an HTTP request gets created, using the standard Spring `HttpMessageConverter` beans to transform the method arguments into HTTP request path variables and query parameters. After all that is done, the request gets sent using a configured HTTP client and the response gets converted into a return type declared on the API interface using the same converters.

Now that we know what `@FeignClient` annotation is all about and what happens under the hood once an API-defined method gets invoked, let's take a look at how to annotate the interface methods that should be translated into remote service calls. Conveniently, and done so on purpose, we can use exactly the same annotations as we are already used to, when declaring controller mappings inside the `@Controller` annotated classes. Each method in our API interface, which we want to map to a remote service, should be annotated with the `@RequestMapping` annotation. The `path` attribute corresponds to a URL path of the remote service we want to invoke.

In our example, we want to call our `BookController.getBook(...)` method, which translates to the `/books/{isbn}` URL path. This is exactly what we put as a value for the `path` attribute, and make sure we also annotate the `isbn` argument in our `findBookByIsbn(...)` method with `@PathVariable("isbn")` to link it to a `{isbn}` placeholder in the mapping template.

As a general rule of thumb, the `@RequestMapping` annotation functions exactly the same as if it were used in a controller, except the configuration relates to an outgoing request instead of an inbound one. It might be especially confusing when configuring the `consumes` attribute of the annotation, that is, `consumes = "application/json"`, because it indicates that it is a remote side that expects JSON as a content-type of the payload.

Service discovery using Spring Cloud Netflix – Eureka

We've already seen how to do service discovery using HashiCorp Consul and integrate it with our application. This recipe will go over an alternative, and a very popular service discovery framework from Netflix-Eureka. Eureka was developed by Netflix to help solve the problem of service discovery, health checking, and load balancing for their RESTful services in AWS.

Unlike Consul, Eureka is solely focused on the task of service discovery, and does not provide many additional functionalities, such as key/value store service or event delivery. It is, however, very good at what it does and should be considered a viable candidate for a service discovery solution.

How to do it...

Before we get to the steps to add Eureka to our application, we need to get the Eureka service itself up and running. Thankfully, the Spring Cloud folks have been awesome enough to provide a sample project that makes creating an instance of Eureka server and running it a breeze. Let's take a look at the following steps:

1. To get things up and running just go to `https://github.com/spring-cloud-samples/eureka` and git clone the `git@github.com:spring-cloud-samples/eureka.git` repository to your machine.

2. After that's done, run `./gradlew clean bootRun` to start the server:

3. Once the server is up and running, we need to add the following dependencies to the `build.gradle` file located at the root of our project:

   ```
   //compile("org.springframework.cloud:spring-cloud-starter-consul-all")
   compile("org.springframework.cloud:spring-cloud-starter-feign")
   compile("org.springframework.cloud:spring-cloud-starter-eureka-client")
   ```

4. Ironically, that's all we had to do, at this point, we just restart our application by executing the `./gradlew clean bootRun` command.

    Make sure the Eureka server is running in the background, otherwise, though the application will start, the `BookPubClient` calls will fail.

5. Once the application is up and running, let's open `http://localhost:8080/client/book/978-1-78528-415-1` in the browser and we should see exactly the same response as in our previous recipe.

6. Just to see that our application did indeed register with Eureka, we can open the browser at the `http://localhost:8761` URL and we should see our service listed under instances list:

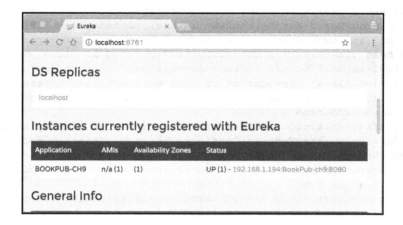

How it works...

With a seemingly effortless change, we have switched one service discovery provider, Consul, for another, Eureka. What looked like not much of a change on the outside actually did quite a bit of work under the hood. The reason we were able to do it so easily is the common set of APIs provided by the `spring-cloud-commons` and `spring-cloud-context` foundational libraries. Automated module loading support via the `spring.factores` descriptor allowed for transparent substitution in the initialization of a different service discovery provider. As long as we retained the `@EnableDiscoveryClient` annotation on our `BookPubApplication` class, Spring Cloud did the heavy lifting, taking care of loading the appropriate autoconfiguration files and setting up all the right beans to get our application working with Eureka.

We had to remove the Consul dependency from our classpath at the very first step of the recipe, and that had to be done in order to disambiguate the `DiscoveryClient` implementation. Without doing so, our application context would have ended up with two different implementations of the `DiscoveryClient` interface, which in itself would not be bad, except that Spring Cloud would have to disambiguate and choose one, and might not choose the one we want.

If we leave the `spring-cloud-starter-consul-all` dependency in our `build.gradle` file, and attempt to run the application, it will fail during startup and in the logs we will see the following entry:

```
WARN 5592 --- [  restartedMain] ConfigServletWebServerApplicationContext :
Exception encountered during context initialization - cancelling refresh
attempt: org.springframework.beans.factory.BeanCreationException: Error
creating bean with name 'jmxMBeanExporter' defined in class path resource
[org/springframework/boot/actuate/autoconfigure/endpoint/jmx/JmxEndpointAut
oConfiguration.class]: Invocation of init method failed; nested exception
is org.springframework.beans.factory.UnsatisfiedDependencyException: Error
creating bean with name
'org.springframework.cloud.client.serviceregistry.ServiceRegistryAutoConfig
uration$ServiceRegistryEndpointConfiguration': Unsatisfied dependency
expressed through field 'registration'; nested exception is
org.springframework.beans.factory.NoUniqueBeanDefinitionException: No
qualifying bean of type
'org.springframework.cloud.client.serviceregistry.Registration' available:
expected single matching bean but found 2:
eurekaRegistration,consulRegistration
```

As you can see from the exception, Spring autowiring can't decide which one of the service registries should be used. This is because both Eureka and Consul automatically have created an instance of `Registration`, and the autowiring wants only one.

Since there is a hard requirement for only having one registry, it is best not to configure multiple discovery client dependency libraries to avoid errors. If, for some reason, multiple libraries have to reside in the classpath, one should use configuration properties to explicitly enable/disable a specific client implementation. For example, both Consul and Eureka provide configuration to toggle the state. We can set `spring.cloud.consul.discovery.enabled=true` and `eureka.client.enabled=false` in `application.properties` if we prefer to use Consul to provide service discovery functionality.

Using Spring Cloud Netflix – Hystrix

Throughout this chapter we have looked at all the aspects that apply to having a successful microservice application running in the cloud environment. We have learned about how to integrate better into a dynamically changing ecosystem, consuming remote configuration properties, registering service, and discovering and calling other services. In this recipe, we will take a look at another very important aspect of operating in a distributed, highly-volatile cloud environment circuit breakers.

The particular implementation of circuit breaker functionality which we are going to look at is Netflix Hystrix. It provides a very powerful and convenient way to annotate our service calls and handle things like remote service failures, queue backups, overloads, timeouts, and so on. By having circuit breakers in an application, developers can ensure overall application stability if a particular service endpoint becomes overloaded by requests, or experiences an outage of any kind.

How to do it...

1. To get started with Hystrix we need to add the `spring-cloud-starter-hystrix` library to our project. Let's modify our `build.gradle` file located in the root of our project with the following content:

```
dependencies {
    ...
    compile("org.springframework.cloud:
      spring-cloud-starter-consul-all")
    compile("org.springframework.cloud:
      spring-cloud-starter-openfeign")
    compile("org.springframework.cloud:
      spring-cloud-starter-eureka-client")
    compile("org.springframework.cloud:
      spring-cloud-starter-netflix-hystrix")
    runtime("com.h2database:h2")
    runtime("mysql:mysql-connector-java")
    ...
}
```

2. After adding the Hystrix dependency, we need to enable Hystrix for our application. Similar to how we enabled service discovery, we will do that by making a change to the `BookPubApplication.java` file located under the `src/main/java/com/example/bookpub` directory from the root of our project with the following content:

```
...
@EnableDiscoveryClient
@EnableFeignClients
@EnableCircuitBreaker
public class BookPubApplication {...}
```

3. Now, let's make a few changes to `BookController.java`, located under the `src/main/java/com/example/bookpub/controllers` directory from the root of our project, with the following content:

```
@RequestMapping(value = "", method = RequestMethod.GET)
@HystrixCommand(fallbackMethod = "getEmptyBooksList")
public Iterable<Book> getAllBooks() {
    //return bookRepository.findAll();
    throw new RuntimeException("Books Service Not Available");
}

public Iterable<Book> getEmptyBooksList() {
    return Collections.emptyList();
}
...
```

4. Due to Hystrix internal functionality, we also need to modify our entity models to have them eager-load the relational associations. In the `Author.java`, `Book.java`, and `Publisher.java` files located under the `src/main/java/com/example/bookpub/entity` directory from the root of our project, let's make the following changes:

   - In `Author.java`, make the following change:

```
@OneToMany(mappedBy = "author", fetch = FetchType.EAGER)
private List<Book> books;
```

   - In `Book.java`, make the following change:

```
@ManyToOne(fetch = FetchType.EAGER)
private Author author;

@ManyToOne(fetch = FetchType.EAGER)
private Publisher publisher;

@ManyToMany(fetch = FetchType.EAGER)
private List<Reviewer> reviewers;
```

   - In `Publisher.java`, make the following change:

```
@OneToMany(mappedBy = "publisher", fetch = FetchType.EAGER)
private List<Book> books;
```

5. Finally, we are ready to restart our application by executing the `./gradlew clean bootRun` command.

6. When the application has started, let's open `http://localhost:8080/books` in the browser and we should see an empty JSON list as a result:

How it works...

In this recipe we have done three things after adding the Hystrix dependency library to our project. So, let's take a look at each step in detail to learn what exactly happens:

- The `@EnableCircuitBreaker` annotation, similar to `@EnableDiscoveryClient`, or `@EnableFeignClients`, which explicitly indicates that we want Spring Cloud to load appropriate configurations from `spring.factories` from all the libraries which have the `org.springframework.cloud.client.circuitbreaker.EnableCircuitBreaker` key defined.

- In the case of Hystrix, it will load `HystrixCircuitBreakerConfiguration`, which provides the necessary configuration to enable the Hystrix functionality within the application. One of the beans it creates, is the `HystrixCommandAspect` class. It's purpose is to detect all the methods which are annotated with the `@HystrixCommand` annotation and wrap them with a handler to detect errors, timeouts, and other ill-behaviors, and deal with them appropriately, based on configuration.

- This `@HystrixCommand` annotation, provided by the Hystrix library, is designed to mark methods which represent `Hystrix-guarded commands`, that is, methods which we want to protect using Hystrix against cascading failures and overloads. This annotation has a number of attributes and can be configured in a variety of different ways, depending on the desired behavior.

- In our example we have used the most typical attribute—`fallbackMethod`, which allows us to configure an alternative method, with matching signature, which can be automatically called if the real method fails the invocation for whatever reason. This is the prime use-case, and it provides the ability to specify graceful degradation of service, using sensible defaults, if possible, instead of blowing up exceptions up the stack.

- We used it to direct failed calls to the `getEmptyBooksList()` method, which returns a static empty list. This way, when the real `getAllBooks()` method fails, we gracefully degrade and return an empty collection, which renders nicely as a response JSON. In the situations when we do indeed desire a particular type of exception to be propagated up the stack, we can configure those explicitly using the `ignoreExceptions` attribute and set it to the desired exception classes.

- To configure the circuit breaker behavior of a particular command, we can set a number of different options using the `commandProperties` or `threadPoolProperties` attributes. There we can set things like execution timeouts, size of backup queues, and many others.

 For a complete list of available properties, see `https://github.com/Netflix/Hystrix/tree/master/hystrix-contrib/hystrix-javanica#configuration`.

One last thing to discuss is the modifications we made to our entity models to set the relational association annotations to use `fetch = FetchType.EAGER`. The reason we had to do so is due to the way Hibernate handles association loading. By default, those are loaded using the `FetchType.LAZY` setup, meaning that Hibernate is only going to establish the relationship, but the loading of the data will not happen until the getter methods are invoked. With Hystrix, by default, this could cause an error that looks something like this:

```
failed to lazily initialize a collection of role:
com.example.bookpub.entity.Book.reviewers, could not initialize proxy -
no Session (through reference chain:
com.example.bookpub.entity.Publisher["books"]->org.hibernate.collection
.internal.PersistentBag[0]->com.example.bookpub.entity.Book["reviewers"
])
```

This is due to the fact that Hystrix uses `ThreadPool` to execute method calls by default, and because the lazy-loaded data needs to access the datastore at the time of invocation, Hibernate requires an active session to be present in order to handle the request. Since Hibernate stores the session in `ThreadLocal`, it is obviously not present in the pooled executor thread that Hystrix is using during the invocation.

Once we changed the fetching to be eager, all the data is loaded during the repository interaction in the original Hibernate thread. We could, alternatively, configure our `@HystrixCommand` annotation to use the same executing thread by using the following configuration:

```
commandProperties = {
  @HystrixProperty(name="execution.isolation.strategy",
                   value="SEMAPHORE")
}
```

While Hystrix strongly recommends to use the default `THREAD` strategy, in situations when we absolutely need to be residing in the same caller thread, `SEMAPHORE` is there to help us.

Alternatively, we can set the same configuration in our `application.properties` file using `hystrix.command.default.execution.isolation.strategy=SEMAPHORE`, or, if we want to be specific to only configure particular `@HystrixCommand`, we can use the value of the `commandKey` attribute, which is the name of the annotated method by default, instead of the default section of the property name. For our specific example from the `BookController` instrumented method, the configuration key would look like `hystrix.command.getAllBooks.execution.isolation.strategy=SEMAPHORE`. This is possible thanks to the Spring Cloud-Netflix Archaius bridge, which makes all Spring environment properties visible to the Archaius configuration manager, thus accessible by all of the Netflix components.

Spring Cloud Hystrix integration also provides a `/hystrix.stream` actuator endpoint, which can be consumed by the Hystrix dashboard for visualizing the state of all the circuit breakers in an application.

To get the dashboard running quickly, Spring Cloud provides a sample application which can be seen at `https://github.com/spring-cloud-samples/hystrix-dashboard`:

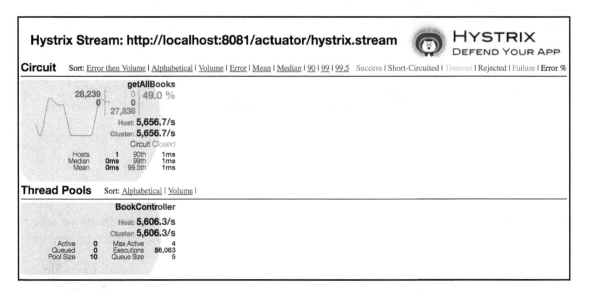

The same stream can also be fed into **Netflix Turbine Stream Aggregator**, downloadable at `https://github.com/Netflix/Turbine`, for data aggregation across multiple instances, which can later be visualized using the same dashboard.

One can also use the `spring-cloud-starter-turbine` dependency library and the `@EnableTurbine` annotation on a basic Spring Boot application, similar to the Hystrix dashboard sample.

Other Books You May Enjoy

If you enjoyed this book, you may be interested in these other books by Packt:

Spring 5.0 Microservices - Second Edition
Rajesh R V

ISBN: 978-1-78712-768-5

- Familiarize yourself with the microservices architecture and its benefits
- Find out how to avoid common challenges and pitfalls while developing microservices
- Use Spring Boot and Spring Cloud to develop microservices
- Handle logging and monitoring microservices
- Leverage Reactive Programming in Spring 5.0 to build modern cloud native applications
- Manage internet-scale microservices using Docker, Mesos, and Marathon
- Gain insights into the latest inclusion of Reactive Streams in Spring and make applications more resilient and scalable

Mastering Spring 5.0
Ranga Karanam

ISBN: 978-1-78712-317-5

- Explore the new features in Spring Framework 5.0
- Build microservices with Spring Boot
- Get to know the advanced features of Spring Boot in order to effectively develop and monitor applications
- Use Spring Cloud to deploy and manage applications on the Cloud
- Understand Spring Data and Spring Cloud Data Flow
- Understand the basics of reactive programming
- Get to know the best practices when developing applications with the Spring Framework
- Create a new project using Kotlin and implement a couple of basic services with unit and integration testing

Leave a review - let other readers know what you think

Please share your thoughts on this book with others by leaving a review on the site that you bought it from. If you purchased the book from Amazon, please leave us an honest review on this book's Amazon page. This is vital so that other potential readers can see and use your unbiased opinion to make purchasing decisions, we can understand what our customers think about our products, and our authors can see your feedback on the title that they have worked with Packt to create. It will only take a few minutes of your time, but is valuable to other potential customers, our authors, and Packt. Thank you!

Index

A

Abstract Window Toolkit (AWT) 41
application properties, Spring Boot reference
    documentation
    reference 61
application
    launching, Gradle used 15

B

basic RESTful application
    creating 29, 30, 31
behavior-driven development (BDD) 79
Bill of Material (BOM) 240
book catalog management system
    creating 10, 11, 12, 13, 14

C

capabilities, Spring Data
    reference 26
certificate keystore
    reference 58
command-line runners
    using 17, 18
configuration
    toggling, custom @Enable annotations used 74,
      76
Consul
    reference 160
    setting up 160, 162, 163
    used, for externalizing environmental
      configuration 164, 166, 167
Cucumber-JVM
    reference 104
Cucumber
    used, for writing tests 104, 107, 109, 111, 113

cURL

cURL
    reference 162
custom @Enable annotations
    used, for toggling configuration 74, 76
custom conditional bean instantiations
    configuring 71, 72, 74
custom connectors
    adding 58, 59, 60, 61, 62
custom health indicators
    writing 170, 171, 172, 173, 175, 176, 179
custom HttpMessageConverters
    configuring 38, 39, 40
custom interceptors
    configuring 36, 37, 38
custom PropertyEditors
    configuring 41, 43, 44
custom PropertySource
    adding, to environment 145, 149
custom remote Shell commands
    writing 195, 197, 199, 201, 203
custom servlet filters
    configuring 34, 35
custom Spring Boot autoconfiguration starter
    creating 66, 67, 68, 69, 70
custom static path mappings
    configuring 52, 53, 54
custom type formatters
    configuring 45, 46, 47, 48

D

Dashing
    Micrometer metrics, integrating with 213, 216,
      218, 222
data repository service
    setting up 22, 25
database connection

setting up 18, 19, 20
database schema
  configuring 86, 87, 89
  populating 86, 87, 89
database
  initializing, with Hibernate 90
  initializing, with Spring JDBC 90
  initializing, with Spring JPA 90
Docker Hub
  reference 130
Docker images
  creating 130, 131, 134, 135
dynamic application restart triggers
  configuring 227, 229

E

embedded servlet containers
  selecting 57
envconsul
  used, for externalizing environmental
    configuration 164, 166, 167
environment
  custom PropertySource, adding to 145, 149
environmental configuration
  about 142
  externalizing, Consul used 164
  externalizing, envconsul used 164
  externalizing, environment variables used 154,
    155
  externalizing, Java system properties used 156,
    158
  externalizing, JSON used 158, 159
  externalizing, property files used 150, 152
EnvironmentPostProcessor
  custom PropertySource, adding to environment
    145, 149
Eureka
  service discovery 254
executors
  scheduling 26, 27

F

Feign
  using 247, 248, 250, 253
Flyway 89

G

Gradle multi-project builds
  reference 70
Gradle-Docker plugin configuration options
  reference 136
Gradle
  used, for launching application 15
Graphite
  Micrometer metrics, integrating with 203, 205,
    207, 209, 212

H

Hibernate
  database, initializing 90
hierarchy 142
Hyper SQL Database (HSQLDB) 19
Hypertext Application Lamguage (HAL) 177
Hystrix
  about 240
  using 256, 258, 259, 260

I

in-memory database
  used, for creating tests 91, 95
integration testing 80

J

Java Persistence API (JPA) 10
Java system properties
  used, for externalizing environmental
    configuration 156, 157
JMX
  Spring Boot, monitoring via 192, 194
JPA component test
  creating 99, 101
JSON
  used, for externalizing environmental
    configuration 158, 160

L

Liquibase
  reference 89
LiveReload

configuring 225
reference 226
loadbalancing rules
reference 252

M

management context
configuring 179, 180, 182
metrics
emitting 183, 184, 185, 187, 189, 191
Micrometer metrics
integrating, with Dashing 213, 216, 222
integrating, with Graphite 203, 206, 207, 210, 212
mock objects
used, for creating tests 96, 98
MockMvc
reference 86
MVC controllers
tests, creating for 80, 81, 83, 85

O

object-relational mapping (ORM) 22

P

precedence 142
property files
used, for externalizing environmental config 150, 153

R

Remote Update
using 230, 234
route matching patterns
configuring 50, 51, 52

S

self-executing binaries
building 137, 138, 140
service discovery
with Eureka 254
with Spring Cloud Consul 242, 244, 247
service testing 80
ServletWebServerFactory

Tomcat, tuning via 54, 55, 56
Signal Handlers
reference 167
simple application
creating 10, 11, 12, 13, 14
Software as a Service (SaaS) 126
Spock
reference 122
used, for writing tests 114, 117, 121, 122
Spring Boot DevTools
adding, to project 224, 225
reference 224
Spring Boot executable JAR
creating 126, 127, 129
Spring Boot starters
using 8, 9
Spring Boot template
using 8, 9
Spring Boot
autoconfiguration 64, 65, 66
managing, via SSHd Shell 195, 197, 199, 201, 203
monitoring, via JMX 192, 194
Spring Cloud 238, 240
Spring Cloud Consul libraries
reference 247
Spring Cloud Consul
service discovery 242, 244, 247
Spring Cloud Netflix
using 247, 248, 250, 252
Spring Data REST service
creating 32, 34
Spring JDBC
database, initializing 90
Spring JPA
database, initializing 90
SSHd Shell
Spring Boot, managing via 195, 197, 199, 201, 203

T

tests
creating, for MVC controllers 80, 81, 83, 84
creating, in-memory database used 91, 95
creating, mock objects used 96, 98

writing, Cucumber used 104, 107, 109, 111, 113

writing, Spock used 114, 117, 121, 123

Tomcat
  tuning, via ServletWebServerFactory 54, 55, 56

Twelve-Factor App methodology
  about 126
  reference 126

U

unit testing 80

V

versions, Spring Cloud modules
  reference 240

W

WebMvc component test
  creating 101, 103

Z

ZooKeeper 241

www.ingramcontent.com/pod-product-compliance
Lightning Source LLC
Chambersburg PA
CBHW080631060326

40690CB00021B/4886